HOW TO MAKE IT IN THE
MUSIC BUSINESS

SIÂN PATTENDEN

D1313104

To Felix
A cat who only seemed to
like Lionel Richie's music

Thanks to:
Everyone who originally took part in this book, those who
survived the edit and those who have recently made a
contribution. Thanks also to Ian Gittins and Barbara Phelan.
Special thanks to Mr Solanas; and the PPs.

This edition published in 2007 by
Virgin Books Ltd
Thames Wharf Studios
Rainville Road
London
W6 9HA

First published in Great Britain in 1998 by
Virgin Publishing Ltd

ISBN 978 0 7535 1243 2

Typeset by Phoenix Photosetting, Chatham, Kent
7 9 10 8
Printed and bound in Great Britain by Clays Ltd, St Ives PLC

CONTENTS

THE MUSIC BUSINESS: HOW IT WORKS

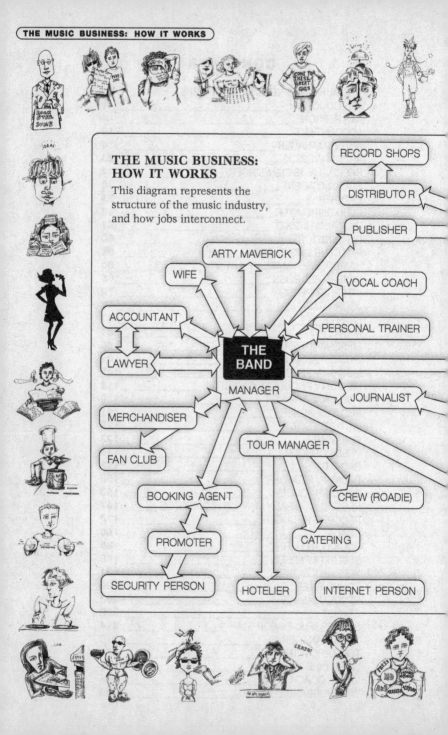

THE MUSIC BUSINESS: HOW IT WORKS

This diagram represents the structure of the music industry, and how jobs interconnect.

RECORD SHOPS

DISTRIBUTOR

PUBLISHER

ARTY MAVERICK

WIFE

VOCAL COACH

ACCOUNTANT

PERSONAL TRAINER

THE BAND
MANAGER

LAWYER

JOURNALIST

MERCHANDISER

TOUR MANAGER

FAN CLUB

CREW (ROADIE)

BOOKING AGENT

CATERING

PROMOTER

SECURITY PERSON

HOTELIER

INTERNET PERSON

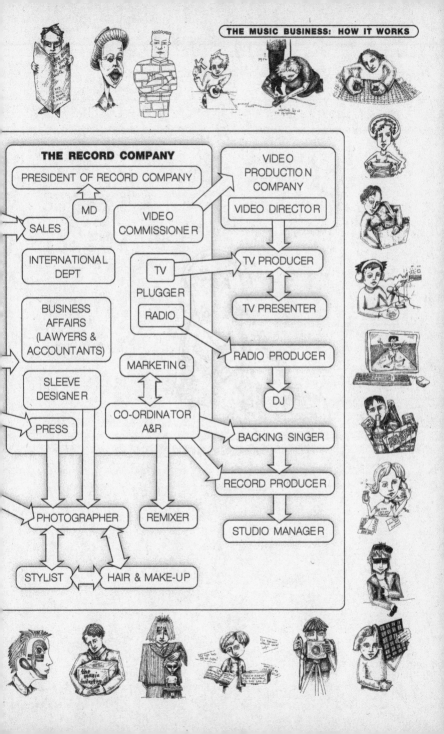

THE RECORD COMPANY

PRESIDENT OF RECORD COMPANY

MD

SALES

INTERNATIONAL DEPT

BUSINESS AFFAIRS (LAWYERS & ACCOUNTANTS)

SLEEVE DESIGNER

PRESS

VIDEO COMMISSIONER

TV
PLUGGER
RADIO

MARKETING

CO-ORDINATOR A&R

PHOTOGRAPHER

REMIXER

STYLIST

HAIR & MAKE-UP

VIDEO PRODUCTION COMPANY

VIDEO DIRECTOR

TV PRODUCER

TV PRESENTER

RADIO PRODUCER

DJ

BACKING SINGER

RECORD PRODUCER

STUDIO MANAGER

A MUSICAL SHREW

INTRODUCTION

In the last nine years since this book was originally published, the record industry and its industry satellites have changed substantially. Things, they say, will never be the same again. The Internet has dominated most of these discussions, and still continues to do so. 'Consumers' have never had it so good, music is available at the touch of a button, and cheaply – or free, if you download illegally.

CD album sales in this country have, according to observers, stayed steady while the rest of the world has seen a decline. But online music sales in the UK will have increased many times over in just a year. People are consuming music in a different way, a way the record companies did not foresee, or at least did not take into consideration. It means the industry is currently in a state of flux, not that the nation's passion for pop music and its sub-stratas has been dampened. When the fastest-growing market is downloadable ringtones, which at the time of writing account for 10 per cent of global music sales and are worth an estimated £3 billion a year, the industry gets worried. Perhaps the singles chart will be based on downloads rather than sales in the near future. Maybe the five major record labels will merge into one, or two, which will spawn a new crop of independents. Then the Arts Council could subsidise some sectors to provide great bands at great prices. Just a thought. What is clear is that people still love music.

The debate as to whether *X Factor* has been the greatest artistic gift to the UK music scene is not relevant to a book like this. Shame, but it isn't. This is the definitive guide to getting a job in one of the most sought-after industries in the world, whether you want to work for a major, an independent or for yourself.

The Internet 'revolution' has certainly proved one thing, that the music world frequently appears to be one in which nobody at all has any idea what will happen next; its internal machinations can appear arcane and extraordinarily impenetrable to outsiders. Clearly, money and sales figures dominate the business, as all others, and yet the ground rules for success are more than just a matter of who's shifting the most records this month: the whole shooting match is as fickle, maverick, unpredictable and fascinating as pop music itself. The music business is not for those who crave safety and security in their career.

The majority of the clichés surrounding the industry are essentially true, for better or worse. Yes, most of the industry is based in London. There is a network of labels, promoters, distributors and venues spread throughout the UK, but the majority of graft is done in the capital – all the major record and publishing companies and most of the magazines are based there, and there's a wealth of venues for A&R people to stand at the back of. You don't have to be in London to survive in the music world – independent labels like Chemikal Underground in Glasgow, and Warp, in Sheffield, have bucked the trend over the last two decades – but you'll certainly find a lot more possibilities in the capital. Or at least people being sick on your trousers who claim they know someone who knows Alan McGee.

The idiosyncrasies and foibles of the music industry are truly legion. It won't take you long to notice that, at parties, far more people than is healthy will call you 'mate' or 'babe' while simultaneously craning over your shoulder to see if there's anybody more famous or interesting for them to talk to. They will also ask you whether you have 'any drugs?' in much the same way as ordinary folk will discuss the weather. The music business is not a 'normal' calling like estate agency or accountancy, possibly because it's staffed almost exclusively by young people. It is also the subject of some fascination – as much as pop stars now dominate the tabloid newspapers, and top the *Sunday Times* Rich List, the business pages are keen to speculate on the share prices of companies like EMI. It's a much-scrutinised world.

Thousands of people long to work in music, and the main reason is that it's a lot of fun. It's *not* like a proper job. Despite how it may look from the outside, it's not impossible to get that first foot in the door. However, a recurrent theme of this book is that, whatever sector of the industry you want to work in, you will have to be prepared to work for very little – or even nothing – to get that initial break.

It doesn't matter if the first post you're offered isn't your dream job: with application and skill you'll be able to change tack later on, and many major figures in the music industry started off working in their spare time while holding down 'straight' jobs or living with their parents. And, remember, despite the extraordinary amounts earned by its top dogs, the music business isn't all baroque decadence and peacocks in the lobby – especially in the current economic climate where share prices in record companies are not especially rocketing.

How To Make It In The Music Business is a guide to taking your first tentative steps in the most exciting, glamorous and compelling industry in the world, whether you want to be a rock star, label bigwig, A&R person, make-up artist or roadie. This is a complete update of the original, and in nine years the industry has changed substantially, leaving some formerly famous names out on their elbow. Harshly, they were flung out in preference for newer, more relevant characters. I talked to the people who know best – or at least think they do – those who've made it to the top of their chosen vocation, whether they be Zoë Ball, Ronan Keating, video director Chris Cunningham, vocal coaches John and Ce Ce, Jamie Cullum, manager Chris Herbert or Stephen Street, record producer. I hope this book is a good read and gives you some vital tips, but also that it shows that the industry isn't so intimidating and nepotistic that a keen individual with a genuine passion for good tunes and several ounces of enthusiasm can't leap in there and start shaking up the fat cats. If you love music – despite what the cynics may tell you – that's the most important thing of all.

The only thing that has changed in the last nine years is that 'acts' and 'bands' are now more commonly known as 'artists', which bothers the irony monster somewhat (I always think of it as an irony monster...), when the Cheeky Girls are still famous.

So, off you go, then. Remember to invite me to the aftershow.

Siân Pattenden, April 2007

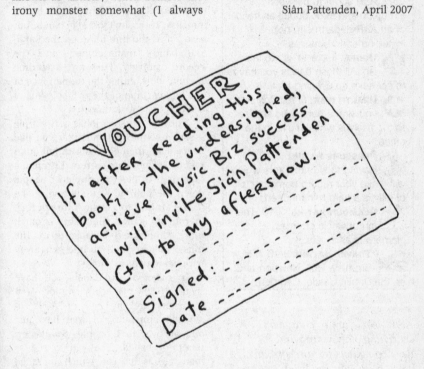

VOUCHER

If, after Reading this book, I, the undersigned, achieve Music Biz success I will invite Siân Pattenden (+1) to my aftershow.

Signed: - - - - - - - - -

Date - - - - - - - - -

All illustrations by Siân Pattenden

A&R PERSON

A&R people are in charge of searching out, signing and developing acts for a record label. They go to gigs and listen to tapes of new bands all the time, and never stop looking for The Next Big Thing. And, when they've found that, they have to look for The Next Next Big Thing. And then The Next Next Big Thing Who Wears A Hat.

The **A&R** department of a record company is responsible for the future of music, no less. They sign new bands to the record label they work for, all of which they hope will create great tunes for years to come, while pushing back the boundaries of rock 'n' roll and **shifting units** in the process. They don't just sign bands, but also act as the link between the band, the band's management, and the record company. They are, according to your view, either the human face of the big machine or the evil colossus of the corporate rock industry.

The A&R person's job is very simple – sign a couple of bands that you like every year, then get them to put out a record. It's not hard, surely. Listen to a tape or two, meet a couple of people down the pub, go to a gig and, voilà! 'Here, Mr MD, this is the future of rock 'n' roll!' Of course, the reality is much more complicated, because this is the music industry and no one gets away with having an easy life.

In major record labels you have scouts, A&R managers, senior A&R managers and a head of A&R; in smaller companies you may have just one or two A&R people. Scouts, er, scout for bands. They go to see as many gigs as they can, which can range from one to four gigs in a given evening, in any part of the country. Scouts listen to tapes that are sent in – sometimes – and are generally the first to meet the bands they like and show their interest. Senior A&R people generally will get involved once a scout has raved about a band. They'll come down to the gig and check them out – they have greater decision-making powers than the scouts. Ultimate decision making is down to the head of A&R and MD, who hear the hoopla from the department and either give the nod or shake their heads. Rarely, a lone MD, or similar top dog, will approach their A&R department with a 'hot' project.

Dan Keeling is head of A&R at Parlophone Records. After a spell as a journalist and club promoter (and with a degree in, er, art) Dan decided he wanted to get into A&R. He sent his CV to various labels and was taken on by A&M Records in 1995 as an A&R scout.

'I always wanted to work with great artists and help put out great music,' he says. At first, he was surprised by the sheer amount of work involved.

'You're trekking round the country, in Birmingham one night, then Leeds, Glasgow the next – it's a lot of hours on the motorway so it was quite hard. You've got to get around and put your face around and see a lot of people. If you're not bumping into people you're not going to find anyone.'

Bands will often give their demo tapes to local promoters, friends, studios (small **demo studios** where new bands record will certainly have a lot of stuff lying around) and local journalists – *before* they thud onto the A&R's desk. You have to go out and make contact with these people. What, in Dan's opinion, makes a good A&R person?

'You've got to understand the creative process of making a record,' says Keeling, who speaks with some authority. 'You have to be aware of what's going on culturally – around the country and the world. You've got to have good taste in music, you've got to understand artists and get them to trust you – it's good people skills.'

One of the problems of A&R is keeping things secret. You want the band to yourself, to record all their best songs for your label and to buy you expensive watches for your birthday when they get rich. If you let on how much you like them, every other label will be standing next to you at their next gig, whispering things down their mobile phones and sending the band little cards: A&Rmanship is like courting. You have to get on their side, smile, buy them a drink (you'll get it paid back as expenses) and express deep love for all of their tunes. Except the one with the rap in the middle. Sometimes you'll be expressing deep love for all of their tunes, except the one *without* the rap in the middle.

What A&R people do when they meet other A&R people – because they are sly and weaselly creatures – is to say how much they love a band they only like, to check whether the other person has heard of them. There goes the peculiar language of the beast. They'll sit for hours talking about some

A&R MAN

AT A GIG, EVEN IF THEY KNOW EACH OTHER, A&R MEN DO NOT GIVE THEIR SECRETS AWAY.

the A&R budget on demoing acts they would never sign. Demoing is also a very convenient way for a cunning A&R person to stall hopeful artists. You get The Tawdrid Antelope into the office, take them for a beer, and promise you'll give them £800 to demo four songs in a cheap studio. Then you don't sign them but instead um and ah (traditional sarky shorthand for A&R) and keep them wondering about your intentions.

However, it is inappropriate to be utterly cynical about a whole, very important, bit of the music industry. *Good* A&R people are passionate about their job, and this shows primarily because they tend to sign better bands, and even if they offer a smaller deal cash-wise they will have gained the band's trust from the start. Also, a band's lawyer will generally caution against merely accepting the biggest record label's cash offer: so such simplistic A&R tactics certainly aren't guaranteed to work.

A&R people don't just spot and sign promising acts: they also work closely with them for the length of their career at the label. Problems can arise therefore when you find that you love the music, but possibly not the people who are making it.

'There was one particular band I worked with who were really hard

band they can't even remember the name of, trying to gauge whether the other person really does like them, while keeping mum about who they're really after. It's all a very silly game.

'It's difficult when a few labels are fighting after the same thing. You can be over-keen or, conversely, under-keen,' says Dan, who failed to sign the Streets and Franz Ferdinand but did sign Coldplay and Athlete. 'You've got to be very clever ... Wily.'

Keeling moved to Parlophone in 1998 and rose up the ranks from junior A&R manager. He now looks after the whole A&R department and oversees other people signing bands as well as signing artists himself.

You *used* to get a fair few iffy A&R types who weren't confident and spent work,' says David Laurie, former head of A&R at Nude Records, now running his own management company/record label Openseason. 'The first time I met them we went out and got really drunk and ended up having a laugh. Then, the next time, they acted like I had never met them before. I thought: Oh, I just can't be bothered with this.'

A&R persons can come up against snotty managers who render a band unsignable simply by being pig-headed and impossible to work with. Dan Keeling thinks this is rare. In fact, he hasn't come across this yet but other A&R people claim different. It goes to show that every case is individual, man. 'The rules are there are no rules,' as Wendy James from Transvision Vamp oft-repeated. Or, as Brad Pitt said, 'The sixth rule of Fight Club is: *No shirts, no shoes.*' Maybe.

A&R people constantly stress that, no matter what hair or which trousers they sport, the band must always have *songs.* 'That's what it's all about,' confirms Keeling.

Rick Lennox, former A&R at Polydor, agrees: 'There are a billion bands out there who have one really good song each. But you can't sign a band because they've got one good song – they need a whole set of them.'

It generally costs around £500,000 to 'break' an album from a new band spread across all record label departments such as marketing, A&R, press and payment for tour support (in itself around £80,000). £200,000 is the slice that A&R receive, which includes recording fees which can be from around £50,000–100,000 for a band starting out. For top artistes, it will invariably cost hundreds of thousands for those who want to record in exotic locales and fly first class (sitting in Sting's back garden comes free – at the moment) but they should have a proven track record and will have recouped all advances. As the recording sessions progress, the A&R person will listen to each new track and give advice as regards potential singles, and those which should remain album tracks. These hints sometimes clash with the band's and manager's own ideas, so diplomacy needs to be one of the A&R person's skills.

A&R people are thus under constant pressure to sign artists who will have hits, and fix them up with the right producer and recording studio and make sure there's a cracking album as a result. The A&R liaise with artist, manager, studio managers, producers and marketing within the record company.

Most A&R people agree that not many good bands come along in a year – 'maybe a dozen' says one A&R type. And you can't sign a heavy-metal act to an indie label, because Ver Kids would notice and think something was up. However, Dan Keeling admits that he doesn't think of the bands he signs as sharing a common Parlophone sound – and to do so might be detrimental.

'I try and sign unique artists who've got songs and will prove to have some longevity, that's my criteria,' he says.

Does he ever write down his ideal band on a piece of paper – John Lennon's voice, Eric Clapton's guitar playing, Keith Moon on drums etc. – and go out and find them?

'No,' he says, not sounding very impressed at the thought. 'It doesn't work like that. I love music, I love buying records. I look at it as the stuff I'd buy.'

Ninety-eight per cent of the tapes sent to Nude were 'dreadful', according to David Laurie. Keeling says he rarely listens to unsolicited tapes – that's not the way it works.

'Everyone in this A&R department has their own contacts, which can be anyone from a music lawyer to other managers, friends, anyone involved in the business. You have to be out there meeting lots of people and talking about music. We do listen to some stuff that comes in and I'm sure you can find some *all right* stuff but *all right* isn't good enough. You need to find the great stuff. When they do come along people talk about them, so then you listen.'

A record company advance is paid out when the band actually sign a contract with the label, and goes towards their living expenses, business costs (lawyer, accountant, etc.) plus buying equipment: plectrums, leather trousers etc. Then, as mentioned, they receive a recording budget – for studio time and producer costs – and are allocated a press, promotion and marketing budget. But this is money lent to them, and they have to **recoup** it, which is why it is known as an advance.

A good A&R person will, therefore, have a thorough musical knowledge and be able to spot a stolen riff or nicked lyrics, or generally contextualise a band's sound, man. You'll see gigs, meet bands and proffer advice. Only when you are very *very* sure will you sign someone. So it sounds like a good sort of life, roaming free around the country, enjoying power and control, with future pop stars as your mates, doesn't it?

Well, it's not all fun. An all-expenses-paid trip round the country can be dull on your own. A&R can be really hard work, and a thankless, almost impossible task. If you are going to do this job you have to be absolutely sure that you want to. A&R jobs are hard to come by and it's difficult to be a success without a slog. You will also find that it totally dominates your social life – and not only your significant other but even your friends will forget who you are because they never see you.

'You've got to have a passion for music,' says Dan, who admits that no pop star has ever been sick on him (when asked). 'If you haven't got that you might as well not bother doing it. You've gotta think about it constantly. Some of our artists, be it Chris Martin or whoever, they're obsessed by music. It's the same with football, if you want to be a footballer you've got to think about football constantly.'

Has anyone ever tried to bribe Dan into signing them? Free drinks?

'No!' he exclaims. 'I've never thought about it like that. Of course I'd accept anyone buying me a free drink but it's not going to make me sign a band.

'If anyone wants to do the job,' he continues. 'I'd say get out to a lot of gigs – whatever music you're into, be it R&B, or bands – meet people, be enthusiastic and just be a general all-round good person. I'm sure if it's for you, you'll be able to get into it. You'll meet the right person who'll give you a job at the time. It's all about making connections with people.'

GLOSSARY
● **A&R**

Stands for 'Artists and Repertoire'. In ye olde days, record companies had artists, who needed a repertoire of songs to sing. Thus the A&R man got tunes in for people with a good set of pipes. It really was as simple as that.

● **Shifting units**

Selling records. 'Units' is the global term for denoting quantity, a word which lawyers and accountants happily use but which profoundly upsets artistes because they don't like to see their creativity being reduced to economics. But that's the nature of the game, chums.

● **Demo studios**

Small recording studios which may not have as much equipment as the fancier ones, but which are used to record 'practice versions' of songs for forthcoming singles and albums.

● **Recoup**

The process of returning to the record company, mainly through album sales (singles and tours don't often make a lot of money), the advance which they lent you when you first signed to them. Advances can take years to recoup, and bands are dropped when the company realises that they'll never get their money back.

SKILLS YOU'LL NEED

Musical knowledge, friendliness, a keen ear for hot new sounds, willingness to get in early in the morning and go home late at night, diplomacy, a pathological obsession with music.

TIPS

● Start going to small gigs, getting to know promoters (the people who run club and gig nights) and cadging in for free. You'll soon start to spot the A&R people.

● Ring up record companies and give them tapes of the bands you've seen (ask any band and they'll vomit C60s over you).

● A lot of people get into A&R via promoting – either fixing up gigs at college or else starting to run a regular night at a local club. Speak to your student union or local venue.

● Talk to managers of local bands. They'll want your impressions of their acts, and can give you contacts.

● Writing for the local paper about local sounds is a good way to start.

USEFUL ADDRESSES

● EMI Records, EMI House, 43 Brook Green, London, W6 7EF
TEL 020 7605 5000
FAX 020 7605 5050
WEBSITE www.emirecordedmusic.com
● Polydor Records, 72–80 Black Lion Lane, London, W6 9BE
TEL 020 8910 4800
FAX 020 8910 4801
WEBSITE www.polydor.co.uk
● Sony BMG Music Entertainment Ltd, Bedford House, 69–79 Fulham High Street, London, SW6 3JW
TEL 020 7384 7500
FAX 020 7371 9298
WEBSITE www.sonybmgmusic.co.uk
● Warner Music, The Warner Building, 28A Kensington Church Street, London, W8 4EP
TEL 020 7938 5500
FAX 020 7368 4903
WEBSITE www.wmg.com

ACCOUNTANT

MONEY: Lots. If you embezzle your client's funds you make a mint, but then you get found out and have to go to prison.

HOURS: 9 a.m. to 5 p.m. every weekday, or 10 a.m. to 6 p.m. You rarely go down the pub with Geri Halliwell. Hurray!

HEALTH RISK: 2/10. Sitting in an office all day passive-inhaling Tippex isn't too bad at all.

EQUIPMENT COSTS: Nothing if you are employed as part of an accountancy firm, but you pay your own costs if you set up your own business. Bought ledger book, fancy Shaeffer ink pen, desk, phone, subscription to *What Suit?* magazine, etc.

PRESSURE RATING: 6/10. Sometimes deadlines loom up, as with any other business.

GLAMOUR RATING: Very low: 1/10. Unless you find adding up sexy. You may receive a Christmas card from Phil Collins every year. So, er, not at all glamorous then.

TRAVEL RATING: 2/10. Apart from your own holidays, not much. And travelling to and from your leatherette office swivel chair with smooth-action height-adjustment and bendy-back springs for those casual 'Look how relaxed I am, Mr/Ms Important Client' moments.

Every single area of the music industry needs an accountant to be in charge of its finances. It is a vital role, yet it can be the least involved in the crazy rock 'n' roll madness. At points you might not even notice you're in the music industry.

Accountants are the Great Unknown in the world of rock. They're not really meant to be there: they wear suits and drink Andrews Liver Salts and complain that the Doberman has just ripped up their prize sofa. Rock accountants rarely differ from the normal type; they've just been trained in the whys and wherefores of record-business contracts and the way the system works. Essentially, they are still talking calculators.

To be an accountant you have to follow the normal route: train for at least three years and apply for suitable posts. Some accountancy firms specialise in music; others handle music and different accounts, like merchant banks. Once you've joined a firm, you'll be given clients and you'll work wholly with them. There will be a lot of balancing of figures and last-minute rushes to send off **tax returns**. Many musicians are self-employed: they are not taxed at source but owe money to the tax person at the end of each financial year. Many have their own company, or companies, and are taxed accordingly. For tax-deductible expenses, such as stage wear and equipment, pop stars are expected to keep receipts. This is all for relevant expenditure: you can't buy a horse and pretend it'll be playing tambourine on the next album.

The accountant's job is to tot up those expenses, calculate gross income per annum and net income per annum (gross minus expenses). You have the task of finding out where that £500, or £50,000 went. A rock accountant may have to be slightly more dogged in the pursuit of an artist's receipts for all those loon pants they want to claim back, but many pop stars (and their managers) are organised and understand the need to file everything away.

If you *are* sensible, like a bit of soft rock and fancy yourself a whizz at sums, then the accountant's life is for you. It's a sure-fire career: every single aspect of the music industry needs an accountant to sort out its finances. It's ideal if you're not a rock renegade but you are looking for **security**. And, once you've had your practice at someone else's accountancy firm, you can take the plunge and start your own! You can make a lot of money as your own boss too, but there's more pressure. Major record companies employ in-house accountants to do the books, as part of their business-affairs department. Sting had a problem with his accountant, in

that he found that he was stealing a portion of his income. He took him to court. That's probably as exciting as Mr Accountant's life gets.

David Moss is a director at OJ Kilkenny, who deal exclusively with rock stars and their chequebooks. After training he didn't have much truck with corporate accounts and wanted to do something a little more interesting. Not being fazed by the thought of sulky rock stars coming in and dropping fruit smoothies on the carpet, he got a job at OJ Kilkenny in 1991.

'I started a long time before that,' he says. 'When the entertainment business was looked after by fewer firms than it is now. While I was too young to make a conscious decision about things, I think I wanted to do a more arts-based job.'

OJ Kilkenny employ around fifty people in London and Dublin (the Dublin office deals with U2 – what one would call a 'nice little earner'). The role, plainly, is collecting cash from various sources – record company, publishing company, live performance promoters, PRS, sponsors etc. The accountant pays the bills and informs the client as to where the money is going. Each accountant deals with a few clients, liaising with the band's lawyer on the band's contracts, assisting with negotiations.

ACCOUNTANT

They make sure the artists put their wonga aside for their tax bills, don't spend too much money on sweets, and can advise them to buy property, start their own record label, build a recording studio, buy art, geese or Iceland, whatever is agreeable with their personal cashscape.

They also deal with the tax implications of working abroad, which the bands invariably do on overseas tours and when they record in other countries. And nice Mr Accountant will even supervise putting your cheques into your account so you never have to stand in a queue in Barclays.

Mr Moss deals with 'problems as and when they arise. My days are not planned in the same way as they might be within a more conventional firm, where you have your audit, accounts preparation and your compliance work, I do very little of that.'

He also deals with 'some intrinsically difficult tax cases'. Sounds exciting. (It might not be.) 'No matter what career they follow,' says Moss, 'and this doesn't just apply in music, there are those people who spend more than they earn.'

Moss cannot advise pop stars to invest in any specific thing, but guides them through when needed.

'There are conventional forms of investment like pension funds but even they seem to have a bad name these days,' he says. 'Property – everyone falls into that at a drop of a hat. Many people have their own plans and they'll talk to us about how to put them into action in the most effective way. Those people who do not know what to do if they have surplus cash, they'll come and talk to us and say, "What are your bright ideas?"'

Is it interesting dealing with creative people?

'Yes, because it's such a personalised business,' the no-nonsense Moss replies. 'But I'm sure you have creative people in more regular types of business. In music it's pretty apparent these people are creative.'

Is it a thrill for those working at OJ Kilkenny to work with creative types?

'We studiously avoid employing people who are star-struck.'

Moss does go to gigs 'occasionally ... but I never want anyone in my firm to be called a ligger.' He wears a suit because he's 'been around since God was a boy'. And, no, the office is not full of rock 'n' roll accountants having a beer in the morning.

'We don't have to follow all the attributes of our clients. We like to consider ourselves as a steadying hand. Hahah!'

One of the frustrations of the job could be the repetitious nature of accountancy: every April (start of the new tax year) the same pattern repeats. And don't get too big for your boots, thinking you 'own' the client because you oversee their spending. Nor is there room for favourites. This is serious. This is sensible. This is accountancy.

Ever had to sack a client because they were so useless at money?

'Hahha hah!' David Moss is very much amused. 'There *are* occasions when you say, "We ought to kiss and say goodbye." Nothing is for ever.'

GLOSSARY
● **Tax return**
Big form which details annual earnings: a 'return' of information about 'tax'.

● Security

Loose term based on the ignoble pursuit of a steady income. You might not bump into such a word very often in the more creative areas of rock 'n' roll. All it means is that you'll have money to go to B&Q after you're sixty.

SKILLS YOU'LL NEED

Being good at sums, organisational skills, suit-wearing, punctuality.

TIPS

● You'll need to get a degree, and then apply to an accountancy firm for a traineeship.
● Do not swindle anyone out of any money.
● Don't get jealous because everyone you do accounts for is having a rare old time swanning off to Chinawhite and getting their picture taken with Lisa Scott-Lee.

USEFUL ADDRESSES

● Baker Tilly, 2 Bloomsbury Street, London, WC1B 3ST
TEL 020 7413 5100
FAX 020 7413 5101
WEBSITE www.bakertilly.co.uk
● Carnmores Royalties Consultants, Suite 212–213, Blackfriars House, 157–168 Blackfriars Road, London, SE1 8EZ
TEL 020 7261 1660
FAX 020 7261 1659
WEBSITE www.carnmores.com
● Entertainment Accounting International, 26a Winders Road, Battersea, London, SW11 3HB
TEL 020 7978 4488
FAX 020 7978 4492
● Nyman Libson Paul, Regina House, 124 Finchley Road, London, NW3 5JS

TEL 020 7433 2400
FAX 020 7433 2401
WEBSITE www.nlpca.co.uk
● OJ Kilkenny & Co, 6 Lansdowne Mews, London, W11 3BH
TEL 020 7794 5611
FAX 020 7792 1722
● SRLV, Kendal House, 1 Conduit Street, London, W1S 2XA
TEL 020 7287 9595
FAX 020 7287 9696
WEBSITE www.srlv.co.uk

ARTIST MANAGER

MONEY: You take between 15 and 25 per cent of your artist's gross income and net of tour income (although this can vary). Promotional budgets aren't included in these calculations. Your salary can therefore range between nothing to many millions.

HOURS: 24 per day, seven days per week. It's not a breeze.

HEALTH RISK: 9/10. The stress means you could be on Lemsip for days.

PRESSURE RATING: 10/10. It's your responsibility if it all goes wrong, and the artist (and others) gets the credit if it's a swinging success.

GLAMOUR RATING: 8/10. Some swanky lunches and some posh dinners.

TRAVEL RATING: 9/10. You get to travel first class with the band and go around in limousines, once your artists get to a certain level. If not, it's renting a Transit van and squeezing in the back with them, or walking.

You sort out everything for your band: which record company they're signing with, what tour they're doing, what pants they wear, paying their gas bill (yes, sometimes), and making sure they ring their mums regularly. It is a thankless and often brutal task, but at least you get a percentage of all their earnings for it.

Managers are notoriously scuzzy, unkempt individuals who make low-down dirty deals with people in suits 'on the quiet' and lie to their bands about how they're not ripping them off. Well, that's the image. Some managers are indeed a little on the grim side, but most of them are quite respectable people who like the music and also enjoy getting shirty with industry bigwigs once in a while.

It's a job that requires absolute commitment. It is the cliché of being the extra member of the band and, while anyone can be a manager, there are very few who are really good at it. Much of the time people start managing because their friends in a band need helping out. Suddenly someone who's not au fait with the workings and evil machinations of the music industry is expected to know what gigs to play, what deals are the best kind, what sort of trousers make you look hunky, etc. Managers are always being flung into the deep end. It takes someone very dedicated to do the job.

Some bands don't have managers, but only for short periods of time. The Spice Girls didn't for a bit when they sacked Simon Fuller. The KLF never had one, perhaps because Bill Drummond used to be a manager himself and didn't like the idea. But these are exceptions. Think of a band as being like a boat with some people in it. They know they're a boat, they look like a boat, sound like one, but they haven't got a paddle. In wades the manager, to help them steer.

There are some really famous managers from history who were just as loony as the bands they managed and hence remembered almost as much as the band themselves, such as Andrew Loog Oldham and The Stones, Brian Epstein and The Beatles and Peter Grant and Led Zeppelin. In those days they did more of the jobs the record companies hadn't invented yet: marketing, promotions, A&R, etc., all rolled into one. Now the music industry is so structured and defined it's hard for the manager to be as creative as s/he would like. Someone else will be paid to do it, or not do it, as the case may be.

Chris Herbert, former manager of the Spice Girls, Five, Hear'say and now Alex Parks and Kym Marsh, started as a pop manager because he wanted a job in a record company. His father had an accountancy practice which dealt with a lot of people in the entertainment industry and he 'dabbled' in management along the way.

NOT OPTIONAL.

'I was brought up in that environment and was a massive pop fan from when I bought my first edition of *Smash Hits*,' says Chris. 'I had another business at the time, which was corporate hospitality. I was looking to get into the music industry myself, and I went for all sorts of jobs but you needed an introduction in. I thought I'd start managing acts ... in the hope that if they were successful it would raise my profile and eventually I'd get a record company job.'

It was 1994. Chris went to his father,

Bob, and suggested he stop the 'dabbling' and join forces. 'I started off managing a solo artist signed to London records, called Maria Rowe. The next project was the Spice Girls.'

The desired job in a record company went out of the window.

Chris's story is a good one for those interested in the, um, *learning curves* involved in music management. He never, he says, felt like a music business insider – he was working without the backing of a record company or producer. He and his father were joined by a business partner, Chic Murphy.

'At the time I was looking at the boybands, Take That and E17 were flying high. I thought, this only appeals to half the potential audience – girls. If you do a girl band and it's sexy but sassy as well – girls should aspire to be like them and boys will follow as well. That was the idea.'

There was not really a template Herbert could follow. Bananarama in the 80s, and American groups the Go Gos, the Bangles ...

'At the beginning I made up a mood board of all the characters we wanted to make up this band. As you would see a gang of girl friends out – a loud one, quiet one, cute one etc. – we wanted every single flavour; it was really to try and re-create that but in a pop band form. So we went out and started looking everywhere from pubs, clubs' talent competitions, performing arts schools, open auditions for other castings – and then I put an advert in *The Stage*.'

ARTIST MANAGER

The ad asked for 'Five lively girls ... R U 18–23 with the ability to sing/dance? R U streetwise, outgoing, ambitious, and dedicated?' Suitably couched in youth-speak, the ad attracted a few hundred girls who auditioned. Chris wanted to find the girls and get them 'up to speed' – i.e. polish off the rough edges a little. Then he'd **showcase** them to writers and producers, build a good production team around them, go on to complete an album and sign to a record company. Chris says he was in at the deep end from day one.

'In hindsight I didn't realise it would take so long to get them at a presentable stage, to showcase them. In some cases the girls were from four corners of the country and had not necessarily considered this as a career; some were modelling, some were going for cruise ships auditions. Having to handle all

that and get them in the same place at the same time took the best part of a year. It was long and painful trying to get that together, getting the correct vocal training and choreography. Now, you'd find people who are pretty much there already, but it was basic materials we were working with.'

Chic Murphy financed the project. Chris wanted to contract the girls, so he and they had security – it would be best for everybody. Murphy had other ideas.

'He was an old-school manager, that kind that manages with an iron fist. At the time the girls were coming to us asking to be contracted – but he liked installing that insecurity, so that they knew he could change any one of them at any time. As has been well reported that all backfired, there was a revolution within.'

It would not be the first time. The Spice Girls (they had changed their name from the original Touch) left Herbert to go to Simon Fuller – who they subsequently fired in 1997. Chris is sanguine about the whole affair.

'I got them to the point where they were ready, and then we showcased them to publishers, writers and production teams, to see who wanted to get involved on a proper project basis. We got them to the point where they were starting to record – "Wannabe" was in the making. But once the girls were exposed to the outside world, people saying how good they were, that was the point where they got that confidence to leave. At the time, I was 21 years old ... now I see possibly why they fled like that.'

That's pragmatic.

'Yeah, we didn't land a big fish, it was one that got away but it did exactly what I intended it to and it opened every door in the industry for me, I've gone on and had success with my company from then on.'

Chris's next project was a boy band, Five.

'The Spice Girls were doing well and everyone was talking about putting girl bands together [e.g. Girl Thing, Hepburn and B*Witched]. I thought let's do the opposite, so I started preparing a boy band. Again, it was the same train of thought – is it possible to make it bit more laddish, less traditional, so that boys can relate to the band as well?'

Five were hipper. A bit. They had muscly Jay and 'bad boy' Abs. Or was that Sean? Apparently, they all grew to hate each other, but that's pop music. Herbert had to deal with the egos. As a manager, he feels he has to wear every hat, as it were.

'You have to be everything from a friend to a psychologist, a solicitor, an accountant, a business manager, A&R ... it goes on. It's such a broad role. Every day I come across another area which needs another set of skills.'

Chris deals with name artists and those **in development.** He details his job day to day.

'I deal with all the logistical stuff, any movement the artist makes and all that surrounds that: arranging cars, hair, make-up, styling,' he says. 'I put myself right in the middle of everything and become the channel through to the artist. An approval process goes on as information is coming through, I filter it through to the artist, having tweaked it – and in most cases arranging all the logistics that go with it. I'm talking to artists – maybe ten times a day.'

Chris is no stranger to being called round the clock, including weekends. 'The role of the manager is 99 per cent problem-solving.'

Honesty is the best gambit in this job, especially if you're new to the role. If you pretend you know what's going on but have no idea, you'll end up making stupid mistakes. Ask what people do if you don't know (even after reading this 'mazin' book). Ask what they're talking about. They'll appreciate your curiosity. You need to understand every aspect of the industry, the circulation of each and every one of the music mags, the viewing demographic of every TV programme, the commission a booking agent takes, the price of a stylist, what **cross-collateralisation** is, the difference between mechanical royalities and PRS ... The manager has to swot up on all aspects of the business, because the artist doesn't want to be bothered about even half of it. Some of them can't even phone a taxi. They have to be left to roam free in the corners of their creativity and come up with some cracking tunes.

'I think management is the hardest job in the music industry,' says Chris Herbert. 'Also, those seeing it as a career are that more savvy to the mechanics of what goes on,' he says. 'We've seen so much more about behind the scenes in the music business. Fans approach me sometimes and ask what the midweek is on a certain single – I wouldn't have known what it was at their age! So artists come in with that knowledge and sometimes that brings another set of problems – they think they know it all.'

Some managers are tempted to get delusions of grandeur (see 'ruling with an iron fist' mentioned above), but the job shouldn't be a power trip. You have to tell your artists everything, keep nothing to yourself, and make decisions with them. The only exception is when they're too busy and not bothered whether their T-shirts are red or mauve, or when the artist has stopped **being objective** and you're the only person who has an overview and can make a rational decision.

Chris says the last time he shouted was 'last week' but he doesn't do it often: 'I think I can get people to do more for me by being friendly towards people rather than shouting at them.'

In the early stages, a lot of unsigned bands will suffer knock-backs from surly record companies and be put off. It's your job to keep them motivated. Herbert thinks there is little difference between a pop manager and a rock manager.

'The basis is the same, but I think you adapt within different genres. Where we have all the problems with more image-based issues, an indie manager will be dealing with sound and technical problems for touring and recording.'

Chris doesn't get many holidays, but there are other perks.

'The high points are when an artist succeeds,' he says. 'And when you're thanked by that artist. When you're pulling up at Wembley and the name of your act is emblazoned across the front of it – they're the little moments that you give yourself a pat on the back for. All those kind of milestones, you share it with the act.'

But the pressure is always on. Chris says the manager is the first person to blame when anything goes wrong. In the artist's world 'if there's one place to point a finger at it's at the manager. My

biggest gripe about management you get the least thanks but the most criticism when things go wrong.'

Egos are fragile because in this particular industry the product isn't a car or a spoon; it's a person's own creative personality.

'If your artist has had a really shitty day, they're sulking, and you know they've got to do an incredibly important interview in ten minutes, what do you do?' asks Alex Kadis, former manager of Mark Owen. 'Your very inner being is saying, "I want to smack you round the head." But the old management responsibility taps you on the shoulder and you have to suppress all your own feelings of anger and insult to think: We have ten minutes to resolve this situation.'

Alex continues. 'Sometimes you'll say, "That's a bad haircut and you look really horrid. I know you're not here to be a fairy on a cake but, my God, make an effort." They complain and fight against it, then eventually they have a rethink and it was now all their idea. And you think to yourself: *That's four months it's taken you* … It's not glamorous. You have to get your hands dirty.'

Chris's advice is, predictably given his early experience, to make it all legal.

'I wouldn't advise anyone to do a handshake deal like we did with the Spice Girls. You put in a lot of energy, time and effort. Like anything you do within business make sure you secure it with a legally binding contract.'

GLOSSARY
● **Showcase**
When new pop bands perform a few songs for interested persons – be they

record company, producers, writers or journalists, this is called a showcase.

● **In development**

Acts often are signed to record companies in a development deal, which means the label invests money in recording and grooming them for success, but is not contractually obliged to release anything yet.

● **Cross-collateralisation**

Concerned with moneys earned not just from record sales but through other means such as merchandising, tours, songs used for the ads, etc.

● **Being objective**

Maintaining a logical and non-emotional approach. In pop-manager terms, this means the art of standing outside yourself and saying, 'Hmm, those trousers are actually rather horrible.' Pop stars don't do this often.

SKILLS YOU'LL NEED

Diplomacy, tact, motivation, discipline, calmness, being good in a crisis, learning to laugh when record-company bigwigs tell jokes.

TIPS

● See as many fresh, new bands as you can, spot one you like, ask if they have a manager ...

● Get to know local promoters and press people who'll give you more of an insight into the way the industry is run.

● A lot of people running record shops get into managing because young bands come into the shop all the time. Record-shop experience is useful anyway. It tells you what people like.

● Management training courses will give you an idea of the basics. The Brits school in Croydon, financed by

the BPI, is an excellent place to study media, management, business and finance – and also dance, drama and music. It takes on pupils of fifteen and over and provides GCSE, A level and BTEC courses. It's the only one of its kind in Britain and is great for making contacts.

● Practise on your friends! Go to the shops for them and pay their gas bills, then demand 20 per cent of their Bristol and West savings account. Oh, only joking. Sorry.

USEFUL ADDRESSES

● Ignition Management, 54 Linhope Street, London, NW1 6HL
TEL 020 7298 6000
FAX 020 8741 3289
● Nigel Martin-Smith Management, Nemesis House, 1 Oxford Court, Bishopsgate, Manchester, M2 3WQ
TEL 0161 228 6465
FAX 0161 228 6727
WEBSITE www.nigelmartin-smith.com
● Principle Management, 30–32 Sir John Rogersons Quay, Dublin 2, Ireland
TEL 00 353 1 677 7330
FAX 00 353 1 677 7276
● The Brits School, 60 The Crescent, Selhurst, Croydon, CR0 2HN
TEL 020 8665 5242
FAX 020 8665 8676
WEBSITE www.brit.croydon.sch.uk

ARTY MAVERICK

> **MONEY**: From living off gruel to thousands of pounds a week.
>
> **HOURS**: 24 per day, seven days per week. It's a lifestyle, man.
>
> **HEALTH RISK**: 7/10. Can be pickly if you want to follow tradition and cut off your ear.
>
> **PRESSURE RATING**: 2/10. It's art, isn't it?
>
> **GLAMOUR RATING**: 10/10. Again, the art is in the glamour, not the glamour in the art.
>
> **TRAVEL RATING**: Irrelevant. All art is travel of some kind.

The arty maverick does arty things within and around the music business. S/he also promotes the idea that the music industry is still fun and spontaneous and cross-cultural, etc., etc. Ha.

There have been arty mavericks floating between the avant-garde and **popular culture**, taking in a bit of pop along the way, since time immemorial. If it wasn't for such cross-fertilisation, half the good ideas in pop would never have happened. There once was a time when everyone who went to art school was also in a band. Art rock was the music-biz cliché, Franz Ferdinand-watchers. The cultural world of rock involved everyone, not just musicians.

Yoko Ono met John Lennon when she was an influential art person of the 60s, involved in the Fluxus movement and similar extremist projects. Seventies 'I am mad' singer Captain Beefheart was a noted artist. Duran Duran keyboardist Nick Rhodes decided he'd take out-of-focus Polaroids of static noise on hotel TVs and published them in a book called *Interference* in 1984. Hm. The tradition has been brought up to date with Damien Hirst directing the Blur video for 'Country House', and Sam Taylor Wood working with The Pet Shop Boys for their live shows in 1997 and directing Elton John's 'I Want Love' video in 2001. Performance artist Leigh Bowery formed his own group, Minty, and live shows included him 'giving birth' on stage. (That was one of the less visceral highlights.) Boy George wrote the musical *Taboo* about Bowery and the 80s nightclub years. Bjork dates modern 'I'm a bit spooky' artist Matthew Barney, creator of the Cremaster series, if you're interested. You could even say that Rolf Harris has been one of the most successful artists/performers/vet voyeurs in history. But only if you were half insane.

Pop stars are often spotted at exhibition openings quaffing Moët with the poseurs of the year. They love the thought that they can transcend the banalities of rock by associating themselves with more profound and elevated artistic disciplines. Jarvis Cocker was always a man who enjoyed an arty gathering or four. The borders of art, pop music and fashion are where the culture vultures bump into each other and spill said champers down each other's Issey Miyake tank tops.

Jeremy Dellar is less pretentious than most arty mavericks, but still highly successful and was nominated for the 2004 Turner Prize. He began his career by making T-shirts which said 'My Drug Hell' on them, which he sold in trendy shops around the country. What followed soon-ish after was the hugely successful Acid Brass project. Like many a great notion, Jeremy had the idea in the pub, but unlike most people he did something about it. The Bluecoat Gallery in Liverpool were asking for ideas because they wanted to commission four pieces of new work which dealt with sound. Jeremy submitted his ideas and they were up for it – mad for it, in fact.

'It just comes out of liking music – that's the basis of my work, as simple as that,' he reflects. 'It's been very straightforward. The idea of the brass band has captured people's imagination.' Acid Brass is essentially a collection of musicians from the William Fairey Brass Band from Yorkshire who stand in uniform and soberly play tunes by 808 State and A Guy Called Gerald, among others. Audience reaction to date has been tremendous. The working-class-liberated-by-brass-band/working-class-people-liberated-by-dancing-to-techno cultural analogy is the main point. It's the kind of arty thing that is a perfect example of the merging of popular cultures and producing something that posh people can paw over.

Possibly the apex of such crossover shenanigans was the KLF 'Fuck The Millennium' performance at the Barbican in autumn 1997. Acid Brass played as the KLF, dressed as old people in pyjamas, whizzed about in wheelchairs, with Bill Drummond holding a dead swan. Fifty sacked Liverpool dockers sang along to The KLF's song 'Fuck The Millennium (We Want It Now!)' and it was chaos. Some of the dockers were allegedly very drunk and no one knew what to make of it. Now that's Art. A few people also said it was a load of risible old tosh, but there you go.

Jeremy thinks the only way to get on as an arty maverick, which is not the most stable of callings, is to do that grizzly thing, 'network'. Go to art-exhibition openings, talk about your ideas in the pub, and then try to do them. 'It's **ligging**, basically. That's how you meet people in the arts,' he says. 'It's like meetings. Accountants have meetings with accountants. In the arts it's a more fragile network, more fluid. When you socialise it's like having a meeting. You bump into people and take it from there.'

Many such, erm, 'visionaries' find it a lot harder to survive, however. Arty types don't mix with the real world too well and some of them sneakily sign on or have to work in chip shops to pay the rent. Art-music is not at its height at the moment – these are the days of Norah Jones and Blue, not Roxy Music and David Bowie, despite the aforementioned Ferdinand and, um,

Canadian uber-femme Peaches, who many claim is rubbish.

Luke Haines has been an arty maverick within music since the release of his first album *New Wave* as The Auteurs, in 1993. He even has an entry in *Debrett's People Of Today*. He has always insisted on doing things his way to the extent of releasing a single around Christmas time in 1996 called 'Unsolved Child Murder'. Spin-off project Black Box Recorder's first record included a chorus that parpled, 'Life is unfair/Kill yourself or get over it'. Haines once boasted in an interview of building a piece of conceptual art out of McDonald's burger boxes. It has yet to be seen in public. Quite clearly the man can only describe himself as an 'artist'. 'I thought in terms of concepts since I was about eight. Maybe before that,' he says, over a cup of tea.

Although aware of the art school tradition in rock music, Haines's own experience was somewhat different.

'My generation was the last to have benefited from the state-subsidised art school ... but it wasn't all I hoped it would be,' he explains. 'It thought it would be people making underground movies in the corridor. Instead it was a hotbed of bores, interested in technical drawing ...'

Haines made the first Auteurs album expecting it to be his last. 'There's that old quote, you have 24 years to write your first album and you don't think much further than that. I made a second album cos I signed a contract with a major label and that's what you do. It was pragmatic.'

The third album, *After Murder Park* was conceptual enough – placed round the idea of infanticide, a subject usually relegated to such non-fiction writers as Gordon Burn and Blake Morrison. Nice. For his fourth album Haines decided to record under an entirely different name – Baader Meinhof. His label, Hut (owned by Virgin), were fine about it.

'The only odd thing about that was that I wanted to call the album "This Is The Hate Socialist Collective", which the MD thought was a bit much – perhaps because it's an anti-socialist sentiment – but otherwise they liked it. They treated me as an artist rather than some little prick.

'I've never took that much notice of what I was supposed to do,' he continues. 'Why would I be bothered to listen to anyone else's idea of what I should be – be that the music press, the record company or anyone in a band – who I don't ever recall expressing any opinion?'

Would the record company not baulk at releasing a record called 'Light Aircraft On Fire'?

'Those things were always OK, and Virgin were the most supportive label I've ever been on,' admits Luke. 'That particular record surprised me, it even got on the Radio One playlist. But I did a video for a song called "The Rubettes" which had a lot of library footage of IRA car bombs and stuff like that. There was a memo from Virgin listing what was wrong with the video – "3.3 seconds, car bomb. 5.4 seconds, IRA demo on beach". There was a phrase at the bottom: *"Luke Haines is under contract as an entertainer, not as someone making a political point."* I wasn't making a political point, I thought it was entertaining.'

Touché. Luke has made twelve albums in all. His artness has not been restricted to musical output. In 2001 he called a Pop Strike. Based on Art Provocateur Stewart Home's 1990–93 Art Strike, Haines asked for all musicians to down tools for a week and all consumers not to purchase any records, but only for a week. Pop Strike coincided with the release of Haines's latest album, *The Oliver Twist Manifesto*.

'That was just playing around with the press,' he explains. 'And ideas of what pop is. It suited a particular quarrelsome record I was putting out at the time. Pop Strike was a big joke, which possibly only I appreciated. Why shouldn't the laziest substrata of society which is the spoilt pop star go on strike?'

Mr H. is pleased with his work.

'I've never pandered to the diluted formula that everyone else veers towards. I just get on with it, because I am an artist.' And tips for the budding arty maverick?

'A trade secret is to try and come up with the most ludicrous idea possible and then build a song around it. We did that with Black Box Recorder a lot. For example, rather than start writing a song about the 80s you'd take something you're not particularly interested in, say Wham! Then you write a eulogy to Andrew Ridgeley but making him out to be the talented one.'

Haines thinks for a moment. 'But by their nature, arty mavericks don't take advice, do they? This is one stumbling block.'

He pauses.

'Argue about everything. That's it. And don't take yes for an answer. Yes is not good enough.'

GLOSSARY
● **Popular culture**
What pop stars are obsessed by. It's the new classicism, you know.

● **Ligging**
Hanging out at other people's events for no other reason than you want to be 'there', because it's so 'now'.

SKILLS YOU'LL NEED
Guts, wild ideas, perhaps wild hair, tunnel-vision, big ego, a thick skin, more luck than you can shake a small copse of sticks at.

TIPS
● Nurture all the above qualities, then go out and do it, friends!
● Hang out at pubs opposite gig venues. The band playing will often drink in the pub closest to their show after the soundcheck. A bit obvious, really, but this is where you can introduce yourself.
● Start an art gallery in your house.

BACKING MUSICIAN/ SINGER

MONEY: Musicians' Union rates are about £100 for a three-hour session, with extra money for overtime. This is a guide, and often musicians get paid a competitive rate instead. This can be around £2,500 for a few sessions with Blue but it can stretch to £5–6,000 a week if you're working for someone like Sting. Or God.

HOURS: From one or two hours a week to every single day. Variable.

HEALTH RISK: 6/10. You might get poked with a drumstick if you're not singing right.

PRESSURE RATING: 5/10. Because you're in the background, in all senses, the pressure isn't so great. The freelance nature of the job can be more stressful.

GLAMOUR RATING: 6/10. You see studios and backstage dressing rooms. You might be able to pat George Michael on the back, sometimes.

TRAVEL RATING: 8/10. Lots of gigs. Then there's foreign touring and exotic climes and papaya skins with cocktails in them. Oh, and being able to take home those shower caps and fancy sewing kits from top-class hotels.

The backing musician, and singer, provides extra welly for artists who may not have a virtuoso saxophone player in their band or may want a nice harmony to go along with their warbling.

Not every band can play all the instruments they'd like to, or sing all the **harmonies** which are bouncing around in their heads. Some of them can't sing at all. Session musicians and singers can do these things, and are in constant employment, augmenting the sound of recording artists from indie to pop to dance music. When a band is recording, or preparing to tour, they'll find out who they need to fill in any musical gaps. The A&R co-ordinator at the record label will then go to the agents of the session people and see who's available.

A lot of musicians get work through word of mouth: a producer will recommend someone good s/he worked with the week/year before and then ring them when they're needed. Most session people have an agent to negotiate fees and help get work. The gigs will vary from album work to commercials and film scores. It's not just rock 'n' roll in this game. The session person confirms that they can come in, goes into the studio when needed, and records exactly what the band and producer want. The more established they are, the more input they can have. When the session's over, our chum goes home. Easy as that: no having to look

BACKING SINGER/MUSICIAN

tonsils of steel. 'One bit of work will lead to other things. A producer heard what I did, and asked, "Can you do harmonies?" I happened to be in the right studios at the right time.'

Beverley has since worked with trillions of folk, including Bill Wyman, Jamiroquai, Eurythmics, Chaka Khan; and Gary Barlow and Robbie Williams when they went solo. She thinks the key to a good backing singer is to be as flexible as possible. A wide vocal range is needed – 'the bigger the better' she says. To be successful you probably have to have what she calls a 'nondescript' voice which won't stand out too much, because you have to blend in: you can't intrude with throat-throttling gusto when the lead vocals are being sung by some lily-livered band member who couldn't blow out a birthday candle.

'I can do nondescript, but I get hired because of how I sound as well,' says Skeete, who also does lead-vocal gymnastics on house records. 'But the skill is mostly in learning how to take a back seat.'

A lot of backing singers want to be lead singers and get frustrated when Ms Lily Liver can't reach beyond three notes and they could sing everyone into buying swimsuits at Christmas. Sometimes you have to lay down the track so the singer can sing over the top, you fill in the cracks, as it were – you ape the singer's voice. A bit of a cheat, eh? Even though your part might be harder, doing harmonies and **multiple tracking**, you have to be humble.

However, this anonymity has its benefits. Yes, it really does. When you're on stage nobody is looking at you and thinking the B flat was a bit

hunky on a record sleeve or anything. Smashin'.

Beverley Skeete started doing trainee accountancy when she left school, for she thought that a life of sums would be for her. Singing was an accident. Her sister-in-law mentioned that she was a great friend of a singer who ran a record shop. He was making a single, asked her to sing, and thought she sounded pretty good. She sang backing vocals on his record.

'It's like when you go to a shop to buy one thing, and you end up buying lots of things,' says Beverley, who has iffy. You can do those funny backing-singer dances, giggle a lot, and wear something saucy. Backing singers always look like they're having a lot more fun than the stars, anyway. Some backing singers were lead singers once upon a time, and enjoy the pressure-free 'ba-ba-ba's much more than spotlight duties.

Session singers have to have a good ear, so playing an instrument helps. The job involves making up harmonies at the drop of a hat, because no one else has a clue. You have to get to places on time, smile, and be prepared to go over things again and again. Having said that, you can go into a studio and do twenty minutes' work. Skeete is used to this: 'Sometimes with house music they'll sample one "Yeah baby!" and that's all they want.'

Backing singers are often replaced by fancy models on video shoots. It happens all the time, and it can be annoying if you see someone else there doing your job. It's not exactly truthful, is it? 'I used to get annoyed,' says Skeete. 'But I recognise if you're making house records you're selling to a certain type of audience. If you want to sell records to five- or six-year-olds, then it's very unlikely they're going to use you. And, with videos, you're escaping a fate worse than death. You get paid a pittance and you have to stand there at six o'clock in the morning, half-dressed and freezing. I'd rather they get models.'

The most stressful part of being a freelance session musician is the erratic nature of the work. You can have no work for weeks or find yourself involved in risible and farcical projects (a Bob The Builder album, for instance). You get no sick pay or holi-day, and often don't know what job is coming up next. Just to make things even better, basic rights, like being paid every time your video is shown on the telly, are also slowly being eroded by the new contracts coming in for session work. This is the toughest part of the job: not having a regular wage, and having the rights that you did have taken away.

Some say session earnings are lower than they used to be and, when a band uses more than seventeen musicians on one session, the record company pays no more in total than the Musician's Union rate for seventeen persons. However, this is balanced out by a change whereby the rules on the use of samples are getting tougher, which means that vocalists are more likely to be paid when a band nicks a line or two from an old song. Such minute shifts in the balance of power are watched like hawks by session people – to them it can mean the difference between poverty and swanky living.

As a session musician, naturally, the amount of work you receive will also depend largely on the instrument you play. Guitars rarely go out of fashion, but trumpets are hip only every other decade, and didgeridoo players may well find they need a back-up instrument for those lean spells. You will also find competition fierce – many session musicians were previously in signed-up bands and moved into session work when their major project failed to make it big.

Tim Weller has been a session drummer for over a decade, working with types including Death in Vegas, Black Box Recorder, Paul Young, Alison Goldfrapp and Aqualung. He learned the drums at school from the age of eleven, but always eschewed the notion of being in a band, preferring to play with different groups.

'I was into bands when I was twelve, thirteen,' he says. 'But then I started noticing how the same guy would be credited on the backs of various albums. Ian Paice drummed with Deep Purple, then Whitesnake, then Gary Moore. It was the same with Cozy Powell – he was *the* rock drummer. That these people moved from band to band seemed much more glamorous than staying put. I thought musically it would be more interesting.'

Tim worked with a few local bands until he saw an advert in the now-defunct *Melody Maker* for a drummer; the band had a deal with Tony Visconti's Unique label. Tim knew Visconti's work as Bowie's producer. 'I was impressed meeting him, but I was very young and I wasn't very good. He was suitably unimpressed with me and I got fired.'

Tim decided to take some lessons and practise. Wise move. He got into the mindset of the session type. It was all about attitude.

IF THE BAND LIKE BEER, YOU DRINK BEER.

IF THE BAND LIKE HAMBURGERS, YOU EAT HAMBURGERS.

'You might not be the most virtuoso musician in the world, but you have to be a good enough player to do the job, the best person to have around, reliable, sober, your equipment works and you don't try and sleep with the singer's girlfriend. You *behave*.'

You also have to have a certain humility.

'When you start playing an instrument it's tempting to *play out* all the time. You're showing off, but *everyone* will hate it. That's the biggest part of the learning curve. The irony is that you spend ages practising technical and fancy stuff, but when you get out into the real world of working no one wants to hear that, they just want you to groove along. And rightly so. You have to learn the discipline of what to play and what not to play, and always remember that you are backing someone else, not soloing.'

Tim can't think of a record that has ever graced the top forty which included a drum solo in it. But nor has there been one where there were no drums on it (not that we can think of, apart from songs sung by schoolchildren. Answers on a postcard etc. etc.)

It's a difficult area to get into unless you have contacts. Bands employ people whom they know, or who are recommended by people they know. Over the years you'll find you get more and more work, and steadier jobs. Once a band does like you, they'll take you on tour worldwide, treat you to the finest hotels, invite you to cheese 'n' Chablis parties, and remember your birthday. You get to the stage where you can be choosy and decide not to work for some types, or take time off because the money you make is good when you are working. One of the most important things is that, while you're versatile, you must know your limits.

'You have to be quite well versed in a few musical idioms,' says Tim, getting a bit technical. 'But the idiom is like a language, there's a different vocabulary associated with each one. When you're young you really think you can play any style of music. Yeah, you can order a beer in most languages, but having three hours of fluent conversation is a bit harder. But if you're honest, and don't always accept every gig, it tends to come back on you in a good way.'

One well-respected session man, who prefers not to be named so he won't get in trouble with any bigwig employers, played trumpet in a chart band in the 80s. He was spotted playing live by someone who needed a **brass player**. The band were sliding down the ladder of success, and Mr Anonymous got two good sessions. 'Once you get one good job, more follow,' he reckons.

Our Mr Anon is paid a retainer by his major employer, which means they reserve the right to use him whenever they like, and he is given a minimum weekly wage so he doesn't swan off with some other group. He used to play with loads of bands, mainly pop acts, but is now restricted to one thing. He's doubly in the pink because the band he works for have a fair few members, who are often off making solo records and need his trumpeting skills for their work. They like him; he likes them. A good situation to be in. However, he does find that he has to play the game and fall in with their rules.

'You have to be reasonably tolerant,' he says. 'Some bands want to do certain things like getting you to go out clubbing with them, for instance. Others want everyone in bed by ten o'clock. You have to suss that out because, if

you don't, then you can get into trouble. You're there to please the artist.'

Bands might like you to look smart, or they might like you to wear a chicken costume. The main trick is getting on with people. If they don't like Marmite backstage, you don't like Marmite backstage. But the difference between you and the band is, according to Tim, that 'you're only ever as good as your last gig. If you do a great show, and the next day the rest of the band want to get coked out of their faces, it'll screw up your performance and you won't do what you're being paid to do.'

But when you do bond, the job is obviously much more satisfying, both personally and professionally. Playing live is the musician's most enjoyable '**buzz**' and you may even get the chance to do a couple of super guitar licks. You've seen those gigs when someone simply announced as 'Mr Funkeee Leeroy on the AXE!' plays some Godawful guitar solo while grinning like someone who's got a lemon in his mouth. It's quite an embarrassment, but session musicians live for those moments. That's **jelling**, man.

Mr Anon also believes things have changed. The record companies don't pay session stars as much as they used to because they don't respect the session musicians, he claims, unlike bands and their management. However, our friend loves the job. It has many pluses.

'It can be a long career,' he says. 'And you can jump ship at any time. If you're with a band that's going down, you think: Crikey! It's going pear-shaped – and you leave that artist. The lifestyle is quite privileged, though – you get the good bits of being a pop star but you don't get recognised.'

GLOSSARY

● **Harmonies**

Playing or singing a musical phrase which tonally complements the main melody line. Pretty obvious.

● **Multiple tracking**

When more than one vocal line is recorded. You can record as many as you want, including harmony lines, and it sounds like a choir. Often used in pop records.

● **Brass player**

All trumpets, trombones and bugles are brass instruments. The saxophone was possibly the most common brass instrument on 80s pop records.

● **'Buzz'**

State of excitement. Sometimes there's a buzz about a band, or a singer. That means they're it, man.

● **Jelling**

Bonding, all coming together in a musical way. Yes, it's often live when this happens.

SKILLS YOU'LL NEED

Being able to play an instrument or sing, not having too much ego, discipline, good time-keeping, being friendly.

TIPS

● Learn an instrument properly if you want to play; invest in some singing lessons if you want to sing.
● Offer to use your skills with local bands.
● Playing on friends' demo tapes will get you heard by producers and the like.
● The Musicians' Union and Equity, the actors' and singers' union, has legal guidelines session people should follow.

USEFUL ADDRESSES

● Musicians' Union, 60–62 Clapham Road, London, SW9 0JJ
TEL 020 7840 5534
FAX 020 7840 5599
WEBSITE www.musiciansunion.org.uk
● Royal Philarmonic Orchestra, 16 Clerkenwell Green, London, EC1R 0QT
TEL 020 7608 2381
FAX 020 7582 9805
WEBSITE www.rpo.co.uk
● Session Connection, PO Box 46307, London, SW17 0WS
TEL 020 8871 1212
WEBSITE
www.thesessionconnection.com

BOOKING AGENT

MONEY: £13,000 p.a. to loads, if you are head of your own company.

HOURS: 10 a.m. to 7 p.m. and out to see bands in the evening. It just never stops, basically.

HEALTH RISK: 2/10. Unless you keep falling over the steps at the Barfly.

PRESSURE RATING: 6/10. If you book Justin Timberlake into the Dog & Gherkin in Doncaster you may have a few problems. Tempestuous artists are often a bit picky.

GLAMOUR RATING: 2/10. Unless you're helping out The Rolling Stones and become their mate and they invite you on their cruiseliner with P Diddy and 45 elaborate cakes.

TRAVEL RATING: 3/10. Yes, it's the Bath Moles Club again, or perhaps Leicester's Princess Charlotte. Hm.

A booking agent gets the right gigs for individual bands and deals with the smooth running of tour schedules in venues from pub rooms to stadiums.

A band plays the Badger and Pineapple a couple of times. They've had a single out and had several letters from Warrington revealing a small army of fans. They've got a new single out soon, which contains a nifty recorder solo, and they want to shout about it. What they need is a tour.

Booking agents are the people responsible for booking a band's dates at the right venues on their whirlwind exploration of the glamorous sites of musical history. You can help fledgling, excited new artists spend every night playing the 'toilets' of Great Britain. Or the stadiums, obviously. All depending on what you, as their booking agent, deem suitable.

There are around five major booking agencies who 'sign up' bands they think will be **hot to trot on the live scene**. A lot of bands are relatively experienced in the trotting business and may not have a record contract. Agents are getting into bands earlier and earlier, and thus have to court managers etc. because there's so much competition. Usually the booking agent will provide the band with an income that is separate from the income that a record-company advance gives. However, the record company are the bigwigs who decide how many dates should be played and all that malarkey.

If the job is done properly, say booking agents the world over, a tour will always be tied up with the marketing process. This means that there'll be an album to promote, a single out, and someone will have actually checked that the band aren't just playing cover versions of wildlife-programme themes (unless that's what they usually do, of course). A tour can also coincide with **in-store appearances**, local-press articles and, erm, other stuff that the

BOOKING AGENT

all your bother. With the many summer European festivals, wot pay a lot of money, it is vital to ensure that any bands taking part have a contract with the promoters and that everything is above board. In virtually every case, if artists don't sign a contract they don't get paid, and issuing these is something that only the very professional booking people can do really well.

Booking agents also scout for bands, by attending gigs and standing at the back with people like lawyers and journos. There's a lot of competition to get the top new acts, and so you need to have an idea of what people want to go and see, as well as **how to make the hi-hat less toppy**.

Many people who become booking agents, or get into the touring side of the music industry in general, come from student unions. Being entertainments officer is good practice for all this sort of thing.

There is one exception to the above way of working: when trying to break a new act, the record company may pay to get the artist a support slot on a tour. They'll fork out up to £5,000 to ensure that their new band gets to play to a large audience first time around, and bypass the whole booking agents' talent-spotting procedure. This is rare, though, and only a pop idea. Genuine indie types have no truck with this. Agents have to understand that indie, pop and rock all appeal to different people, and book the tours appropriately. A successful tour is congratulation enough. And you might get to stand in the same room as Someone Who Used To Be In Gene at an aftershow party.

record company makes sensitive artists do which makes them turn to heavy drinking.

'We're the bit in between,' says our person from a booking agency, who is shy and doesn't want to reveal her name. 'There's always some debate as to whether a booking agent is superfluous. If you're a smaller band it's vital to have an agent. We can wangle them a **support tour**.'

A booking agent also protects young bands from 'dodgy promoters and ropey venues'. Not every promoter is a nice, smiling chap in a windcheater who'll give out free crisps. Some are money-grabbing scumbags who'll try to charge bands a load of money for gracing their wobbly stage with their presence. As booking agent, you'll send such wide boys off with a flea in the proverbial ear.

As an agent, you'll ensure that bands get paid for each gig they play, then take 10–15 per cent of their fee for

GLOSSARY

● **Hot to trot on the live scene**
Rather good at wowing an audience –
making them dance, sing or clap
along. Many bands build up a loyal
'live' following after only a couple of
singles – and sometimes even before
they have a major release (e.g. Suede,
Oasis).

● **In-store appearances**
Whereby a band goes to an HMV
store, sits behind a wobbly table and
signs copies of their new release.
Either that, or else the odd midnight
'gig' at which a band plays three songs
off a new album on the day before it's
released, and all of the drunken
people in the audience get to appear
on Sky News the following morning.

● **Support tour**
A tour – nationwide or worldwide –
by a band playing as 'special guests' of
the headlining band. People spill lager
over each other during their set as the
band flail sensitively but are
sometimes ignored.

● **How to make the hi-hat less
toppy**
One of the profoundest conundrums
in the realm of recorded sound. The
hi-hat – a cymbally-drum thing –
either sounds 'toppy' or 'bottomy' and
absolutely never 'right in the mix'.

SKILLS YOU'LL NEED

An eye for the next live sensation;
organisational abilities; an
understanding of the current live
scene, man; a mistrust of promoters
(in case they're dodgy); obliviousness
to standing in a pool of cider while
watching some losers try to play their
instruments.

TIPS

● If you're at university, approach
student-union entertainments and
offer to help out.
● Managing a local band might help
you get to know the local venues and
the art of booking a good night.
● See as many bands as possible.
Writing for a college magazine/local
paper helps with getting freebie
tickets.

USEFUL ADDRESSES

● Asgard Promotions, 125 Parkway,
London, NW1 7PS
TEL 020 7387 5090
FAX 020 7387 8740
● International Talent Booking, Ariel
House, 74a Charlotte Street, London,
W1T 4QH
TEL 020 7379 1313
FAX 020 7379 1744
WEBSITE www.itb.co.uk
● Primary Talent International, The
Primary Building, 10–11 Jockey's
Fields, London, WC1R 4BN
TEL 020 7400 4500
FAX 020 7400 4501
WEBSITE www.primary.uk.com
● Solo Agency, 1st Floor, Regent
Arcade House, 252–260 Regent Street,
London, W1B 3BX
TEL 020 7009 3361
FAX 0870 749 3174
WEBSITE www.solo.uk.com
● Value Added Talent Agency,
1 Purley Place, Islington, London,
N1 1QA
TEL 020 7736 5925
FAX 020 7226 6135
WEBSITE www.vathq.co.uk

CATERER

MONEY: From around £12,000 p.a. to loads if you run your own catering company. Especially if you run it from home and have no office overheads.

HOURS: If you're on tour or at a video shoot you can start at 6 a.m. and go on through the night providing bacon butties for all. Even if you're preparing a posho meal for an awards ceremony, you'll be up the markets at dawn with your string bag.

HEALTH RISK: 9/10. You could scald yourself, set fire to your hands, poison yourself, or fall into a freezer. So, very dangerous, really.

PRESSURE RATING: 7/10. Getting grub to the table on time in cramped conditions, for people who think their basslines are the best thing ever, can be a little tiresome.

GLAMOUR RATING: 4/10. You do a lot of washing-up, even if it is for Paul McCartney.

TRAVEL RATING: 10/10. You never stop! Those smashing European tours, holed up in a tour bus for days. Those British tours, holed up in a Transit next to a portable fridge that's leaking. Mm-mm.

Cooking food for band and crew is ever such big business nowadays, and there are specific companies that cater solely for the entertainment industry. Everyone needs grub, after all.

Catering can be as impossible as it is rewarding. It can be impossible to satisfy the demands of the fussy pop star who, to all intents and purposes, is five years old and has decided not to eat anything beginning with the letter B. It can be rewarding, consequently, to see said pop star tuck into a large plate of bananas 'n' beans.

Caterers are employed by the band management to provide food for the artist and crew during video shoots and on tours. There are thirty companies who deal exclusively with the whims of the music and TV/film industry. So, if you like food and enjoy hearing people discuss how bottomy the hi-hats are on the single or during the encore, this could be your pigeon.

Catering firms employ chefs who've already had some training. Colleges provide basic catering courses which give you a shiny City and Guilds qualification if you get through the rigorous egg-boiling exams. Finding work at a restaurant or a local catering company will help a lot. Ringing up Rock Scoff Ltd and getting your mum to tell them how good your bubble and squeak is will not do the trick. These people want a proper CV.

Tony Laurenson is the MD of Eat To The Beat caterers – one of the first music-business catering companies to spring up in 1984 (before then your John Lennons had to run to the corner shop to get a pie before a sell-out arena show). And yes, people do apply for jobs at his company thinking they'll be drinking Hooch with Katie Melua instead of cooking up a mean gnocchi.

'It happens on occasion,' he says, 'but we're quick to discover them. We don't put people out on tour before we know what they're like. We try them out for a few weeks here first. Being on tour you're with the band all the time and become part of a family. Personality is almost as important as being able to cook.'

But it's not all fun with lentils. You also have to wash up, buy the food and cart around portable hot cupboards and fridges. Eat To The Beat also deal with the band's **rider** and so have to lug cans of Hofmeister up to dressing rooms. Plus, you have to deal with pop stars. Some of them are vegan, some macrobiotic, some only want halal food and others want three portions of everything. Some don't like eating at all. Kylie's not going to

CATERER

trouble her caterers for more rice pudding. Mark Owen, from Take That, is a vegetarian but has admitted he 'doesn't really like food'. The elfin French chanteuse Vanessa Paradis once pulled out of an interview because she was ill, and the PR admitted the only foodstuff she would allow herself was sweets, hence the sudden collapse. Meat Loaf obviously doesn't have that problem. You have to deal with this sort of caper on a daily basis and it ain't easy.

Catering companies send two or three chefs to accompany a band on tour. Eat To The Beat also carry their own equipment with them, including cumbersome fridges, etc., as **venues** have notoriously poor facilities and sometimes don't even run to a sink. Washing-up has been known to take place in the shower.

As a music caterer you'll have to know your crème caramel from crème anglaise and keep abreast of current cooking trends. 'When we started we made things like shepherd's pie, because it was about quantity rather than quality,' says Tony. 'It was a success just to get a meal out. Now, in this marketplace, it's far more competitive.'

You need to be able to produce a cut-price tuna swirl that's accessible to both the lowliest roadie and the poncey guitarist who is getting into fine cheeses. Eat To The Beat provide mushroom cassoulet and veal peppercorn terrine to such diverse folk as Daniel Bedingfield, Whitesnake, UB40 or Duran Duran. They also deal with supplying **after-show** party drinks, and cater for festivals and all the hungry crew there. It's nonstop – breakfast, lunch and dinner. Plus snacks. And drinks.

Tony Laurenson says it's worth paying the cash for a caterer because the band stays 'fit and healthy and can perform six shows a week, rather than three, which pays for the catering'. This means there'll always be a job for a good chef and everyone thinks they can be a Jamie Oliver these days – Eat To The Beat receive one CV per day and try out all promising people. So that's OK, then.

GLOSSARY
● **Rider**

Order of food and booze for the artists' dressing room. All bands have a rider per night when they go on tour. They all complain it's not big enough, then their so-called friends come into the dressing room and nick it all for themselves. Indie band Smog have Monster Munch on their rider. True.

● **Venues**

No, you don't have a special place to cook in: you have to make do in a back room near the electricity meters. You don't have a banqueting hall to eat in, either.

● **Aftershow**

Party after a gig and usually a byword for free beer and top gossip. People go to aftershows and talk about other people in the room without wanting them to hear. Then they fall over and 'go on' somewhere else. 'Going on' is very music business.

SKILLS YOU'LL NEED

Being able to cook; being able to cook under pressure; being able to cook for people who'll have tantrums if there's anything red on the plate; being able to stand all that bacon that the road crew will want every mealtime (and for snacks); being fit – to carry all that grub and bottles of booze; not getting car sick.

TIPS
● Go to catering college to learn your trade.
● Try working at a local restaurant.
● Practise on your friends – invite thirty around and see how you get on.
● Practise with your mum or dad.
● Don't become a caterer just because you want to poison Ocean Colour Scene. You'll be found out and go to jail. Even though you may feel it's still worth it.

USEFUL ADDRESSES
● Eat To The Beat, Studio 4–5, Garnet Close, Watford, Herts, WD24 7GN
TEL 01923 211702
FAX 01923 211704
WEBSITE www.eattothebeat.com
● Saucery Catering, Watchcott, Nordan, Leominster, Herefordshire, HR6 0AJ
TEL 01568 614221
FAX 01568 610256

CLUB DJ/REMIXER

> 💰 **MONEY**: Bundles. Although fees can start at a few hundred quid, they have been known to leap to around £5–10,000 for one single remix, although rates are a lot lower than they were at their height in the late 90s.
>
> 🕐 **HOURS**: 12 midnight to 6 a.m. – that sort of nocturnal living.
>
> ➕ **HEALTH RISK**: 6/10. You might accidentally scratch yourself with a stylus.
>
> **PRESSURE RATING**: 6/10. Making sure the floor is full of jostling torsos ... That's about it, really.
>
> 🍸 **GLAMOUR RATING**: 6/10. You get to sit in dank clubs with other DJs.
>
> ✈ **TRAVEL RATING**: 8/10. Nipping up the country, to Europe and Japan and wherever else, to DJ those stormin' beats.

The top club DJ swizzles round other people's tunes, plays tunes to people in tight tops and writes his/her own stuff a bit.

Remixer/producers are now an established breed. Time was, back in the early 80s, when a swish US producer from the New York or Chicago House scenes might dabble with a chum's tune and give it a porkier beat. This was rare, or reserved for very special releases. By the mid 80s 'extended version' twelve-inch singles were quite common, and white soul bands and fluffy pop groups commissioned fancy types to extend their records by putting a drum solo in them. Then the **indie-dance crossover** 'revolution' made dancing more mainstream again, and types like Paul Oakenfold remixed records so he could play them at his DJ nights. The record companies of the original artist would get wind of this and ask him to release them. Now remixes are standard, if not a little passé in rock circles. No single is complete without some trendy type in bangin' trainers cutting 'n' pasting, swizzing 'n' switching different bleepy sounds and making the hi-hats, that were once so very toppy, very bottomy indeed.

Remixers used to be able to sneeze on a record and make a mint. For sitting in a studio half the night eating chips and talking about the football, then just removing the guitar bit from a chorus, they used to rake it in. But now (at the time of writing) the music industry has Less Money and it's not such an easy ticket. However, if you're a name DJ you will be asked to do remixes and get to go to swanky parties. Perhaps you'll appear in a reality TV show, or release your own compilation CDs like Tim 'Eyebrows' Westwood, as he's not known.

'Most of us are quite ugly, boring people,' says Rollo, the man behind Felix's massive anthem 'Don't You Want Me', who regularly remixes types such as Bjork, The Pet Shop Boys, Donna Summer and Gabrielle – he is also the publicity-shy guiding light of dance band Faithless. 'You sacrifice a huge amount when you're a DJ remixer or producer. You drive to DJ at three or four gigs at the weekend then see loads in the week, and spend the rest of your time in the studio. You don't get to see films, read books, or see people. The idea that we're supercool human beings is rather misguided . . .'

Rollo went travelling the world in 1990 and met up with a keyboard player in Australia a year later. They made a series of demos together then met producer, Martin Thomas, by chance at a party.

'We hassled him till he just said "ring me" to fob us off.' Rollo rang him four times. Mr Producer had just started going out with a model who wanted to be a singer and said that he'd help them record their tunes if she could sing on them. They soon found out that the bird just couldn't sing. Nonetheless, Rollo and chum got a record deal from the vocal-less tunes they made. If you're involved with a name producer, someone whom record companies have heard of, they will automatically assume that you're the tops – whether you are or not.

Rollo got cold feet after he landed his Australian deal and decided to move back to London with his **advance money** and set up a studio with another mate. They got together a sampler, a module, and a couple of keyboards, and hoisted the lot into Rollo's bedroom. From that came Felix's 'Don't You Want Me', which sold two and a half million copies worldwide.

This, however, is a rare case. Many dance producers are studio boffins who've been hanging around sequencers for years making hip-hop

sounds and getting very little recognition. Roni Size, for instance, the 1997 Mercury Music Prize winner, has been going for several thousand centuries and remembers Pompeii before it was cast in lava.[1] Is Howie B still making records? Probably, but he has slunk back to from whence he came, hitwise. However, once you do have a big hit around the world, and penetrate the upper echelons of the US charts, you are probably a millionaire, so long as you hold the publishing rights to your tunes.

Dance music caused a mini-revolution in the music world, with many people setting up their own home studios cheaply and creating their own tunes. The big studios have suffered because of the wider availability and cheaper price of new technology. More people have a home set-up than ever before, and everyone knows someone who's got a pair of decks. Play your tunes to someone friendly at one of those vibey, independent labels that are called things like Bangin' Trainers and wahey! If you're good enough you can release stuff – just persevere. Or, save some money and put out your own record. People are more convinced when they see product, whatever label it's on. What matters is you like music – dance types are quick to spot impostors who look like they're in it for the free flights to festivals in Norway. Label mates might ask you to remix their tunes, and so the fun begins. Be aware that everyone donates their services for free at the start. It's all for the experience and the love of it, youngsters.

After the Felix hit, Rollo was

1. Not entirely true

immediately besieged with requests to remix this and twiddle with that. The general procedure is that the record company will ring you, the label, or your management up, and pop a tape in the post for you to hear the original song to see if you're interested in making a remixed version. Many record companies try out people they think will be good producers for up-and-coming bands by giving them test remixes – in the dance world, even when artists have already had a massive hit, there's still the danger it could have been just a one-off.

'When we agree to do a remix,' says Rollo, who works closely with fellow Faithless member and DJ, Sister Bliss, 'it's because there's something about the track which we like.' They attempted a Spice Girls remix once, but couldn't get into it and had to waive their fee.

According to Rollo, there are two kinds of dance producer.

'One is a technical producer and, at the other extreme, there are people with untrained ears. Technical producers are hired for pop groups and are employed to make a sound for a particular market. I'm the other sort of producer: I don't have the patience or the

knowledge to make a track fit into a specific genre. I go with what I like.'

That's the difference between your more underground sounds, **man**, and your professional dyed-in-the-wool producer. The latter tend to work with bands they like, and often work with engineers who do the fiddly bits so they can be more personally friendly with the band. Rollo, on the other hand, finds bands 'problematic' because the process is far more diplomatic and the drummer is always having to have her/his say. He leaves the DJing to Sister Bliss, who is world-renowned for spinning the wheels of steel.

Top-flight DJs do not earn as much as they did in the heady days of the late 90s. There is not so much money about, and the cult of the DJ grows less as there are more and more DJs. However, if you get any EasyJet plane to Ibiza at any point in the summer season you'd be forgiven for thinking that the world is made up entirely of disc-spinners, such are the numbers on every flight. Oh look, Mr C! Hey, Andy Weatherall! Blocko!!! Argh!!! etc.

DJ REMIXER

Trance type Paul Van Dyke, who has made four albums and DJed all over the world, has tips on what makes a good DJ.

'You must have a very clear idea about your own sound, and be confident in the music that you play ...' he says. 'You have to interact with the crowd.'

He loves it when he's playing (even though he rarely uses decks – he has everything stored on a laptop) to an eager audience. As a DJ you get the same adrenalin as when you're singing or, er, dancing in front of a huge crowd. 'The feeling you have when it's working – it's so exciting,' says Paul. 'It's the payback for the schedule.'

Van Dyke, who lives in Berlin, runs around from airport to airport almost every day – he never stops. He is In Demand. He wears Posh Clothes. All this from buying a faulty pair of decks from a fleamarket when he was a teenager.

Beavering away on your decks is a good start, but you have to be dedicated – you have to practise how to mix, or you won't make the grade. Another way of getting your face around, as it were, is to loiter around friends' studios, or friends of friends' studios.' Sister Bliss first met Rollo when she came down to a studio where he was working. She 'criticised everything', mentioned she played keyboards, then the next time Rollo was stuck for a keyboard player she drove from Cornwall to join the session. Such dedication can pay off. Rollo has likewise signed to his label a chap called Skinny who hung about and was able to prove his drumming skills when someone didn't show up for another session.

Rollo's ultimate dream is to semi-retire in a few years' time and produce two albums a year. As long as sampling hasn't been replaced by knitting as the nation's coolest pastime, he could be in with a chance. The opportunities are there on every level.

'If you're a DJ, your whole job is to find a hot new record and play it, and that's how you get kudos,' says Rollo. 'Kids in their bedroom are producing stuff all the time and dance music is essentially self-perpetuating. If you're good at what you do,' he concludes, 'you will get discovered and bankrolled, whether you're from Essex or Nigeria or wherever. You only need to make one good record and everyone starts talking about you. Oh, and the other factor is that you can make lots of money after years of suffering.'

GLOSSARY
● **Indie-dance crossover**
Early-90s movement which is also called 'baggy'. Lots of surly indie types decided that dancing was good again and got matey with DJs.
● **Advance money**
The money which artists are paid when they sign a record deal. It is effectively lent to artists by the record company.
● **Man**
Contrary to what you might think, musicians and producers still use this term of affection/punctuation in everyday speech. Especially if they 'smoke'. Ahem.

SKILLS YOU'LL NEED
Initiative and a bit of guts, perseverance, patience when the hi-hats are still too toppy, the art of looking slightly aloof, a vague bit of technical knowledge.

TIPS

● The Prince's Trust can provide grants for arts projects if you're under 25. It may be worth contacting them for studio time and/or equipment money if you're serious.

● Magazines like *Future Music* explain new developments in studio technology and have details on home studios and good equipment on the market. Ace.

● Potential DJ-types will spend a lot of time in record shops listening to the latest imports and meeting useful contacts. Er, other DJs.

● Hang around mates' studios and try to meet up with people who have bedroom studios to get tips from them. Perhaps you might try slyly mentioning your great keyboard/mixing skills.

● Start DJing at friends' parties. Practice is always essential, and your name will get around. No, it will.

● If you're cool and have already done all of these things, remember to walk around looking a bit surly. Propagate that mystique. Man.

USEFUL NUMBERS

● The Prince's Trust, 18 Park Square East, London, NW1 4LH
TEL 020 7543 1234
FAX 020 7543 1200
WEBSITE www.princes-trust.org.uk

● Musicians' Union, 33 Palfrey Place, London, SW8 1PE
TEL 020 7840 5504
FAX 020 7840 5599
WEBSITE www.musiciansunion.org.uk

DIGITAL WHIZZKID

MONEY: 10/10 if you're the new Bill Gates (richest person in the world for the 193rd year running). Starting out might be somewhat harder, but the cost of running a site is relatively small at first if you are keen on word-of-mouth promotion – something the social networking sites have taken advantage of (before being sold for huge amounts).

HOURS: 9/10. Quite a lot of time will be spent running the site, sitting at the screen. Get out for a walk. Pop out for a pint of milk, why don't you?

HEALTH RISK: RSI, anyone? Googly eyes? Server fall on your head? This is not a rock 'n' roll liver-failure type of job (in most cases), but you do have to watch for those new physiological ailments.

PRESSURE RATING: High. Competition in this sector is fierce.

GLAMOUR RATING: Hm. 1/20. Unless Demi Moore walks past your office in the morning, you might be limited to looking up pictures of Kylie on Google in your 'lunch' 'break'.

TRAVEL RATING: Er, 2/10. Travelling to the Internet café when the server's down. And perhaps to see your auntie to shower her with scented soaps wot you have bought with your pots o' cash.

A digital whizzkid sets up and maintains music/social networking sites. This can include working as part of a team for a corporation – to starting your own company using a laptop, a heap of wonderful ideas and a canny vision of the future. You might know some programming but you can always find someone to help ... It's the knack of finding Ye Olde Gappe in the Market which will serve you well. A tall order? It can be done ...

There are many jobs in the varied world of the digital music industry, but most of them will include sitting in front a computer screen for hours on end, a world away from real things like buses, people, trees, shops etc. However, if you are setting up the next Myspace.com – or another similar money spinner – this may only be of minor concern.

This chapter will give you an overview of the way the music business has changed; and a brief insight into how this too has affected bands, managers and the tech genius who wants to make a mint.

The download sector – providing digital music files for consumers to play at home – has grown in stature and credibility in only a few years, and it continues to move on at a frantic pace. Download sales were 20 million in 2005. In 2006 they were 50 million. But what is new technology one season is soon replaced the next. The – ahem – 'digital revolution' has transformed the way people purchase and consume music. Without stepping foot outside the house you can preview the latest songs, buy a whole album – old or new – and watch music videos at the click of a mouse. The instant gratification society is here, and technology is its lapdog. You can have what you want, anytime, if you have the money to pay for it.

Of course, record companies and retailers have been quaking in their boots for many years now – worried that artists can sell their wares direct to fans thus cutting out the need for traditional marketing and manufacture completely. But the bigwigs can rest easy for a while yet. While singles downloads outsell CDs four to one, it is not the same for albums of which downloads make up only 1.4 per cent of sales. For these, consumers still want *product*. The artwork, sleeve, lyrics and extras are important when making a purchase. CDs are considered something of value, to keep – whereas singles are still deemed throwaway. But downloads *have* rejuvenated the pop charts.

The first single to be included in the UK singles chart on download sales alone was Gnarls Barclay's 'Crazy', which was number one in May 2006 – garnering more sales, perhaps, on the hype that it wasn't released on a real, tangible format. (Social commentators might argue that the songs didn't actually exist. The late philosopher Baudrillard and similarly ponderous music journalist Paul Morley would have had a field day.) But it is not *just* hype that keeps a record afloat. In the olden days, records hopped about the top forty – sometimes taking weeks to reach number one then slowly going

down again. Now the pattern is similar as singles enter the charts, leave, then come back again ... simply because the way people buy downloads is different to buying CDs.

The rules changed in April 2005 when legitimate downloads were deemed eligible for the Official UK Singles Chart by the Official Chart Company (formerly CIN – Chart Information Network). On 17 April 2005, Tony Christie and Peter Kay's '(Is This The Way To) Amarillo' was the first chart-topper of the integrated chart (slightly confusingly, the first number one in the Official UK *Download* Chart in September 2004 was Westlife's 'Flying Without Wings').

Anyone with a song which is available to download can reach the top forty, regardless of release date, if enough people have bought it. Chris Moyles from BBC Radio 1 is amused by this randomness. In January 2007 he urged listeners to download Billie Piper's 1999 hit 'Honey to the B', exploiting the new chart system, to see if it would make the top twenty. The following week, it was number seventeen. Gennaro Castaldo at HMV said that Piper's performance showed how it is now 'so easy' for fan groups or the media to propel an old song up the charts: 'It's further evidence of how bit by bit the charts are going to broaden out,' he frothed. It makes Thursday night's *Top of the Pops* and the excitement of new releases 'hitting the top spot' seem a very distant memory.

'Just a few years ago the singles market was on its last legs,' says Tom Wiggins, Online Junior Writer at *Stuff* magazine. 'But with the help of iTunes sales have doubled in the last two years.'

For the uninitiated, iTunes is Apple Computers' music download site, which launched in the US in May 2003 and in the UK, France and Germany in June 2004. By January 2007 the iTunes Store had sold over two billion songs since launch. It has an 80 per cent market share – that's a lot. The iTunes Store currently sells over 5 million songs a day – that's 58 songs a second of every minute of every hour of every day.

Yet you can only download music onto an Apple iPod – no other mp3 player will work with iTunes (for this reason some European countries claim it is trading illegally – a complicated and ever-changing legal issue we do not have time to explore here ...). Steve Jobs, co-founder and CEO of Apple, claims he would gladly change the technology if it wasn't for record companies stressing that this helps protect their artists' copyright. Some might call it an iMonopoly.

DRM – Digital Rights Management – is the way the mp3 is coded to prevent copyright infringement. It means, as hinted at above, that you can only play downloaded tracks on certain equipment. It limits use far more than any other format.

In an updated version of the 'fight' against home-taping, file-sharing has been the industry's bugbear since Napster started in 1999, when it was an illegal site where people swapped tracks without buying them. To cut a long story short, Metallica took the site to court, it eventually folded and a new, legal Napster was launched in 2003. Within that time, iTunes was up and running ...

So what is each UK site's unique selling point? How does the so-called consumer differentiate one virtual record shop from another? Spencer Kelly, from BBC's flagship technology show *Click*, discusses. 'It's like the competition between supermarkets. The price for downloads is the same but some sites work in different ways. Napster has a subscription service. You can download as many songs as you like from its database for a monthly fee but as soon as you cancel your subscription all your downloaded music stops working.'

This is like renting rather than buying your favourite tunes. This suits the dabbler; the fan of a broad range of music. Whereas with iTunes you purchase each song for your iPod and it sits on your computer for a lifetime. (If indeed your computer lasts for such a period.) You can keep the songs forever.

'But what is there to keep?' ponders Kelly. 'A load of zeros and ones ...' Smaller indie sites, such as subscription-based emusic.com, is DRM-free – you can play yer downloads on any device (and keep them, they aren't licensed to you like Napster). The thinking behind it is, perhaps, because indie music needs honest-to-goodness word-of-mouth to promote itself, sharing music is not seen as the most heinous crime. Big acts, conversely, don't *need* that sort of promotion.

Some sites such as bleep.com provide CD-quality mp3s. Other sites offer exclusives: Napster will have an album up to three weeks before release in yer real, actual shop and iTunes might feature acoustic versions of top hits. These important details *do* breed a certain loyalty with the customer. iTunes has already gained a great deal of loyalty, despite the iPod user at the behest of the DRM.

Apart from Sony BMG, who have a roster of global artists and a whole load of people inventing and manufacturing the technology to listen to them with, no record companies have direct investment in the sites. Indeed, it took a long time for the industry to come to terms with online music stores.

Record companies were notoriously uneasy about the whole digital revolution. It took years for the major labels to come to an agreement with iTunes – some would say the mistrust was without real foundation. But when shares in Napster were bought by BMG and the site started to get sued by other majors. 'It all went a bit pear-shaped,' according to one insider. The labels' own subscription sites failed to take off and they were wary of 'giving' tracks away to a third-party online store – hoping that perhaps iTunes might just disappear if ignored for long enough ...

It was the DRM issue which eventually quelled their fears and, at present, there appears to a very happy relationship between record companies and online music stores. But let us stress that there *appears to be*. It all changes in an instant; especially as labels are so paranoid about piracy – and pleasing the shareholders.

Microsoft, never one to miss a trick, has launched Zune in the US, its own online music store and mp3 player. It will soon be launched in the UK. 'It's similar to Apple,' says Tom Wiggins. 'You can only play songs on the Zune player that were bought from Zune marketplace. For a lot of people, it helps if the provider of music is also the provider of the gadget.' Tough competition.

Myspace.com is perhaps the best-known of the 'social networking' sites.

It was launched in 2003 by Tom Anderson and Chris DeWolfe in Los Angeles. Musicians can build up a collection of virtual friends – some of whom they may actually know and others who might just want to post suggestive pictures on their comments page. Myspace (and, to a lesser extent, YouTube.com – where you can see artist interviews and videos online) has radically changed the artist/audience interface. Users can listen to a band's tracks instantly, read the artist's blog, find out when they're playing, keep informed of their new releases and contact them (they might even reply). Now you can buy downloads from artist's own pages.

Garry Boorman is a music biz manager at CEC Management in London, working with such acts as Luke Haines, Ben Parker and Dee Adam. He previously worked as A&R for BMG publishing. He thinks that sites such as Myspace are 'an advert for artists': 'We're always looking for new acts and Myspace is almost a *Yellow Pages* of bands. Within seconds you're hearing their music. You don't have to wait days to get a demo in the post.'

For musicians, this direct link to the outside world is invaluable. Through the contact pages, songwriters such as Dee have been introduced to other writers and producers. 'It's generated a lot of work for her,' says Garry. 'Another of our acts has garnered a fanbase who turn up to all of his shows, purely through Myspace. It's a useful tool.'

The fact that it doesn't cost anything to set up keeps managers and record companies smiling alike. But you have to invest the time going through and adding your virtual 'friends', contacting other like minds and writing your blog. You might not have time for driving up and down the country in a battered Mini, you're spending so much time at the computer.

Boorman is sanguine about what the future holds for record labels. 'Where, in the past, labels would sign, develop and tour bands over a period of time, bands are now doing this themselves. So record companies as we know them today will become marketing companies, waiting for the bands to develop, produce and record their own music, then move in with the big money. It happened with the Arctic Monkeys. They built their fanbase themselves, then took the top dollar.'

This isn't about the end of the record company completely. 'Most people like a big cheque being waved in their face. This will be the label's role – to help with some financial clout. Touring is very expensive, which is where record companies can help. 'But what you may find,' continues Boorman, 'is that the big acts come to the end of their record contract and may say, *we don't need to renew*. This is what Simply Red have done. REM, U2 ... ostensibly they can do it them-

selves. It may well prove difficult for the majors to retain the big-selling acts.'

Much has been made of Arctic Monkeys and Lily Allen's ascent to chart-topping toppingness, thanks to their many 'friends' on the Myspace site. However, now Ver Monkeys are downplaying the role the site had in their success. Could the 'Myspace route' now be a cliché? With Rupert Murdoch's involvement (his company, News Corp, bought Intermix Media, owner of Myspace.com, for $580m [£332.85m] in July 2006), it may lose its credibility as it cannot now pretend that it is *not* a money-making tool for The Man.

'Some people feel it's had its moment,' says Nick Fowler, musician. He plays with bands Goldrush and Tough Love and is a Myspace aficionado. Many users are becoming cynical – rumours are rife that some record labels purchase 'friend adding' software to create that all-authentic 'grass roots buzz'.

Record companies are more reliant on finding acts who have created their own 'buzz'. 'Labels want the finished product,' says Nick. 'To an extent, they are becoming manufacturing and distribution services. Atlantic Records had great success by simply licensing ready-made [already recorded and produced] debut albums from The Darkness and Hard Fi. When the label A&R-ed the second Darkness album it was far less successful.'

Managers trawl Myspace and the web to find new artists. They do not have to charge round the country in an old Datsun. One example is a 'freelance A&R man' in LA who saw the success of New Zealand band The D4

WARNING:
A BIT
LIMITED.

and wanted to find a fledgling version that he could bring to a label. He dutifully typed 'bands, New Zealand' into Google and found Steriogram, an unsigned act. From his office in LA, he got them a record deal with Capitol Records for $650,000. The group had not met anyone from the label until the deal was done and a limo greeted them at LAX to take them to their new label's offices ... They have since been dropped.

What Myspace is good for, reckons Nick, is the live circuit. 'Particularly for bands trying to get gigs and/or gig-swapping. My band, Tough Love, met another through the site and we got them two support slots in London – and we played in Oxford with them. It's good for small bands to get offered gigs directly. While record sales have dropped across the board, a concert in a festival in Turkey or Russia will get you a decent fee.'

Are record companies scared of the power of Myspace? 'They all try and put a brave face on it, saying that these sites are something that they can harness, but the truth is that it will make things more difficult for them.' Others suggest the opposite – the fewer new bands for the record companies to deal with (especially when many bands are so keen to set up their own labels and do everything themselves), the greater emphasis the labels have on their back catalogue – the big sellers. It doesn't cost anything to develop and market old artists – the job has already been done.

Back catalogue is not bad for online music stores. The biggest omission in terms of this is a little-known combo, The Beatles. Apple Corps. (the Fab's company) versus Apple Inc. (the computer persons) went on for years, with yer remaining Liverpudlian moptops battling over the use of the name and logo. Now a settlement has been reached, and the Beatles may soon be available to buy in one click. Speculation is, as they say, rife. 'Then the top ten singles would just be Beatles songs,' says Spencer Kelly, delightedly. Oh no.

The web can't do everything. It can't make your mother a cup of tea, nor can it help with childcare costs (unless you're selling Jimi Hendrix's old toenails on eBay for funds). Internet gigs, while garnering a lot of press (for example, Sandi Thom's notorious 'tour' from her basement), do nothing for the punter.

'It's a tiny picture on screen, and if the "gig" is really popular then the server would be overloaded,' says Kelly. 'You wouldn't be watching a quality picture, it would be jerky, blocky – not high resolution enough. I think that's just a wacky bit of promotion.'

Despite the increase in the popularity of downloads, only 5% of music on the average iPod has been bought from iTunes. People are burning their own CDs. It shows exactly how far behind CDs downloads are. Customers will have to be persuaded. Statistics from Entertainment Media Research claim that 72 per cent people still think CDs have 'more value' than digital downloads.

'There's something about going into a shop,' says Wiggins, 'and looking through a stack of CDs, getting your purchase home, looking through the artwork and seeing who played cello on track four ... They haven't quite got there with downloads – they sometimes offer digital booklets with lyrics and photos, but do you print it all out?'And Lord help you if your printer is a bit rubbish or the paper jams.

So, after this lengthy overview, how do you *become* that digital whizzkid? The Steve Jobs from Apple? The 'Tom' from Myspace? Or perhaps the new Rupert Murdoch? Erk.

'If I knew that I'd be doing it,' says Spencer Kelly. 'These people are my age, they started ten years ago and they spotted potential. You have to be able to predict how people will be using technology in ten years' time. You need to define the trend.'

Hm, doesn't sound that easy, really. But as TV's Duncan Bannatyne would probably inform you, making multimillions is hard work. You may not necessarily need computer skills. Tom Anderson, who co-founded Myspace, has a degree in film from UCLA. When he wanted to cross-promote his indie band Swank on the web, he created the site with friend Chris DeWolfe (who dealt with the business side). With the help of a few web programmers, he was away. Now bands could communicate with each other, share their music and ... oh, you know the rest. Now he is very rich.

The job is not nine-to-five – to be successful you have to work many hours and, perhaps, put your life into it.

The future looks bright for e-commerce (*and* bands who can play the game and self-promote), but competition is cut-throat. If the big companies get it right – that is, supply what users want *and* keep up with the changing pace, man – they can ensure their continued success in this still burgeoning market. Tom Wiggins is sure that the current wrangles about copyright will be solved.

'There will have to be an end to the DRM system, it is and will become too restrictive,' he laments. 'Consumers are not being given a choice. If enough users get annoyed with it, things will change. It's down to people power.'

Another boom market, thinks Wiggins, will be downloads sent direct to your mobile phone. It's very big in Japan, apparently. 'You pay a small fee a week, £1.50 or so, and you get a set amount of songs. The problem at the moment is that data charges for downloads can be very expensive. Some people like to carry round a phone that can do everything, and soon there will be big enough flash drives to hold a decent amount of music.'

Zune, for example, has a feature where wifi is built in – and you can share tracks with your friends by sending files to their phone. You either have it for a few days, or for a certain amount of plays, and after that it expires. 'But most of the time,' adds Wiggins, 'I'm not sure I like a song in that short a space of time.'

Spencer Kelly is not certain that the vast majority of people want a mobile which does everything. 'What do you want your gadget to do? Surf the web? In that case you need a big screen. There are exciting new technologies coming up – screens which roll out like a mat but we're years off that yet. Most people want their phone to make calls and send texts. One gadget doesn't fit all, plus the connection speed on a mobile is just pants.'

One site offers music insurance, in case your files implode or you drop your mp3 player down the toilet. A good idea, *non*? 'Music insurance is a con!' Kelly is riled. 'Back your files up! Or you can copy them to another computer, then if your computer blows up, you can get them back. Also, get an mp3 with flash memory, so if you do drop it, it won't break.'

Sensible advice. What the online music stores need to do to sell albums is make sure they are competitively priced. If you can buy a chart CD from Tesco for £8, it seems a trifle obstinate to sell those tracks online for the same price collectively.

But all this could be grim for commercial radio, thinks Kelly. Once people are playing their mp3s in their car and at work – for an iPod is a ready-made jukebox – there's no need for the more populist radio stations. "And there's no adverts," he comments.

HMV have reported a slump in sales and have revamped their own online store. Other UK retailers such as Woolworths – part of whose core business is CD sales – have also reported a dive in retail sales. Could this be the end of the record shop, with iTunes, Amazon and Play.com all in the top ten of 'e-tailers'?

Creation Records head Alan McGee, writing for the *Guardian* newspaper online, is vehemently pro the new technology. The last record shop he visited, he says, 'felt like a museum. All the music I want I can get off Amazon or go on MySpace to hear. There's no real need for record shops any more ... As for MTV, YouTube has destroyed it,' he continues later. 'I can't even remember when I last watched it. Why would you, given that everything appears on YouTube within a day of it

being broadcast? I feel more love for my iPod than the CDs I buy,' he concludes, ever a man who can face the future.

EMI Records, too, has recently reported a sales dip and other labels are feeling the pinch. The company blamed 'continued and accelerating deterioration in market conditions in North America where, in the calendar year to date, the physical music market ... has declined by 20%'. However, in the UK market things ain't *so* bad – for the short term. Flagging album sales in Britain have been slowed by the emergence of a new wave of British acts, although international sales have continued to plummet.

Steve Jobs never stops. As bigwig at Apple, he likes to get his hands mucky and wade in about a whole heap of things. He oversees everything that Apple do, and likes to comment about his and Apple's role in the global marketplace as much as possible. He published his 'Thoughts On Music' speech in February 2006, trying to address the whole DRM issue. Jobs started at Atari as a technician, back-packed round India in search of enlightenment and came back to Atari. He then co-founded Apple Computer Co. at the age of 21 in April 1976 with Steve Wozniak. (They are, yes, very rich.)

It is certain you need a bit of charisma if you're going to be at the creative 'end' of the process. You need your business-minded mate and some techy pals (to sort out the server etc. and the pages and, um, going 'live') behind you. You need a good idea that yer rivals have not even dreamed about yet. It's not necessary to live in the San Fernando Valley, LA, where all the tech stuff seems to happen – oh no. Friends Reunited (don't laugh) was created in Barnet, North London.

Finally, a word from our insider: 'This is an era of change, to be honest, no one knows what's around the corner. The popular sites are getting very arrogant, and the industry is in flux – some are quite scared. Perhaps the record labels will all get into gaming, leaving bands to do it all themselves. This could be the new punk rock ... or all restrictions on copyright will tighten up and the music business will become even more corporate.'

The problem with copyright and the net

In March 2007, enormo entertainment conglomerate Viacom took out a writ against YouTube – owned by web search engine Google – for $1bn (£517m). It claimed that YouTube used its shows (footage from MTV and Nickleodeon) illegally.

Viacom alleged that about 160,000 unauthorised clips had been uploaded onto YouTube's site by users. The amount of times the clips had been viewed runs into billions, it said. However, Google said it was confident that YouTube has respected the legal rights of copyright holders.

This is just part of the crackdown on unauthorised sharing of content, which reflects the way the record companies swooped on illegal filesharers a few years ago. The problem still is that if someone thinks they can get something for nothing, they're not going to pay for it. The Internet is seen as somewhere you can get a bargain, or indeed something for free. When companies and artists try and enforce copyright – ensuring people are paid for what they do – they are seen as bad eggs. It's an odd situation. We're not throwing clogs into the machines, here. It *is* stealing, kids.

'There is no question that YouTube and Google are continuing to take the fruit of our efforts without permission and destroying enormous value in the process,' said a Viacom press release.

But YouTube argue that through its site, rights holders have 'the opportunity to interact with users; to promote their content to a young and growing audience; and to tap into the online advertising market'. Hm.

DISTRIBUTOR

MONEY: Around £7,000 p.a. for telesales or £6,000 if you work in the warehouse. Can zoom up to £60,000 if you're high up. There is a lot of room for part-time staff.

HOURS: 9 a.m. to 5.30 p.m. in telesales, really early and really late if you work in the warehouse, and then there are gigs and things.

HEALTH RISK: 5/10. You could end up trapped in the warehouse under a pile of cassettes, or in the pressing plant by accident. Argh!

PRESSURE RATING: 7/10. If pressed-up discs don't arrive at your warehouse in time, things can get sweaty.

GLAMOUR RATING: 4/10. You *might* have Aretha Franklin come and check the hole in her new CD is in the middle, but it's a fairly remote possibility.

This is the actual 'getting the product into the shops' job, from liaising with record companies to making sure that HMV has enough copies in all of their stores to sell.

Glamour! Excitement! Swanky high-rise living! These are none of the things that people associate with being in distribution. Yet, obviously, distribution is a completely vital part of the 'Let's sell records' process. Without distribution, the records that you like (and also the ones that you

hate, granted) would be sitting in a cold warehouse with nothing to do. They're not going to the glittering world of shop lighting, in-store displays and listening-posts if no one's there to put them in the shops. Distribution is vital, and the way that it's done is precise and calculated. It's far more interesting than putting a CD in the back of your car and driving around with it. Like any job, it has creative elements to it.

Record companies are in charge of recording and pressing their artists' wonderful tunes, on CD and vinyl – then they have to physically get them into the shops.

A single and/or album is finished, mastered then scheduled for release. The major record companies get their own distribution department to ring up HMV etc., tell them about the hot new product a couple of months (on average) in advance, and get it to them by the release date. Big releases by yer megastars will be scheduled further in advance to plan window campaigns and **racking** – especially if it's Madonna and Beyoncé going head to head. The main difference with independent labels is that they go through their independent distributor.

Susan Rush is the general manager at Pinnacle Records, UK's biggest independent distributor that has been operating since 1986. Susan finds new business, and deals with labels through their label manager. She is the main point of contact between the labels and the sales team, who get the record into the shops. She makes sure the records are scheduled properly: for instance, there should be no debut singles by wee garage skiffle bands released at Christmas – they would simply be swamped by all the big releases and thus never see the right end of the charts.

The lovable non-corporate distribution company will treat a new release as follows. Imagine that a new band, Dowdy And The Bears, has scheduled a release date for their single 'Flippers' on Hairy Records in nine weeks' time. The record label inform the distributor and supply advance copies of the product, and all the information about what the title is, the correct spelling of the artist's name, plus what gigs are coming up, what press they're doing, any telly appearances, etc. The distributor makes sure this information gets to the retailer. The retailers then pore over this sales note, consider the facts, and decide whether they want to put the record in their shops. Believe it or not, the shops can be as fussy as that. If they think a record won't sell very much, for whatever reason, even if the artist is breaking all boundaries of conventional thought and has produced the Theory of Relativity in record form, Mr Important-Record-Shop Owner will still umm and ahh. This 'fussiness' has become a lot more pronounced in recent years, with supermarkets – who now sell records when years ago they didn't – trying to dictate the market, simply because they can offer products at a price far less than conventional record shops – independent or otherwise. There are all sorts of issues to be dealt with.

'Supermarkets have had a massive impact on sales,' says Susan. 'The knock-on effect is that specialist stores have to look at what their stock is selling at, and if they're not competing on price in the way the supermarkets are, they have to come up with a different proposition for the customer. If someone makes that impulse purchase at the checkout in Sainsbury's, what need do they have to go to a record store any more?

'Stores require you to provide them with a record that's going to be sold, that won't sit there on their shelf and gather dust,' she continues. 'They need to be assured there is enough marketing and promotion behind the record.'

Also, the shelf life of records has become shorter and the market has shrunk, according to Susan.

'Sales of back catalogue are increasing – slightly – units are being shifted, but my feeling is that people are buying their favourite artists whose CDs are down to £4.99 or £5.99. You don't see the figures you used to on new artists.'

Hm. The national account manager at the distributor's deals with national retailers: HMV and Virgin. S/he gauges what the retailers make of a record, and reports back to the label. More information is then fed to these retailers over the next few weeks: if there's additional TV and press lined up, any radio interest, if the artist is turning on the Christmas lights in Bolton, etc. Three weeks before release, the final promotion details are given. Then – then – the independent record shops nationwide get a promo CD of the new release.

Pinnacle work with Network, around 250 privately owned indie record shops, but they focus on the 105 'Selecta' stores which have a Pinnacle 'listening post'. Said post holds five album releases which are rotated every fortnight. 'There are fewer and fewer good indie stores now,' says Ms Rush. 'Stores have been closing over the years, the whole area has diminished.'

Pinnacle's **strike force** will drop off promo CDs at these friendly stores so shop manager and staff can all hear the releases properly, tap their indie feet while reading the pertinent information on the sales note, and then order a whole load to sell to smiling revolutionaries who like their rock *on the bone*. All through this process, Pinnacle will report back to the aforementioned Hairy Records (marketing department, label manager, etc.), who need to deliver stock to Pinnacle ten days before the release date. Release dates shift about like nobody's business, so this is always a sticky point.

On the Monday before the week of release, the computer at Pinnacle collates orders – some of which are placed over the phone via the telesales staff; some are emailed or faxed in. From Tuesday morning it's picking and packing: a team scurry around the warehouse, packing the new releases into boxes which then go to the Securicor regional warehouses for in-store delivery on the Friday before the release date. This gives the retailers two days to price up the new product. At that point, the strike force also bung a load of releases on all formats in their cars and hop around to the smaller shops to boast about the **presale** figures and ask whether these stores need any more. They report to the field sales manager (in charge of the sales team) who in turn reports to the sales director. The sales director completes a report which is given to the label manager, who reports to the label. Phew.

The dealer price for a single is set by the label, which can be any amount, although it has to be within certain parameters if eligible for the UK singles chart. A two-track CD single has a minimum dealer price of £1.20. If you have more than two tracks, it's £1.79. There are rules about packaging singles with posters and free guff. The buy-one-get-one-free offers are not so common because the dealer price has been reduced. Some record companies offer up to 50 per cent discount of the price of a single if they want a store to stock, and thus sell, more.

All record labels want their singles to compete price-wise with releases from other record companies, so the indie distributors have to play the subsidy game, or else fight very hard for the retailers to take their records at the proper price – which the stores are loath to do as they'll make less money, having been spoilt by the majors. If you do sell your record at full price, then some wee indie charlie might come along to the record shop with two purchases in mind, but come out with the cheaper one because wee indie charlie can't afford the pricier one as well. It's a hard and really quite unfair game.

Pinnacle receive around fifty tapes and CDs per week from labels seeking distribution. If a label manager thinks the project worth following, they suggest the proposition to other label managers. If they like it and feel they can do something with it, they offer a distribution deal to the label. But it's getting harder for individual artists, according to Rush, to get such a deal.

'It's easier to make records now,' she concedes. 'But it's harder to distribute them, so there's a bottleneck of artists recording their own music at home, without an outlet. The stores haven't got elastic walls, they can't stock everything.'

Currently (and taking as our example June 2004) a record needs to sell around 600 **units** across the counter to get into the top 75. Selling around 3,000 gets you in the top forty. The biggest-selling single in the week beginning 7 June 2004 was Frankee's 'F.U.R.B.' which sold 36,000 at number one. Eamon's 'F**k It (I Don't Want You Back)' sold 55,000 in a previous week at number one. The singles market slumped in 2003 by 30 per cent. The biggest selling single of the year, Black Eyed Peas' 'Where Is The Love?' shifted 625,000 copies. In comparison, UK album sales rose by 7.6 per cent. Dido's *Life For Rent* sold 2.1 million in 2003.

Some people in distribution find that not only do labels frequently fail to deliver the stock in time, but some are unrealistic about sales and blame the sales force if their record doesn't go to number one. Breaking new acts is a bugger, too. The retailers want to have full confidence in a record, and if they've not heard of the act they get sniffy about stocking it. This is where the indie shops come in – they're far more likely to take a chance with new groups because they read

NME and know what's what. If they stock a fine new band who the big shops don't, more cool kids will go to hang out at their funky dive. And no one has to wear an HMV sweatshirt either and read booklets on the consumer–retailer interface.

Vital are the other main independent distributors, although they no longer own their own warehouse. Pinnacle distribute on behalf of Shellshock, Cadiz and New Note – they deal with music right across the so-called board, from Katie Melua to The Strokes; Justin Timberlake to Black Sabbath. They also sign labels and give them either one- or two-year deals or sign them on specific releases. They take a percentage of every unit sold to the shops. The company also sells computer games and DVDs, which has been a growth market (unlike CD singles, as mentioned a million times now, those at the back).

Times they are a changin', as someone once spluttered. It's that ole devil called the Internet.

'It's certainly had its impact,' says Rush. 'The singles market has taken a nosedive. Ringtones can be more expensive but more desirable than buying a CD single. Consumer tastes have changed but, business-wise, if you don't adapt you die.

'The role of the distrib-

To SHOPS — THROUGH DISTRIBUTOR — FROM POP STAR

DISTRIBUTOR

utor is to be the interface between record label and the retailer,' continues Susan. 'Whether that's an Internet retailer or a digital service provider – they're not going to be able to deal with every label face to face, there's always a need for distribution in whatever shape or form.'

You can make a career of distribution. Susan started at a local recording studio while she was at university in Liverpool in the early 80s. She's been at Pinnacle since 1995, starting as label manager.

'It's extremely busy, extremely varied – you just don't know what's around the corner. When you start off with a project you have hopes for it, but then sometimes things just gather momentum. We had Gary Joules's single 'Mad World' at number one for Christmas 2003 when everyone thought The Darkness would get there. It's an exciting time for independent distribution – we've proved many times that it's equal to major record company distribution. We have more flexibility.'

GLOSSARY
● **Racking**
Very important – makes sure your artist is seen in the shops in … a rack. May be racked with similar artists, or that week's new releases or other such concepts.
● **Strike force**
The people who drive around the regions of Great Britain, taking orders from shops. They are better paid than telesales because they have to do lots of legwork.
● **Presale**
The number of records bought by a shop before the record's release. These

figures give an indication of how well the record might do eventually.
● **Units**
A single record is referred to as a unit. 'Shifting units' means selling a lot of records. Sounds heartless, but the industry often is.

SKILLS YOU'LL NEED
All-round knowledge of the industry; firm bargaining skills; communication skills; being able to drive, normally; organisational ability, tidy desk, that sort of thing.

TIPS
● Try working in a record shop to get to know the distribution side. You can meet reps and strike forces and see how they work.
● As in all trades, work experience can be a good way in – call a few distribution firms and see if they need office help. Practical experience is more important than a degree.
● Know your tunes.
● Being able to drive is good for regional reps.

USEFUL ADDRESSES
● Pinnacle, Electron House, Cray Avenue, St Mary Cray, Orpington, Kent, BR5 3JR
TEL 01689 870622
FAX 01689 878269
WEBSITE www.pinnacle-entertainment.co.uk
● Sound & Media, 3rd Floor, Landmark House, Hammersmith Bridge Road, London, W6 9DR
TEL 020 8237 1500
FAX 020 8237 1300
WEBSITE www.soundandmedia.co.uk
● THE, Head Office/Export, Rosevale Business Park, Newcastle-Under-Lyme, Staffordshire ST5 7QT

TEL 01782 566566
FAX 01782 564400
WEBSITE www.3mv.com
● Windsong International, Heather
Court, 6 Maidstone Road, Sidcup,
Kent, DA14 5HH
TEL 020 8309 3867
FAX 020 8309 3905
WEBSITE www.windsong.co.uk

FAN CLUB ORGANISER

MONEY: Either from £4 to £10 per hour, approx, or a full-time wage, if there's a lot of work to do.

HOURS: From a few afternoons a month to full time: again, it depends on the size of the band. But it can be flexible.

HEALTH RISK: 5/10. Impaled by a stapler? Poisoned by the glue on a stamp? Could do too much photocopying and go blind.

EQUIPMENT COSTS: The band's expenses should generally pay for all printing and running costs, or the membership fee might cover it.

PRESSURE RATING: 6/10. The fan club magazine has to be out on time and you have to think of interesting things to write in it, try to keep membership figures up, and get the band to be involved when they'd rather be lazing around swigging pints of stout etc.

GLAMOUR RATING: 4/10. If you like speaking to the drummer's wife on the phone, trying to locate the errant sticksman.

TRAVEL RATING: 6/10. You do spend time addressing envelopes and updating websites but if you're lucky you get flown around the world by a generous group ...

Runs the club that the fans of a particular band join. Sorts out website, membership, postage, newsletters, nice badges and baubles.

There are many routes to becoming a fan club organiser. You might be just a friend of the band, or an experienced administrator. There are both official fan clubs, and not-so-official ones. Anyone can start one up, and charge any sort of price for over-enthusiastic fans to join. However, if you run a crummy, expensive outfit people will wise up to it, won't renew their membership, nor recommend it to anyone else. You've got to be quite good. Few fan clubs make extra cash for the band. Most membership fees cover costs and that's it. It is for fans, after all.

Jacky Smith runs the official Queen fan club with her sister Val. She answered an advert in the *Evening Standard* 23 years ago, when EMI decided they needed someone to run a fan club for a 'top rock band'.

'They didn't put that it was Queen because they didn't want someone who was too much of a fan because they wouldn't be able to do the job,' says Jacky. 'I liked their songs when I was younger, but I wasn't obsessive.'

Jacky had been a production assistant for a film company who made TV commercials. She had experience of administration and co-ordination, so she was right for the job. She inherited thousands of fans (at the fan club's peak in the 80s the membership was 20,000), instantly having to deal with the queries and quandaries of the legions of Queen nutters.

The membership now isn't quite what it was – around 6,000 – because, according to Jacky, 'if you look up

Queen on the Internet there are hundreds of fan-based sites giving out information, and some fans aren't prepared to pay.' But she does have a loyal base of members who, for £15 a year, receive four newsletters a year and get exclusive offers. All the extras in the 'Radio Ga Ga' video were fan club members. When tours are announced by either Brian May or Roger Taylor, the fan club does its utmost to secure the first tickets.

YOU WILL BE ASKED ABOUT BRIAN MAY'S HAIR, FOR YEARS.

The morning we speak, for instance, Jacky has 151 emails to answer – although it has numbered almost 1,000 after the Christmas holiday – and postal enquiries. These range from Brian's shoe size to how to get tickets for the *We Will Rock You* musical.

'These days we don't get many deep and dark queries,' says Jacky. 'People now know so much about them. In the past we had so many people writing, wondering whether Brian does have a perm or whether it's curly naturally, but we put those facts in a flyer.'

The band get sent cuddly toys, T-

shirts, scarves, books and sometimes gifts for their children. Jacky makes sure everything gets sent to the group – she would never dream of nicking anything meant for someone else. However, if one of the band has no need for it, and it's especially nice, they might offer it to her. And still she won't take it!

'We tend to keep them in the office, then put them in charity auctions, saying "Roger wore this" and he'll happily write a letter to say, yes he did.'

Fan clubs start up after there is a sufficient number of people on the band's **database** who've already written to the record company asking for information on the band. There's no point if there are only three fans. As well as doing admin, you need to be able to know the rudiments of website maintenance, so that you can update your pages as often as you need. There have been many more unofficial fan clubs since the advent of the web, because setting up a site is easy, and cribbing facts from other sources is simple too. Official sites have to be wily – access to exclusive information (diaries, special events, concert tickets) must only be available for members only. Ooh, it's a harsh world.

Every fan club will have its fair share of complainers. Someone will always want something more. Jacky finds that the annual convention at Pontins, Presatyn Sands, brings a huge

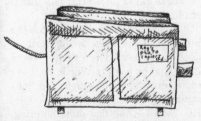

A PHOTOCOPIER, ESSENTIAL.

grin to 1,499 fans and a big frown to the one demanding type who isn't happy with anything. The UK Queen convention offers music, auctions, raffles, games, messages from Brian and Roger and a talent show among a million other things. It's been going for nineteen years, so Jacky and Val know what they're letting themselves in for.

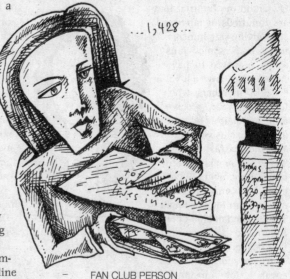

...1,428...

FAN CLUB PERSON

'The person who complains will make a beeline for you and make sure you know about it, so that can be stressful. Some people want to be entertained 24/7.'

It's Jacky and Val who find that they're the stars of the weekend, as much as Queen. 'Yes, I guess I am a figurehead, I have to talk myself to death!' says Jacky. 'I make sure that everyone is having a good time.'

During the weeks that precede the convention, Jacky eats, drinks and sleeps Queen. One imagines 'Bohemian Rhapsody' and 'Bicycle Race' are on a perma-loop inside her head. Bicycle! *Bicycle!* BICYCLE! Hm.

The travel, she says, is good. She has flown around the world doing the job, going to the USA, Japan and Australia – all for conventions. She's been to many concerts in the UK, and also Marbella. She was even flown to Ibiza for a party that Freddie held. Rightly, she concludes, 'the perks are fantastic'.

She has a lot of contact with the band when she needs photos signed or things to be approved.

'We get as much involvement as we need,' she says. 'If I need something I can call; they make time. I only have to go down to the Dominion Theatre [where *We Will Rock You* plays in London] because Brian spends his life there. He doesn't ever consider his role is over on the musical, he's always changing lines or adding new songs. And he's instant with an email reply, he's taken technology on board and he loves it.'

Roger Taylor, however, is a different matter.

'It's hard to track him down. He's rarely at home, he's on his boat or down in Cornwall, I never know where he is. And he has a terrible habit, if it's more than five autographs, to start signing as "Mickey Mouse" or "Noddy". He – and I – find that quite amusing, but the fans don't.'

Management advise on – among other things – all merchandise sold through the fan club.

'It needs official approval, because we're upholding the Queen name. I've sometimes had an idea for a T-shirt and they've said it wasn't right or we can't use a particular image, which often happens in regard to Freddie Mercury. They don't want it to be like the Elvis phenomenon, where he's on key-chains, plates, what have you.'

Jacky and Val's office is open to visitors – another perk is that they might come along for a chat and bring a bottle of wine, or some nice chocs. Other fan club organisers have spoken about a less polite type of caller.

'Someone once found out where I lived and turned up at the back door,' says Alex, who ran Pulp People for seven years until its close. 'I knew who she was immediately, strangely enough. Of course I had to invite her in and she stayed all afternoon, talking. She turned up again a month later, having brought across a photocopier on an old pram from Northern Ireland! I was staggered. She thought we needed one.'

GLOSSARY
● **Database**
Now that computer technology is in full swing, every person who writes asking for information, a photo, or where Brett buys his cat food gets their name and address put on to computer for future reference. Once there are a couple of hundred names, it's time for a fan club to start.

SKILLS YOU'LL NEED
To be organised; ability to file things; ability to write – the newsletter and reply letters; friendliness towards fans who are a bit barking; firmness with the band so that they will sign things and answer readers' queries.

TIPS
● Get to know up-and-coming bands who don't have a fan club.
● Get to know the people at fan clubs and offer to write articles for them. Large fan clubs have more than one member of staff, or need people to help a wee bit once in a while.
● If you work for a management company you might be asked to help out with such matters. Managers set up fan clubs which are completely independent of record companies.
● Running a fan club shows you how the music industry works. It is good experience and can be a stepping stone into other things.
● It might even get you into a pop group. (Mark Webber from Pulp started by running Pulp People.)

USEFUL ADDRESSES
● www.queenworld.com
● The Official International Queen Fan Club, PO Box 141, West Horsley, Surrey, KT24 9AJ
TEL 01483 281995

HAIRDRESSER/ MAKE-UP ARTIST

MONEY: From helping out for nothing to the likes of £1,000 per day if you're a snoot person who works on adverts.

HOURS: From a couple of hours a week to a twenty-hour day at a video shoot starting at 6 a.m.

HEALTH RISK: 8/10. You have to look after your back. Carrying your heavy kit around is hard work on the joints. You also have to be able to sit your pop star down on a high-level seat to avoid bending over. If you don't do this, after five years it will take its toll.

PRESSURE RATING: 6/10. Rivalry being the main stress – the world of the lipliner being very competitive.

GLAMOUR RATING: 6/10. If you like trying to remember what the drummer's called and then trying to tell him he's got a shiny chin.

TRAVEL RATING: 5/10. Mostly studios around London. You might be asked to go to Birmingham, but you have to be really in with a band for them to take you anywhere further than Glasgow.

Make-up artists and hairdressers are responsible for your pop star looking good in photographs, videos and on telly. The job entails standing around a lot, waiting for a stray hair or a shiny forehead to pop up.

Apparently, if you floss your teeth regularly it has such a beneficial effect on the gums that your face doesn't droop so much when you're older. Already knew that? Then you must be a make-up artist. For make-up artists aren't just a dab hand at putting on blusher. They, and their fellow cosmetic compadres, hairdressers, are a fount of knowledge on all things around your head.

There are make-up courses up and down the country which train people to put on mascara properly. They also teach the basics of beauty training: plucking eyebrows, manicures and applying false eyelashes. A good course teaches day make-up, evening make-up, catwalk make-up and bridal make-up. You also get taught 'men's grooming', which is really just make-up for men. In The Old Days, people got their training at the BBC.

Magazines like *Vogue* and *Elle* advertise these training courses, and they can be very expensive: from £1,500 for a two-month course to as much as £8,000 or more for a shorter one. However, many further education colleges provide similar training for less pence.

Patricia O'Neill is a top make-up artist to the stars, working on photo shoots and record covers. At sixteen, she had an interest in fine art, but saw a course at the London College of Fashion for a BTEC National Diploma in Design Fashion Styling For Hair And Make-up.

'The course was very good,' says Patricia. 'It was practical, plus we learned about the history of fashion, art and illustration. It was like doing an art foundation but a *fashion* foundation.'

In her second year, Patricia was offered work experience. 'A make-up artist came in to teach and said, "Does anyone want to assist on *The Big Breakfast* on Fridays? There's no money in it, it's just for experience." No one else in my class put their hands up, but I wanted to do it.'

It was there that Patricia was flung in at the deep end. She had to waft her brush over pop stars and film actors a few minutes before they were due to be on screen. 'It was chaos,' she says. 'Take That came down when they were presenting for a week. There were screaming girls outside saying they'd give me money for my make-up puff.'

Patricia was still earning nothing, but it was the experience she needed. After the job at *The Big Breakfast* she got a job on the last series of yoof programme *The Word*. Her training came in useful – the course had placed a strong emphasis on cutting and colouring hair, unlike some, and when

HAIRSTYLIST/
MAKE-UP PERSON

Supergrass would walk in the door and need a quick trim, she was confident in wielding the scissors.

There are other ways to get a foot in the door. After completing training, many make-up artists ring round the model agencies, who do test shots of all new models – taking their picture with lovely make-up on to show around prospective **clients**. Often *all* parties do these shoots for nothing, just because they can each get a nice picture out of it to show other people in order to get more work – it's good for the **portfolio**. The more work you do for these agencies, then the swankier the models get and the better the photographers get, etc.

There are also make-up agencies you can approach when you've got more experience. These are the people who will want to see your portfolio, and if you sign up with them they'll haggle for the best rate for you while also taking between 10 and 20 per cent of it for themselves.

You don't have to have an agent, but the first thing a make-up artist will ask is 'Who's your agent?' according to Patricia, who doesn't have one after eleven very successful years of freelance work. 'In not having an agent I go on my reputation and my quality of work,' she says. 'I send my portfolio and my showreel out just like an agent except I don't have 20 per cent taken off my earnings.'

That's not to mention the VAT. However, you have to do your own paperwork if you don't have an agent but that ensures, if anything, that you are more efficient. You'll have to chase up invoices and keep an eye on your incoming money and your outgoings. Remember as a freelancer you have to put some of your earnings by for tax: 20 to 40 per cent depending on earnings – and if you earn over £66,000 p.a. you need to register for VAT. You will need an accountant.

If you work with a band who like you and your style, they may ask you to do more with them and in that way you'll become part of their team. Like most jobs, you don't start earning lots of money immediately. You may initially find it hard to get work, so £500 for one job might sound a lot but you could have to make it last three weeks.

Putting a bit of powder and paint on a virtual stranger may sound like a dull old business, but make-up artists are powerful individuals. They know all the industry gossip. The make-up chair acts as some sort of psychoanalyst's couch. Anything can come out.

'I have no interest in other people's tragedies, gains or losses,' says Patricia frankly. 'But people confide in complete strangers, it's a mutual trust thing. If you're a make-up artist and you've got a mouth on you, that will be found out. I know there's people out there who do sell things to the papers but you won't last.' Ooh.

Your reporter once met a make-up artist who recounted a very long story about how Harrison Ford had found her so preposterously attractive that he asked her out, my goodness etc. She gave me her business card and I threw it away. That's what you get for showing off, people.

Sometimes you'll be dealing with an artist's ego. Boys, it appears, don't mind a touch of powder 'but once they're out of the make-up room in front of other people, they don't like it,' says Patricia. 'Sometimes you get girls who are very conscious of themselves. Then you get the fidgets ... they're on their phone, or having a cigarette, or there are a million people talking to them ...'

Once you have established a relationship with an artist or band, and you get on the telly and perform at dubious roadshows in Germany, things can be good. They will want their own make-up artist with them for everything: photo shoots for sleeves, magazines, video shoots, TV appearances and PAs. You'll be in regular work, and thus regular pay. That £800 Prada rucksack will not dent your bank balance. But there are pitfalls. The artist can be dropped, for instance, or the record company want to shake things around (not literally) and use different people. Some years you'll be in with a record company, some days you'll be out. You can't take it personally, but need the wisdom and patience of a Buddhist recluse sitting in a cave. At least you'll have a rucksack to take your packed lunch with you. And, invariably, a lot of cosmetics.

An obsession with the latest colours, tones and textures is a prerequisite. You will start with a little make-up and end up with cupboards stuffed full of 386 types of foundation. It's an expensive business: a complete kit might have to be insured for between £5,000 and £10,000 – although you may get a discount on some lines if you credit the company.

So what makes a good make-up artist?

'Tact,' according to Patricia. 'And don't be gushing over stars – don't ask for autographs, it won't do you any favours.'

Hairstylists work in a similar way to make-up artists. After training as a junior in a hairdresser, some hair-dabblers follow a similar route in that they help model agencies to do test shots of models in order to get experience and work with a make-up artist. The make-up agencies also deal with hair folk, and once you're established someone will take you on, upping your fee (as agencies do) and taking their percentage.

Ben trained at Vidal Sassoon and met Madonna's hairdresser through a colleague. They got on straight away and he assisted her on a shoot with a new model called Kate Moss. As soon as you start to get to know someone in the music biz you find they know someone else who knows someone else – and everyone has a split end or a flyaway fringe to be seen to in this business. As ever, **networking** is the way that a lot of people get on. You can be the best hairdresser in the world, but if you're shy or only want to cut hair in a revolutionary, 'I am an alien' sort of way, then you're going to have to find a pop star who doesn't mind. It's not the 70s any more – Blue don't appear to be pushing back the artistic boundaries.

Ben has worked for all pop types. He loves his job and finds that nowadays he can do many varieties of interesting haircut because everything is so 'diverse'. Ben does actually have an expensive Prada rucksack, but is likeable nonetheless.

'It's a bit like cutting hair in a salon,' he says. 'You talk about everyday life, but you ask what someone's been up to and they answer, "Oh, just been to Acapulco" because that's their everyday life. Plus, sometimes you do a great haircut in a normal salon and it walks out of the door and you think: No one's going to see it! On shoots, I know someone's going to take a picture of it and everyone will see it, which is great. I love my job. I couldn't think of doing anything else.'

GLOSSARY
● **Client**
Posh word for the person employing you, in this case advertising agencies, pop stars and record companies. Note: in our privatised age, hospital patients are called clients as well. Funny that.
● **Portfolio**
Collection of your work, neatly arranged in a folder, which you can show to prospective employers.
● **Networking**
The art of talking to the right people at the right time. Takes place at industry parties and you can also spot it on the streets of Soho, London. You used to be able to spot networkers because they wore puffa jackets. At the time of going to press, it's beards.

SKILLS YOU'LL NEED
Being able to cut hair, being able to do make-up, talking about hair and make-up, patience when someone blinks while you're trying to put mascara on them, communication skills.

TIPS
● For make-up, try to take a course – either at a local college or a well-established independent course. Look

at *The Stage* or health and beauty
magazines for details.

● For hairdressing, ring the best local
salon, and train as a junior.

● Get in touch with other make-up
artists through make-up agencies –
model agencies have the number.
They will give advice, and maybe take
you on to assist. The same goes for
hairdressers.

● Practise on your friends – it's a
good way of getting experience, even
though it sounds a bit naff.

BEARDS ARE NOW TRENDY
(SO IS HOXTON).

INDIE-LABEL BOSS

MONEY: From zero or minus figures if you 'own' a flexi label and are funding everything yourself, to lots of casheroo when you've just sold your label to Sony or someone for a couple of million quid.

HOURS: All hours. All the time. Even weekends.

HEALTH RISK: 9/10. Wining and dining The Casual Trout in order to woo them onto your label is fair rotten for your liver.

PRESSURE RATING: 7/10. Not too bad – you can do things under your own steam for a while, until all your acts get lured away by the prospect of 'proper' money and you have to consider selling out to The Man.

GLAMOUR RATING: 6/10. Well, fanzine writers will quite like you. At first.

TRAVEL RATING: 7/10. Mostly to the Dublin Castle in Camden.

A label boss runs their own label, having started absolutely from scratch. Running a label was actually a tremendous idea they thought of in the pub one night and slowly it has turned into a 'serious concern'.

Being an indie-label boss is a different job from being an MD of a major record company, although the principle is essentially the same – you are the boss of a company that produces records. However, major-label MDs have to report to all the bigwigs who virtually own the world. You, on the other hand, are either starting out with a few bands or you're at the stage where you might have sold some of your company to a major in order to keep afloat, but you are still in charge of most of the financial and creative decisions. There are fewer departments to walk around and nod to. Sometimes there are none at all.

It is no exaggeration to say that most indie-label bosses start out as passionate music fans who like hearing tunes so much they decide that the world needs more, and will sign artists they like in order to release the idiosyncratic collection of notes which float their personal boat. Ivo Watts-Russell at 4AD, Daniel Miller at Mute, and Alan McGee (Creation/Poptones) all began this way. However, every single label runs in a different way. Some labels release one single by an artist and then move on to the next act, while other bands might stay loyal for years. Some deal exclusively with dance music; others are across the board. Some last a few months; others years. It's a bit like discussing taxi firms. Yes, they carry people about for money. Other than that, there are no rules at all – the music business in microcosm.

In my youth, I once co-founded a record label, Trolley Records. We released one **flexi-disc** single and it cost us about £100. The band we'd released went on to be signed by Creation in another guise, but we couldn't find any more acts we liked after that, so we gave up. However, the thought that Trolley could rise again is forever in our hearts – for better or worse.

On a rather more elevated level, Alan McGee started Creation with a couple of mates who were in bands and ended up signing The Jesus and Mary Chain, Primal Scream and Oasis – and making a mint. A lot of the well-established smallish labels were started in the mid 80s and have been sniffing around the feet of the music industry since then. The newest labels are mostly dance labels, and their independence provides credibility. A lot of hardcore dance-music fans wouldn't even glance at a club cut released on EMI.

As stated, each smaller label is run in a different manner and it's somewhat hard to generalise about their modus operandi, so we'll begin by focusing on an indie-guitar-style label. Fierce Panda Records is run by Simon Williams, who wrote for *NME* for over ten years. He started the label with two fellow journalists at the beginning of 1994, when they were all **drunk in the pub**. They wanted to release an EP featuring their two favourite bands at the time, who were yet to sign proper record deals. These bands were termed 'New Wave of New Wave' – they had songs with three chords, looked a bit punky and went on about smashing the system. Suddenly, Fierce Panda had six bands – people find out about such ventures quickly in this business – and a DAT of each song they wanted to put on the record.

Simon had a friend at Damaged Goods Records, who was his business partner for seven years, and he was able to sort out distribution fairly sharpish. Distribution is one of the hardest things to get when you're trying to set up your own company. If you don't have a track record, or anyone really famous on the label, then distributors won't put out your records. Or they might try, but find it difficult to get the record into the shops because the bigger stores deal with major releases only. But more of this anon.

Now celebrating their tenth anniversary, Fierce Panda's launch party was at the Powerhaus in Islington, London (now an All Bar One), at which all their bands played. They soon sold out of the initial thousand vinyl singles they'd had pressed – not a bad start, as some singles on major labels never even reach that mark. Five months later they released their next record, an EP with all the young bands that seemed to be swamping the scene at the time.

'Then it got addictive,' says Williams. A couple of EPs later – new girl bands, new mod bands – and Simon thought he'd take the process a stage further: 'It was time for proper releases.' That meant finding new bands and paying for them to go in the studio. First release was by a band called Scarfo in the spring of 1995. It sold a thousand singles. Press was relatively easy to get (they had a foot in the *NME* for a start) and Williams's close buddy Steve Lamacq liked the bands and played them on the now-defunct Radio One *Evening Session*.

Fierce Panda still find it difficult to get their records in the shops, however. Most major record companies employ creative marketing and do discount deals when they're selling singles to retailers. They give them a quantity of records at a tiny price, so the shop can sell them on cheaply and the record can go into the chart. Unfair, but true. Devastatingly true. Obviously, small record companies can't afford to do this, so The Kids are tempted into buying major releases and albums because they're cheaper, which is ultimately what makes the money for the majors.

'We can't give singles to retailers at a special price because we lose money on a lot of releases anyway,' moans Williams. There are ways to survive, however. A lot of younger record labels make money through 'Best Of' compilation CDs of previous releases. These sell to Japan and other fancy **territories** abroad. Or, you can press a thousand vinyl singles which then sell out, then reissue five thousand or more CD copies of the single a few months later and make some money that way.

Fierce Panda has, to date, released early recordings by Idlewild, Coldplay, Keane and all sorts of other guitartastic types who have since been snapped up by major companies. Panda knew that these were one-off singles, but the big fear of some indie bosses is that artists they want to keep will leave their lovely little label, lured by the big £££s that major record companies will invariably offer once they've seen that the band sells records. If you're strapped for cash, you can't afford to offer groups long deals that tie them to the label – so they can up and go when they wish.

Some indie labels are essentially doing a **free A&R job** for a lot of majors, and this is difficult because you never make any money at all. One fanzine writer wrote that Fierce Panda was The Devil because it was subsidised by IPC magazines, publishers of *NME*. Of course it wasn't subsidised directly, but *NME* paid Williams's wages, which enabled him to keep the thing afloat. Running an indie label full time, without the help of a major record company buy-in or other external funding, would be nigh on impossible. You need good ears, business acumen – and the luck of The Devil.

However, when a small label like Fierce Panda has a very good track record, people in the industry know that it can often break a new band, and so canny press officers and pluggers will often donate their services free to help promote a release. It is a gamble, but they know they could be in with the band after they sign a cash-plenty deal with a major.

Williams doesn't really bother much with artwork and at the moment Fierce Panda, a bastion of the indie industry, is still run from 'a secret HQ in North London' (it used to be his living room, perhaps it still is). Simon listens to every tape/CD he gets sent. He turned down Bush when they asked if they could be on Fierce Panda, as well as one chap whose demo tape was entitled 'Richey Manic is Dead'. One bod got so excited at the thought of being on the label that he pressed up his own record and turned up with it in a pizza box, at a pub where he thought Williams would be. The record was cut and ready to be copied up and pressed into thousands. He'd even given it a **catalogue number**, which actually clashed with another record. Tragically, the disc was never released. Simon also runs various Panda-related Club Fandango gig nights to showcase new bands. He works with new scamps who want to be stadium megabeasts such as Agent Blue, Atlantic Dash and Cablecar. He means it, man.

Other problems indie-label moguls will encounter are bands going into the studio and **running over time** or some piece of equipment blowing up and causing the project to balloon over budget. You have to get used to people messing up. Williams had to learn quickly: 'I used to think, It's my fault! The sleeves aren't pressed in time! The man who prints sleeves must be a very professional person and he wouldn't ever make a mistake. Then you realise they're all flaky old tossers like yourself, and you learn to anticipate there'll be some sort of problem with every release.'

Mark Jones runs Wall Of Sound Records, who put out records from the likes of Propellerhead, Röyksopp, Zoot Woman and others. He started up the company in 1993 when he was working at an independent distributor, Soul Trader. 'We had no master plan,' he says. He would hear tracks by trendy types working in bedroom studios, which were released by Soul Trader. Jones thought the tunes needed to be heard by a wider audience, so got his favourite tracks and released them as a compilation album, *Give 'Em Enough Dope*.

Jones says Wall Of Sound has been through its 'ups and downs' since its conception, though it has still maintained its independence despite being offered a fair few tantalising major deals. He's also managed to keep his acts to the label. He reckons that, if a band wants to stay credible, they will stay with their UK indie label, then sign major deals in other territories in order to stay afloat. Mark was able to start the label on a practical level because he knew about distribution – the 'unglamorous' side of the business.

Mark started running Wall Of

LABEL BOSS/LABEL MANAGER

Sound from home, then set up an office. Staff numbers grew, but now it's back to a team of seven.

'We got to a point where we had around twenty staff,' he says, ebullient as ever. 'We had an office in New York and three offshoot labels. I found myself with a huge roster, so I had to take a big step back and say, "What is it I'm doing here?" The key is having a core team of people that you can trust. We're now focused, everyone knows what they're doing, I prefer it like this.'

There is a phrase that was bandied about when Creation Records 'slimmed down' its organisation in the mid 90s, whether it was true or not. It was called 'get that junkie off the phone'. While this has nothing to do with Mark Jones's experience but for the fact he slimmed down his own operation, it is a music biz rule of thumb. When you start making money, your staff grow and they're often too busy having a good time to bother to do any work. As mentioned, keen lawyer types, this does not relate to Wall Of Sound. And probably not even Creation Records, who have a great track record as employers and upholders of everything this nation holds dear.

Right. Back to the subject.

Mark Jones is all too aware of what he refers to as the 'digital revolution'.

'Music is much more open than it's ever been, but it's harder for independent labels to succeed,' he admits. 'The last few years have brought massive changes to the industry, you have to be able to move quickly and adapt. Hopefully we can do that quicker than the lumbering dinosaurs can. But the number of record sales of a twelve-inch single are dramatically down from

what they were. That's got a lot to do with the technology.'

Smaller labels can feel the Internet pinch harder than the majors, because they simply have less money to cushion them in hard times. Although the website is stocked with tunes Mark knows that 'it still doesn't stop people burning CDs or downloading tunes when they shouldn't'. He continues, 'But my take on it is that it's like when the gramophone player was invented – I'm sure the performers at the time thought it was the end of the world, that the industry was over and they wouldn't be able to make a living. It was the opposite of that, it was embraced and went on to take music to the four corners of the world. The major labels have been in their ivory towers so long they didn't embrace the technology. Sure enough, they're not in control of the hardware, they've shot themselves in the foot.'

Hm. Still, Wall Of Sound have the platinum-selling Röyksopp and they run a regular club night, called (sic). [confusing, eh?], at Fabric in London, plus their DJs play round the world etc. etc. All this socialising is very important. 'It helps to know people. It's good to get out to gigs and try to get as much help and advice as possible. Be yourself, don't be anyone else: that's the key.' People like Damien Harris at Skint started in a similar way. But Jones is sceptical about young upstarts (i.e. you! You people!) starting their own 'mazin' record companies.

'I don't see where the next Wall Of Sound, Ninja or Warp is coming from,' he says, frankly. 'Nothing is allowed to develop any more. If a label like mine existed now and we had a successful act, a major label would come in and they would try and sign the band – if that didn't work they would try and sign the label, which is what happens. I think market share is too important to these people. And it's such an expensive business to run – depending on what kind of music you're releasing.'

He thinks.

'I'd say, if it's your destiny it's going to happen. You have to stick to your guns and release music that you love. You do it for yourself, your friends and because you want to do it, not because you think you're going to make a ton of money out of it.'

Simon Williams agrees – tunnel vision is important. 'You have to have a complete and utter belief in your own tastes and never listen to anyone else. So many people will say, "I think that's shit," but 90 per cent of those people will eventually say, "You were right," and the other 10 per cent will never like them anyway – so why try to convince them?'

A bit about label managers for small record companies:

Label managers work for smaller record companies, sorting out the general day-to-day running of the label, and any bits the boss has forgotten. Small labels do need a lot of help, and this job can often develop from a work-experience posting or it can suit a new person starting out on the ladder.

Stephanie worked for St Etienne's label, Emidisc, in the late 90s. She used to write to Etienne band members Bob Stanley and Pete Wiggs when they wrote a fanzine. Stephanie kept in touch as the duo became pop stars and, when Bob noticed the band manager was overworked, nearly jumping out of windows and singing Northern Soul songs down the phone to pensioners,

he asked Stephanie to come into their office and help. Once Stanley and Wiggs had formed their own label through EMI and had signed up bands such as Kenickie and Denim, Bob and Pete needed help to run their label, too.

'I did the general office work: answered phones, sent out post, filed press clippings, and all that stuff,' says Stephanie. 'I arranged the St Etienne diary and kept things ticking over. I also sorted out tour transport and guest lists.' Being a label manager is full time and a lot of work, but Stephanie went to Tokyo, Paris and Sweden among other places as part of the job.

Working at a smaller label you have a clear understanding of how everything operates, but it's not less stressful – especially if you are working with friends. It doesn't always work. But Stephanie says she didn't like the thought of working at a major label and she could be a lot more honest when things went wrong.

'I liked working with friends. If I got pissed off I could tell them so. It wasn't like a normal job.'

GLOSSARY
● Flexi-disc
Vinyl disc that is pressed on such thin plastic that it is flexible. Very cheap to produce.
● Drunk in the pub
A time-honoured ritual and a breeding ground for top ideas. The pub is traditionally the best location known to Homo sapiens for creative brainstorming and lateral-thinking sessions.
● Territories
All the countries of the world split into sales target areas called things like 'Germany' and 'the Far East'.

America is the biggest territory, and sells a lot of records. Then it's Japan and Germany, Britain, and fast-emerging areas such as South East Asia.

● **Free A&R job**

Some critics say you are finding new talent and nurturing bands until they are 'ready' to be signed by major companies. All major-label A&R people know what the small labels are doing. Crafty.

● **Catalogue number**

Every release on every record label ever is given a catalogue number. You can also give catalogue numbers to all sorts of daft stuff. Factory Records gave its office cat a number, for instance. However, they didn't remix the cat and re-release it in extended formats.

● **Running over time**

If you take longer on a track in the studio, you will be charged by the hour. Williams pays for all Panda recordings: thus he gets disgruntled when this happens.

SKILLS YOU'LL NEED

Diplomacy, a long-term view, single-mindedness, organisational skills, friends to give you a hand, lots of time.

TIPS

● Speak to people with labels to see what advice they can give, as they might know people to help you.
● Fanzines often produce demo CDs etc. Buy some copies (there are always ads in *NME*) and weigh up the competition. Bear in mind that some major-ish labels started this way. Then start your own.
● Decide if there's a gap in the market – if you or your sister have a great band with a moose on trombone and your dad is head of a distribution company, then it may be time to release a record. Use all the opportunities you can spot.

● You don't have to have an 'industry' job to start your own label. Many people have more 'normal' occupations while releasing vibrant tunes from an office in their kitchen.

USEFUL ADDRESSES

● Fierce Panda, 39 Tollington Road, London, N7 6PB
TEL 020 7609 2789
FAX 020 7609 8034
WEBSITE www.fiercepanda.co.uk
● Rough Trade Records, 66 Goldborne Road, London, W10 5PS
TEL 020 8960 9888
FAX 020 8968 6715
WEBSITE www.roughtraderecords.com
● Wall of Sound Recordings Ltd, Office 2, 9 Thorpe Close, London, W10 5XL
TEL 020 8969 1144
FAX 020 8969 1155
WEBSITE www.wallofsound.net

INTERNET PERSON

💰	**MONEY**: Pots. If you design websites you get lots of cash.
⏱	**HOURS**: Varies. Depends what you're doing.
➕	**HEALTH RISK**: 1/10. Might get repetitive strain injury.
✊	**PRESSURE RATING**: 2/10. Main stress is waiting for pages to download.
🍸	**GLAMOUR RATING**: 1/10. Geek chic might have been hip once, but now ...
✈	**TRAVEL RATING**: 0/10. That's, er, the point. You can traverse the globe from your desk. Great.

The information superhighway is a busy road filled with opportunity and stuff like that. Thousands of jobs have been created, from website design to Internet consultancy, on-line magazines and services. We are children of the future. Ahem.

Technology is a big and marvellous thing. It is – yes – the Revolution. Many aspects of our lives have been touched by the whirling dervish that is the Internet. The music business is no exception, and has been *fairly* keen to jump upon the latest growth industry. The Internet provides many different jobs for people writing music, writing about music, slagging off American songstresses, selling CDs etc. It is a furious beast that some fear might change the industry for good, taking away some of the power the multinational record companies have over the commercial side of record-selling – distribution, copyright and sales. Hurray.

Anyone can use the Net to buy CDs. Right-ho. Anyone in the world can use American websites to buy CDs. American prices can be around £5 cheaper than they are here. If you have a credit card, and can wait a few days, you can get a good old bargain. This, of course, won't register in the UK as a sale, and, hence, won't affect chart placing. This is only one of the reasons why record companies are worried.

Illegal downloading is worrying the record companies (see Record-Company MD chapter for more details about the record company's view) flouting numerous copyright laws. While it is starting to become regulated, there is still a way to go. MP3 players, including Apple's iPod, are the new Walkmans.

Furthermore, your rebellious megastars, such as the artist formerly known as 'Prince', have dabbled with Internet-only releases. Some such as Madonna play the game a little more – with tracks available to buy online for fans only and real CD releases too. Other artists who aren't getting any younger and have lost record contracts sell through the Net and enjoy the greater profit margin. What was considered a bit tragic a few years ago is now a viable business alternative.

Fans also have greater access to information about their preferred artists. Official sites can include the drummer's diary, informal tour

YOU TOO CAN DANCE ON THE
INFORMATION SUPERHIGHWAY.

pictures and 'specials' which make the fan–artist interface more direct, boyo. For instance, when Chris Martin from Coldplay and celluloid squeeze Gwyneth Paltrow had a bouncy baby girl, Apple, Chris and his bandmates made a dinky video which they streamed on the website for a week. The three-minute film of Chris dressed up as a heavy metaller, singing a song about changing nappies in *homage* to his new sprog, was not the most professional of promos, nor was the song any cop, but it was funny. A bit. And thousands tuned in. The web allows you to update your news as and when you like, so the fans feel in touch. It also allows pop stars to get in touch with their old chums. Geri Halliwell's name is on Friends Reunited, although the

details have been removed that she was a bit 'lonely' or something.

If you've got your own unsigned band and would like to retain artistic control, you can just release toons on the Net, and you don't need much capital to do it. This will give you more profile – although if you want to get signed labels really want to see more than what can amount to vanity publishing.

'When the Internet popped up,' says Tamsin Hughes, Internet boffin, 'the big record companies wanted to take it outside and chop its arms and legs off. They were really scared. It means they may have less and less control.'

Record companies, at first, did not include web rights in their contracts, but they soon wised up. Nowadays every contract has a section on the Internet. Normally, merchandise profits go directly to the band, not the record company – unless you sell on the Internet, where your label gets a cut. Bah. *Anything* sold through the sites and the record companies will want some cash. Similarly, music press journalists have been asked to sign away their rights to royalties arising from magazine and newspaper articles reprinted on Net sites. No union has yet been powerful enough to stop this.

The Net is by nature cheeky. It was through the web that an infamous Mariah Carey hoax was perpetrated. An interview was circulated, purporting to be a genuine discussion with the first lady of squeaky singing, in which Carey 'said' words to the effect of: 'I'm really envious when I see pictures of Ethiopians, they're so nice and skinny.' Finding the perpetrator/s, who could be sued for libel, was impossible. Although it's getting harder for computer users to remain anonymous.

Hate sites, so beloved of teens in the 1990s, are even targeted by major US record companies. You could be in the doghouse with your **server**, and have to give it up. There are lots of Britney Spears hate sites called things like 'Can we hit her one more time?' and 'Britney must die'. If you are the one who did this, Britney's people can find you and send you a nasty letter. They can tell your server to cancel the account you have with them. But you can't go to jail. Not that we know of. Good.

Papery magazines like *Web User* are good at all-round advice. A good starter book is *The Rough Guide to the Internet*, which is only £6. Of course, there's more advice about the Internet … on the Internet. To state the bleedin' obvious, broadband access to the Net is useful if you want any job in the music industry, anyway, because the number of sites with music news and industry connections is increasing all the time. So swot up and get moving.

Website design and consultancy remain two of the highest-paid Net-related jobs, although they are not in demand as much as they were since everyone started to train in web design a few years ago. (Unless you have a site selling paper doilies in the shape of Abba and business is brisk.) Designers working freelance or for a team help record companies create their band sites, or magazines to create theirs. In-house designers formerly working on sleeves etc. are also now being trained to do the job. You can teach yourself website design using software like Microsoft Front Page, or Dreamweaver. And you can download and pay for it (or get a free trial) on … the Internet.

Consultancy firms make a mint telling people how to make money out of their own sites, how best to advertise, what looks good etc. Consultancy always pays. But you may have to wear a suit.

One great fact Tamsin found out during work on Digital Update was about artist web pages: the chat rooms prove very popular with fans who want to talk about how great their favourite pop star is. On 'robbiewilliams.com', accessing the chat room led to a very interesting conversation with a 'Robbie' who appeared to share the same joys and sadnesses as our doe-eyed pop friend. Afterwards Tamsin discovered there was a computer program called 'The Bot' (as in Robot), which tries to replicate the intelligence and character of a person. Allegedly, the company in charge of 'robbiewilliams.com' must have planted the fake pop star in the chat room. No record company has yet made a comment.

A bit about Internet magazines:

There are plenty of Internet magazines which contain shorter features and include links (either part of the website or sponsored external links) for downloads, ringtones, merchandise etc. Also, NME.com is the inkie's own website which is run as an off-shoot. Matt Mason is the editor of *RWD*, a free, glossy monthly 'urban' magazine and corresponding website. In 2001 he was working at Emap, marketing youth titles, but he had 'always been interested and involved in the underground music scene, DJing on pirate radio, putting out my own records and all sorts of things'. He saw *RWD* and loved it, and contacted the editor. He was invited to join the team – 'I took a risk and a pay cut. I haven't looked back since.'

The difference between papery magazines and websites is immense. Fewer words, for a start, and content that can be updated many times in one day. It's quick to track how many people have visited the site, how many regular users you have, and what keeps people interested. People are queuing round the block to write for *RWD* on the Net.

'It's very difficult to find someone who understands the whole scene and is a reliable, efficient, *good* writer. Few people in my experience seem to be able to combine both. The most important thing is to understand the attitude of a title; any title you're working for.'

The 16–24 age group is a huge market, but Mason feels it's being 'under-serviced' by advertisers who do not understand what young people want.

'The market is changing and evolving all the time,' he says. 'In terms of the amount of money around, it's in rude health. The music industry as a whole is really suffering, but within the urban industry music is just one part of it. In terms of revenue on the magazine only half is music-related; the rest is fashion, lifestyle, DJ gear, trainers, ringtones ... Someone who buys into urban music is the kind of person who always wants a new pair of trainers. It's a lucrative market and it's not going to disappear.'

GLOSSARY
● **Server**
The service provider which enables Internet access, i.e. Tiscali, Demon, Tesco.com etc.

SKILLS YOU'LL NEED
● 'To start your own website,' says Tamsin Hughes, 'you don't need a computer studies degree. Every art media course now has an online component. All you really need are good ideas.'
● For design, you'll need that ol' visual eye. For consultancy, a nice suit and impeccable Net knowledge. For your own home page/Net record label/Steps Doily Production line, you'll need a bit of imagination and lots of time and patience.
● Technology: you need a fast modem, a modern computer, access to telephone line/rental, specs, sci-fi paperbacks etc.

USEFUL INTERNET ADDRESSES
- www.musicnewswire.com
- www.ubl.com
- lsp.fortunecity.co.uk
- robbiewilliams.com

JOURNALIST

MONEY: A staff writer on a magazine or newspaper earns £14,000 to £30,000 p.a. Freelance journalists are paid a word rate or block sum per feature or per column. A freelancer who works a day in a newspaper or magazine office will be paid a fixed, agreed day rate.

HOURS: 10 a.m. to 6 p.m. for a staff job, more or less. Freelancers working from home may have spells of intense activity followed by long periods without work, and will also find they have to sacrifice a lot of their weekends.

HEALTH RISK: 9/10. All journalists are in the frontline as far as supping too much free ale at ligs is concerned.

EQUIPMENT COSTS: You need a tape recorder, and perhaps a couple of pens. Magazines will provide the rest of the equipment in the office. Freelance journalists working from home will also have to get themselves a computer, biros and a notepad, as well as a phone and a liver of steel.

PRESSURE RATING: 8/10. Deadlines. Brr. The dreaded word. Deadlines are revered and hated – they make your life a misery, but if you didn't have them you'd spend your life polishing the fridge.

GLAMOUR RATING: 8/10. You may meet the hunks of pop but they're the ones who are having their toenails buffed and ordering the bubbly while you have to tape their words of 'wisdom' and are lucky to be offered a seat.

TRAVEL RATING: 8/10. Leicester! Perth! Holland Park! Yes, journalists scoot all over the nation in the search for that story. You may also go abroad reasonably often and be treated to the sights and sounds of foreign climes. However, bear in mind that most pop stars tend to venture no further than McDonald's, the Hard Rock Café and the hotel bar.

The journalist is perhaps one of the most high-profile music-industry jobs, second only to pop star. As long as people can read, journalists will be able to write their frothy, often dreadful, prose about J-Lo 'n' her latest squeeze till kingdom come. And then they can write about kingdom come, and what Posh Spice will be wearing when it happens.

Being a music journalist is one of the greatest jobs known to Man. You get to write down what you think about music: a privilege that most people would give their knees for.

Unfortunately, most people who write for a living do not hold this view after six months of being in the job. Journalists are always complaining about something or other, and this is probably because they meet pop stars for a living and hear them complaining. Also, because they're always trying to write that semi-autobiographical first novel but end up having to write live reviews of German family bands for a ha'penny (or less) instead. There is, after all, rent to be paid.

A journalist's job is to report the latest music news, interview pop stars, review all products related to music such as albums, books and DVDs and contextualise the current 'state' of 'music' every three days, all for the delectation of the **readers**. You can also join the National Union of Journalists which has a strict code of conduct. No making up 'My mother's a herring!' quotes, no malicious comment upon the silliness of your interviewee's hair, or other such cruelty. Needless to say, many journalists of the tabloid-paper profession fail to follow these rules by the letter. Or the full stop. Hence all the court cases about intrusion and 'public interest' etc.

So! What happens? Well, most rock writers get a very early idea that music journalism is the sort of thing they would like to do. Very few people simply 'fall into it'. A few rock writers study journalism (the London College of Communication provides a famous course) but are more likely to be doing their homework at the School of the Live Gig and in the HMV shop. Many start by writing fanzines: their own little magazines will interview local bands (and sometimes the stars, if they shop at your local Homebase), then get photocopied and sold at gigs. School and college magazines also serve that purpose – they're good practice, and you can do whatever you want. No one's going to tell you to cut the jokes out and you can rabbit on about what you like with a Joycean sense of the ridiculous.

'When I left university,' says Chris Heath, who's an internationally renowned music writer (*Rolling Stone*, *The Face* and others) and author of two Pet Shop Boys books, 'I asked the local free paper if I could do a pop column, because I wanted free records. I got £5 a week. Then they announced they couldn't pay me and I did it for nothing, because it was a shameless device to get free records.'

If you ring or email a magazine, telling them you want to write, they'll ask you to send in some examples of your work, including some reviews written in the style of the magazine. You have to know what sort of music the magazine covers and what sort of person reads it to be able to write for it. A *Smash Hits*-style piece won't fit in the *NME*. Editors receive a lot of **unsolicited work**, and the best ones read through everything, no matter how long it takes. Some writers have started this way, but more often than not the best idea is to specifically contact the reviews editor, whose job is to find new writers to pontificate on the relevance of all the guff that's released every week.

One reviews editor says he likes to commission reviews by both experienced and not-so-experienced writers. 'It's not always the experienced writers that are the best,' he says. 'You have to keep an eye out for writers who've become complacent – their ideas aren't up to scratch or they're bad at keeping deadlines.'

Next up, on your way through the magazine structure, is to bag a **feature**. To do this, you need to impress a features editor, who commissions all pieces – after a feature's meeting with the editor and staff – and makes sure

JOURNALIST

essentially means being self-employed. Chris Heath started at *Smash Hits* this way.

'The first job I was given was to spend a month getting Christmas messages from the stars for a phoneline they were doing. I met the forty most famous pop stars on the planet – Wham!, New Order, Duran Duran, Depeche Mode ... Sade had to say her sentence fifteen times because she was tired. Then, just before Christmas, I went on tour with Wham!. They gave me the job because no one else wanted to do it due to the time of year. George Michael put his back out and they cancelled one date. I was terrified because I'd been meant to cover the two dates. In the end I went back to London with them on the bus, and went to George Michael's mum's house for tea. He was saying, "Another cup of tea, Mum?" and from that moment on I was golden boy at *Smash Hits*.'

If you get on well, your next step is to get a job on the staff of a magazine. Staff writer is a job in which you can find yourself writing everything from the contents page to features, news pieces, reviews, competitions, and editing letters. You tend to be thrown in at the deep end, especially on **'teen' titles** where new staff can be inexperienced and expected to learn the ropes as they go along.

A lot of people aren't told the whys and wherefores of how the system works when they first begin writing. For instance, it's a journalist's job to hear as much new music as possible, in the interests of the magazine. Therefore, journalists are given free records. If you review a gig, the press officer will give you at least one free ticket. Caitlin Moran, author, ex-TV-

the writer knows the **brief, deadline and word count**. The idea is that there is a balance in the features – in a magazine like *NME* they feature indie, but also pop and some hip-hop/'urban' pieces while keeping the core audience happy.

'I remember being in the first editorial meeting,' says Helen Lamont, pop writer who started at *Smash Hits*. 'I thought it was like *Absolutely Fabulous*. They were saying, "I'm thinking Take That, I'm thinking Boyzone..."! The first gig I went to was for the man who used to be in Yell!, at the Atlantic Bar and I got a free CD as I left! I thought this was incredible.'

Most writers start freelance – which

presenter and journalist for *The Times*, didn't have a clue how things worked when she started writing for *Melody Maker*.

'My reviews editor never told me I could get in for nothing at gigs, so I used to pay at every one I was reviewing,' she says. 'The other big mistake I made was letting my dad take me to a Smashing Pumpkins gig. I thought that if you reviewed a concert you automatically went backstage to meet the band afterwards. I took my dad and we somehow got into the dressing room. My dad leaned over to the singer, Billy Corgan, and said, "You're a tight little combo and your bassist isn't bad looking either." Now that was embarrassing.'

Caitlin Moran has conducted twelve-hour interviews with Courtney Love, been sick next to Kirsty McColl while Kirsty was playing acoustic guitar in her bathroom, and has had a Teenage Fanclub song dedicated to her live. 'But I put in a lot of legwork,' she says. 'I promised to buy them drinks for a year.'

Most writers hop about from paper to paper – as editors change, so do the staff. An editor either comes up from the ranks via being features editor then assistant editor at the same magazine, or else gets drafted in from another publication (often a **rival**).

The editor's job is to oversee every working of the magazine, from editorial through to design and production (the latter being schedule-keepers and spelling-correctors). It also involves lengthy marketing meetings, scheduling meetings, advertising meetings, meetings meetings, and any other discussion where a representative of the editorial side is needed. Some editors like to do a bit of writing, too – just to

keep their hand in – because they get envious of writers who don't have to go to so many meetings.

A lot of editors, and particularly features editors, take great pleasure in cutting out particularly good jokes or adding phrases which they think may explain ambiguous passages. Sometimes they are very good at this and sometimes they are appalling. As a writer, one must be prepared to accept this, and realise that one is not a pop star and cannot have a tantrum. Bah.

After editorship, the more officey-inclined might choose to be promoted to the role of publisher. This involves wearing a suit (you have to meet a lot of other bigwigs in 'em) and making corporate decisions about the overall direction of your **title**, the profile it has, the readership, the advertising, the page thickness, etc. This is only for the steely – it is very corporate, and you rarely get the chance to go down the Dublin Castle and watch Low Flying Owls.

Publishers like making lots of rules, so the editor can blame the 'no jokes' policy on someone else. Publishers worry only about selling magazines and could often give nary a bat's wink for intricate vocabulary or lofty metaphor. The most precious sign of a writer worth their salt is that they've either managed to squeeze in a few jokes, or else they've produced a spectacular and imaginative analogy – likening a well-known rock star to an historical figure from the Repeal the Corn Laws Campaign, for example. I don't recommend that you do this too many times.

A bit about magazine bigwigs ... and what they do next:

Mark Ellen is the editor of *Word* magazine, the first magazine from independent publishers Development Hell. Mark started out working for *Record Mirror* in the late 70s, then worked for *NME* before joining the fledgling *Smash Hits*. Ellen was a top pop scribe during the Adam Ant, ABC, Human League and Soft Cell electropop years – but his aim wasn't to become a venerable music writer. 'I wasn't in it to be a rock journalist,' he says. 'I wanted to work on magazines. I was excited by seeing how magazines were put together.'

Ellen presented BBC2's *Old Grey Whistle Test* with his buddy Dave Hepworth from *Smash Hits*, who had been doing stuff for Radio One then 'drifted into editing magazines' mainly because most of his colleagues couldn't be bothered – preferring to hang out with Paul Weller. Ellen's success in the role led to him being given the chance to work in a senior position at Emap overseeing all new launches. Mark began this new remit by being part of the team that invented *Q* and has also launched *Mojo* and **relaunched** *Select*, *Mixmag* and various other titles.

When Development Hell was set up by Dave Hepworth and Emap publisher Jerry Perkins, Mark was asked to join the team. He was back in the fray, writing more than he'd done for years and getting real enjoyment out of it.

'I started off in Emap in 1981, working in a tiny room in Carnaby Street,' says Mark. 'When I left 21 years later, there were 200 people in the building I was in. In a big company, you spend a long time working on things that might not necessarily result in anything, including launches. I now edit, proofread, write and research the magazine every month. We're pretty good at what we do, we've collectively had a lot of experience, we know each other well, so if we think something's a great idea, great. If we think something's a bad idea we can tell each other, and hopefully we won't be offended. I've nothing against big companies but you find that everything's wading in treacle.'

In 2003 Mark won the British Society of Magazine Editor's Mark Boxer Award – for making an outstanding editorial contribution to magazines in this country. So there you go.

A bit about celebrity journalism:

Celebrity and tabloid journalism works slightly differently from magazine journalism. For a start, tabloid pop hacks wear smarter clothing because they're always going to lunch with press officers and 'a close friend of the band'. They have a daily deadline by which they have to get in stories, and thus the pressure on them is a lot greater.

Tabloid pop journalism relies on getting stories, and there are many ways to go about finding them. Sometimes there may be an initial phone call from a 'stringer' – someone who supplies stories, or leads to a story, for a one-off fee. Sometimes there may be vague industry rumours to follow up. Often the press officer of the artist in question will try to give the tabloid a story – probably worried that the hacks will simply make something up if they don't. Some stories are blatantly nicked from music magazines, particularly in the summer when there's nothing happening. At other times the journalist will just stride up to a pop star at a function and ask them if there's anything going on.

'There are many ways of doing it,' says Matthew Wright, former showbiz editor on the *Mirror*. 'I went out most evenings and always had to aim to come back with something. Sometimes you felt stupid talking to people but, generally speaking, 95 per cent of celebrities are charming and they knew I had a job to do. It was easier for everybody if they speak to me – they got the publicity and I went home happy.'

Mark Frith is editor of *Heat* magazine. He started on *Smash Hits* in 1990, after editing *Overdraft* – the student paper of the Polytechnic of East London. He edited *Sky* magazine and then worked on *Heat* for two years before its launch.

'*Heat* is part of the British tabloid tradition,' he says. 'It's big headlines; headlines that grab you. The subject matter changes from week to week. We follow up the stories the tabloids cover – and we compete with them for big stories.'

There's this thing called *Heat* culture now, y'see. Celebrities are everywhere and we can't get enough of them. Has journalism turned into curtain-twitching? Is there a real, national sense of shame at our failure to keep up with the Zeta-Joneses?

'It isn't just people being mad about celebrities,' says Mark. 'Ant and Dec's manager was recently talking about *Heat*-type TV. What does that mean? It is celeb-based, but it's also cool, cheeky, young, fashionable. It's picture content over words, a sense of humour, we do

things differently. But I can't say we planned it – it started as an entertainment magazine for men . . .'

Some stars like *Heat*, others hate it. With articles about how orange celebs' faces are, they might not see the 'cheeky' side.

'We print pictures of celebs without their make-up on – some don't like that at all. They're the ones we're never going to please but we do it for the readers. We do hear from PRs, so and so's not pleased . . . but some are really supportive. But if you're going to look bright orange we'll put it in the magazine.'

There is no established route to learning music journalism until you start doing it. Most writers will claim they 'didn't have a clue' before they were published, and felt they were muddling through while hoping that nobody would suss them out. Interviewing styles vary from magazine to magazine, and writers alter their style accordingly, if only very slightly. The best writers are always after something more than they think anyone else will get and a way to find a different side to the interviewee in question.

'Good times, bad times, hard liquor, soft women, weird sex, exotic cocktails, good friends, bitter enemies, creative fulfilment, a punch in the cakehole – you could get absolutely everything you wanted with-

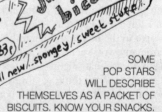

SOME POP STARS WILL DESCRIBE THEMSELVES AS A PACKET OF BISCUITS. KNOW YOUR SNACKS.

out ever stepping out of the office,' said Tony Parsons, somewhat baldly, of his stint at the *NME* in the 70s. Magazines have changed a lot in the last couple of decades. Originally, music writing was closer to creative writing than journalism. Those that wrote about music wanted to be writers, not journalists. The adjective was your best friend, the concept was your crutch and the pop star might actually just be a passing troll in the fable of your own spiritual, musical journey.

Paul Morley personifies the old-school, creative music writer. He started writing in his bedroom – music reviews just for the pleasure of it – then after school he produced his own fanzine *Out There*, and sent it to the then editor of the *NME*, Nick Logan.

'They had just printed their "Hip Young Gunslingers" ad and it seemed too obvious to apply for that,' he says. 'Instead, I sent this fanzine with the typically arrogant line: *I can do better than you*. I happened to be in Manchester and things were about to happen there, so I had something to write about. I'd always loved the *NME*, it was the biggest thing. It was the one place that if you wanted to write you thought of going.'

Morley wrote preposterous things about preposterous pop stars and

thrived on the competitive spirit within the *NME* team.

'You had Danny Baker, Parsons and Ian Penman and if they wrote a great piece then you wanted to. It was a constant fight, but it was healthy atmosphere. We were all trying to outdo each other, not really knowing it was having any impact at the time but gradually you noticed it was becoming very entertaining.'

Paul went on to work with Trevor Horn as part of the ZTT (named after futurist slogan Zang Tumb Tumb) label – crafting his creative circumlocution around such colossi as Frankie Goes To Hollywood, Art of Noise and Propaganda.

'At the time when I was thinking I was getting too old to write about music [25], I wanted to do something creative rather than parasitical,' he says. 'I carried on writing in a way ... it was like a magazine in my head. The way I organised the label, every sleeve, poster and advert was like a page out of a magazine. The magazine had a point of view, an editorial stance, it believed in something.'

Mr Morley agrees that some of the creative element within music journalism has been lost. It has, you know. (Could come back, eh?? *Eh????*)

'Because of the word processor everybody thinks they can write,' says Morley. 'Truman Capote said about Kerouac, *he doesn't write, he types*. Lately I've noticed people don't write, they just word-process. If you want to write about music as a *writer* – a sense of being a creative literary writer about music – there's few places to put that now. Everything's got to be a guide, everything's got to be an extended caption, or have almost a fanzine enthusiasm. It's not necessarily about developing an argument or giving space to do proper interviews. You often read glorified press releases, nothing is decoded.'

Morley wrote a piece about Duran Duran which made its members out to be Princess Di-loving Tories rather than a New Romantic Art Machine at the forefront of rock's lost tea-towel. They hated it, and never forgot it. He's had Lou Reed looking like he was ready to hit him.

'His manager literally dragged him back and apologised saying, "Lou's had a hard day,"' says Paul, sounding resigned. 'Meatloaf tried to hit me with an acoustic guitar once, on the seventeenth floor of a skyscraper in New York. He came charging towards me but got stopped halfway – which was good. Youth out of Killing Joke tried to punch me, but he was too drunk.'

Often the 'worst' interviews are the best to read. Sylvia Patterson is a master of asking highly individual questions of every star she meets. At *Smash Hits* she was renowned for getting the most from top pop stars by asking apparently spectacularly banal questions. Jon Bon Jovi, after being asked posers like 'Can you cook up a mean spaghetti bolognese?' and 'Have you ever thought life is like an ironing board?' confiscated her questions and ran towards his fellow band members, shouting, 'Guys! Guys! You'll never believe what I've just had to go through!' Similarly, LL Cool J put the phone down on Sylvia when she asked, 'Do you have a goldfish?' Such incidents give an insight into pop-star behaviour which 'How long did it take to record your album?' simply doesn't.

Many journalists go on to broadcasting, and Steve Lamacq, Mary Anne

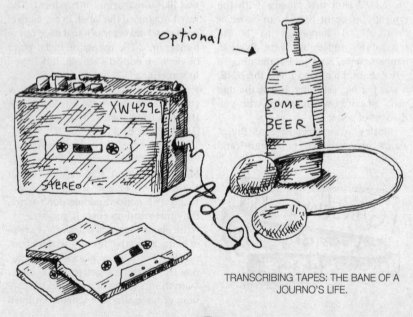

optional →

SOME BEER

XW429c

STEREO

TRANSCRIBING TAPES: THE BANE OF A JOURNO'S LIFE.

Hobbes, Miranda Sawyer, Andrew Collins and Stuart Maconie are just a few examples of this. Some go on to write books, both fiction and non-fiction. Some even become pop stars, including Neil Tennant, Chrissie Hynde and Bob Stanley from St Etienne.

Very often pop journalism can be deeply frustrating, especially when you have to deal with short deadlines, need to rewrite copy to please the editor, have to transcribe hours of tape (thirty minutes of tape takes over an hour to transcribe), and – worst of all – need to meet silly pop stars (Sylvia Patterson: 'I don't have a problem with pop stars being stupid. But Sonia took banality into the next dimension.').

Overall, pop writing is just about the next best thing to actually being a pop star. You can sit back and enjoy the travel, the free gigs, the records, and getting to meet hundreds of interesting people. The very best thing is that, unlike pop stars, you don't get the sack if you're not good-looking enough.

GLOSSARY
● Readers
The people who buy the magazine and dictate what you put in it. They write letters complaining if you don't like Shakin' Stevens or Bon Jovi, and all journalists are obliged to bow down to their infinite knowledge and wisdom. Sort of.
● Unsolicited work
Articles written by a writer without being commissioned. A lot of writers try this and fail because they think a piece on Jimmy Nail will suit *Private Eye*.
● Feature
All articles, interviews and overviews

are referred to as features in the magazine world. Reviews are called 'downpagers' because they run 'down' the 'page'.
● Brief, deadline and word count
These terms are all intrinsic to the awful business of writing a feature. A brief is the angle that your editor wants you to pursue when interviewing a pop star – which line of questioning, which angle you are going in at, which answers the editor wants. The deadline is the day and time that the piece has to be in by – and is notoriously rarely observed by journalists. The word count is the exact length of the feature or review. Again, this is often wildly overlooked by the idiosyncratic writer. Ha ha.
● 'Teen' titles
Smash Hits, *Big!*, *Top of the Pops* magazine and *Sugar* are some of the magazines that have a predominantly teenage audience. Overlooked by pop snobs, teen mags can sometimes contain the best pop stories.
● Rival
Smash Hits and *Top of the Pops* magazine are rivals. You cannot work for two rival papers: you'll get the sack from one or both.
● Title
Publisher-speak for magazine. Posh publishers always speak of a 'meat and potato' title when talking about a magazine that people tend to buy regularly. They are mad.
● Relaunched
When an existing magazine is given a severe makeover: redesigned, different sorts of features, perhaps different writers and a more specific content. Sometimes successful; sometimes not.

SKILLS YOU'LL NEED

Being able to spell, being able to walk
into a room and get on reasonably
well with people you've never met
before, being able to write coherently,
organisation, coping under pressure.

TIPS

● Writing your own fanzine is good
practice in the basic arts and skills of
music journalism.
● Working for student magazines will
give you experience of getting your
work published.
● Reviews editors are the first port of
call for novice freelancers
approaching music magazines. Send a
few examples of your work then call a
few days later for the editor's response.
● Suggest live gigs you can review for
live editors. You have a far better
chance of being given a commission if
you live outside London: *NME* is
always short of stringers in
Manchester, Birmingham, Leeds, etc.
It's a good way to start.

USEFUL ADDRESSES

● *NME*, IPC Magazies, 25th Floor,
Kings Reach Tower, Stamford Street,
London, SE1 9LS
TEL 020 7261 6472
FAX 020 7261 5185
WEBSITE www.nme.com
● Q, Emap Metro, Mappin House,
1st Floor, 4 Winsley Street, London,
W1N 7AR
TEL 020 7312 8182
FAX 020 7261 5185

LAWYER

MONEY: Between £10,000 p.a. and bucketloads. Lawyers are traditionally very discreet about their earnings. But they're well off.

HOURS: 9.30 a.m. to 6 p.m. most days. A gig once a week or so, standing at the back, briefcase in hand.

HEALTH RISK: 2/10. Unless someone decides to trip you up after a particularly nasty court hearing.

PRESSURE RATING: 9/10. Going to court is quite heavy. Then again, you are a lawyer. Sorting out warring managers, record companies and bands can also be pretty tricky.

GLAMOUR RATING: 8/10. Transaction lawyers, as they're known, have to meet clients and earn their trust, so they do get quite close to them.

TRAVEL RATING: 3/10. To and from the court if you're a litigation lawyer. Perhaps up to Donnington if your client is playing a hot gig.

Every aspect of the process of making records and playing live involves contracts, and lawyers are the folk to deal with them. They also sort out the disputes that every band has: mainly fighting the system and each other for cash or credit. They earn a lot of pence for doing so.

'It's all run by lawyers!' Such is the tormented cry of the record industry purist, the soulful individualist who is a bit 'indie'. Lawyers are people for whom 'dressing down' is loosening a tie, or wearing brogues. Lawyers, like accountants, are not known to be very rock 'n' roll. Lawyers like writing things out in neat.

If you fancy yourself as a dazzler in litigation, a sly fox in the world of who owes what to whom, then you'll probably be interested in being a lawyer – or solicitor, as they also like to be known. If you like good tunes and fancy something a bit more exciting than the usual run-of-the-mill suity job, then the music side of the profession is certainly one to think about. In the olden days, musty old lawyers invariably believed that albums always had photographs in them. However, as the entertainment industry grew and grew, some clever firms realised that they could take on these new creative clients and get to have a glitzy night out once in a while. Money could be made out of it. And that is, after all, what these types are rather interested in.

To be a lawyer you need to start with a spell at university. You don't necessarily have to plump for the strict law degree as you can always take a conversion course afterwards which lasts a year. Once you've got your law degree, however, you have to do a legal practice course for a year. This covers the practical aspects of the business and subjects like advocacy in court and how to deal with clients. You have to

i lasts hours

ii there's more to come

iii really difficult

iv you won't finish

v it's really sunny outside

P.T.O.

YOU HAVE TO ENJOY THESE.

parts of their body. This doesn't just involve being able to recite all the Smiths' B-sides in chronological order, including catalogue numbers. You have to understand the way record contracts are constructed and the way that they change every bleedin' moment depending on whether two-single deals are in, or whether it's five-album deals. Your job is to get your client – the band/artist – the best deal possible for them at the time. Knowing who's got what recently, and persuading a record company to give your client the best deal, is imperative. You've got to know your onions, seeing that, for instance, the current Sony contract is around 75 pages long – actually, now it's probably longer.

Ann Harrison runs her own company – Harrison's – after twenty years as a top music business lawyer for other firms. She represents artists such as Moloko, Bernard Butler, PJ Harvey and Tim Westwood. Initially, Ann did a basic training and then decided that she'd like to work on the entertainment side of things. She started with litigation, which specifically deals with disputes that reach court. She decided to move to the contracts side after six years. Why did she decide to be a lawyer?

'It was the intellectual challenge behind it and the recognised career path,' she says. 'I'm interested in the idea of helping people. You can help a small band who have made mistakes.'

Bands often get the raving hump with their record companies, their managers, with each other, with famous songwriters who think they've nicked their songs – everyone, really. Up pops a lawyer, making sure no one has to go to court and … kerrching!!

enjoy studying in order to be a lawyer, as you can probably gather.

Then you have to do two more years on a trainee contract with a solicitors' firm although, if you've been working on the business side of a record company for a while, the Law Society may reduce your trainee time to a year or so. These two years see you covering the fascinating depths of conveyancing (for buying and selling property know-how), litigation, and company and commercial work. If you've already specialised for your training contract, you'll be taught the intricacies of being an entertainment lawyer. Oh, and there are accounts courses, practice in **client care**, and other practical stuff. Then, and only then, you start looking for a job.

There are now many solicitors specialising in entertainment – and some only deal with music. There are litigation lawyers who take disputes to court and transactional lawyers who do the negotiations and the contracts. Bands and recording artists rely on the latter, who must know the music industry like the back of their hand and all other

Most lawyers either work as partners in a company and share the profits and the losses, or as employees of those companies. Some lawyers work in-house for record companies, trying to make sure the record company gets the best deal and that the band can't release twelve mixes of one single whenever they want to – obviously a marvellously creative project, but one that might cost quite a lot of cash. However, record companies are eager that every artist gets legal advice, because if the contract they're offering is unfair and the artist signs but then gets disgruntled, the artist has a far better case against the cruel record company.

A new development is the growth in the number of independent small boutique companies like Harrison's who specialise in transaction work and occasionally also civil litigation, but are niche firms who don't offer an all-embracing legal service but bring in that expertise when needed by referring it to other firms or specialists. Phew.

Copyright problems, including sampling and now the use and sale of music on the Internet, are some of the biggest lawyer headaches. Copyright laws are more complex now that Britain is subject to European as well as UK law. Most record companies have a system for clearing samples, and a standard rate to pay the geniuses who've had their basslines nicked by some goon making a summer snogging record. Again, this is to try to ensure that not many cases end up in court.

Ann Harrison sometimes does put her leather jacket on to go down the Water Rats to watch her clients play. She also goes to other gigs to 'see what's happening out there'. She doesn't pick her bands because she likes their tunes: 'If I wanted to do that, I'd do A&R ... If I knew what made a number one I wouldn't be sitting behind this desk.'

Pop stars are, she warns, a little different from your average client. 'You can't expect them to keep to an 11 a.m. appointment. It'll be 11.30 if you're lucky. But it's good fun. You do get tantrums and egos – you're not allowed a beer in my office – but I enjoy it. If I'm seeing a client for the first time we may meet in a pub because it's more relaxed. I can imagine it's quite tense for them going to see a lawyer. It's a non-smoking building, but I do let them have a cigarette if they want one.'

It's not just pop stars who need lawyers. One (female) journalist was pictured in a tabloid newspaper with the caption 'Alex James from Blur's girlfriend'. A lawyer took on her case – as this was a clear untruth – and won £1,000 in damages.

LAWYER

89

Yer lawyer faces lots of competition for clients, so another stress of the job is the getting and *keeping* of the artists. It has also become a very popular area for young lawyers to qualify in and so demand is high for just a few jobs. If you've done some intellectual property courses or secondment at music companies you might stand a better chance of getting at least an interview for a job.

And so, is the music business really run by lawyers, Ms Harrison? 'Hm ... There are a lot of lawyers at record-company management level – legally trained people. Some companies are more lawyer-led than others, but lawyers are, to an extent, indispensable. We oversee contracts for bands, producers, album mixers, publishing, merchandising, managers, tours ... I guess we're part of every single element of the music industry.'

GLOSSARY
● **Client care**
Diplomacy and customer relations. Difficult stuff.

SKILLS YOU'LL NEED
Interest in paperwork and small print, being able to communicate formally and informally with the suits and mohicans alike, interest in money, sense of justice and fairness for all, patience.

TIPS
● A law degree is an absolutely essential first step. There are no short-cuts.
● Try to do your training with the entertainment division of a firm.
● You can pick up a nice suit in the high street these days, and it won't cost you an arm and a leg. Arf arf.

USEFUL ADDRESSES
● Clintons Solicitors, 55 Drury Lane, London, WC2B 5RZ
TEL 020 7379 6080
FAX 020 7240 9310
WEBSITE www.clintons.co.uk
● Denton Wilde Sapte, 5 Chancery Lane, Clifford's Inn, London, EC4A 1BU
TEL 020 7320 6516
FAX 020 7320 6571
WEBSITE www.dentonwildesapte.com
● Harbottle and Lewis, Hanover House, 14 Hanover Square, London, WIS 1HP
TEL 020 7667 5000
FAX 020 7667 5100
WEBSITE www.harbottle.co.uk
● David Wineman Solicitors, Craven House, 121 Kingsway, London, WC2B 6NX
TEL 020 7400 7800
FAX 020 7400 7890
WEBSITE www.davidwineman.co.uk

MARKETING

MONEY: From around £18,000 p.a. for a marketing assistant job at a major company to £40,000 for head of marketing and up to £90,000 for marketing director.

HOURS: 10 a.m. to 6 p.m. minimum, then a few gigs per week to catch up on the latest vibes.

HEALTH RISK: 7/10. Stressful, and a whole box of posters might fall on your head.

PRESSURE RATING: 8/10. If the whole corporate strategy doesn't work, people seeking a scapegoat often point the finger at marketing, and then laugh cruelly.

GLAMOUR RATING: 6/10. Ringing up and ordering posters isn't exactly the top end of the fancy stick.

TRAVEL RATING: 7/10. Not bad, if you're into going to gigs up and down the country, but you may grind your teeth if you're stuck at your desk while the international executives jet off to Paraguay.

The marketing person (can also be called a product manager) plans and co-ordinates all adverts in the press and on the TV and radio, as well as poster campaigns. Also oversees the long-term strategy of a particular artist – which can be a detailed plan over a period of up to twelve months. He or she decides how the band is perceived, man, and now is at the helm of the good ship Viral Marketing, which – although it sounds like a coldsore or something – is very important in our information-based culture etc. etc.

B rian Epstein, the legendary Beatles' manager, was once asked how he did what he did with The Beatles. He replied, 'I imagined them at number one, and then worked backwards.' Ultimately, this is the job of the marketing person.

The title doesn't exactly conjure up any mental images of vast, spectacular rock 'n' roll excess or high-octane-'Let's stop work this afternoon to play Rummikub!!'-style anarchy. Yet marketing is like management – it can be highly creative. Malcolm McLaren, the Sex Pistols' manager, knew how to make four modest young boys from London into a real threat to the moral fabric of 70s Britain. It was the 80s that saw the marketing and managing become two definable roles. Obviously it's very important and high-powered and responsible and everything, but it's also essentially challenging and creative. And there are no dodgy greengrocers involved.[1]

Marketing, or product management as it's also known, is a job which is in actuality very closely linked to the band or artist it is promoting. The sacred triumvirate who have the task of promoting and exploiting the artist's

---

1. A very poor joke about markets, for which the writer is very sorry indeed. A bit.

hot tunes is made up of their management, the A&R person who signs the band to the record company, and the record-company marketing people. These three work together. The artist is signed, their material is recorded and mixed, and thus a grand strategy needs to be created. Press and publicity people are then involved further down the line.

The marketing person is in charge of placing adverts in the right places, positioning well-appointed posters around the country, leafleting gigs, etc. There may be a TV **campaign** to plan. S/he is essentially in charge of **exploiting** the special appeal of the band and working out how they are going to pick up millions of potential fans – or, if the artist already has a large fanbase, keeping them happy and excited.

There are as many different marketing campaigns as there are types of artist. If the look is geeky, then product managers will geek the band up even more and festoon the nation's buses with the words 'Geeks are cool!'. If the look is ancient-grizzled-old-rocker-croons-the-hits, then the target is all the old rockers who still have an ounce – or a memory – of rock rebellion in their souls, but have to be up by eight on a Monday. Ideally, the marketing exec will love the product they are working with and say, 'Wahey! This band is great – but how do I let everyone know that?!'

Jo Power started helping out at the entertainments office at her university and helped to book and promote touring bands. She saw a job advertised for trainee product manager at Sony Records and swotted up all she could before the interview – she went to the library to read *Music Week* and marketing magazines as well as ringing anyone she knew who was even vaguely connected with the business. Jo also found out all the departments at Sony and learned who the company's main rivals were, and read all the music magazines and watched TV so that she understood which publications and programmes were right for which artists. After one initial interview and a day and a half spent plotting a test marketing campaign for a

MARKETING MANAGER

single release, she was given the job on a Friday – and started the following Monday.

Jo's first major project, after a few months in the job, was Liverpool band The Real People. She also worked with Kris Kross, whom she 'just knew would happen', and Julio Iglesias, which was a relatively straightforward marketing job as old Julio already had a ready-made audience of ardent laydees willing to snatch up his every record. However, she still had to work within a budget to place adverts, talk to the press and promotions people about the campaign and who they would target, liaise with designers about logos and record sleeves, talk to **sales executives** about getting the CDs into shops, and place a couple of TV adverts. Television used to be a luxury reserved for only the highest-selling acts. Now it is much more commonplace.

Marketing comes with its own built-in frustrations. You have to try and work well with A&R people as it's good to have a vision when working as a team – but, as A&R execs are notoriously opinionated and have their own agenda, personalities can clash. It's also frustrating if you love the band but don't have a big budget to promote them, or if you have to spend your time dealing with American acts who already have their people giving your people a load of gyp about what they think is right. Then there is the artist's management, who vehemently believe that a full-page colour advert in the *NME* is the right way

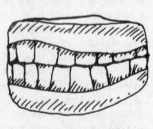

IF YOUR BAND WEAR THESE, YOU HAVE TO MAKE THEM A TRENDY LIFESTYLE ACCESSORY.

forward and don't appreciate that's not always the only way to do things. You should also get used to the fact that, when the album's number one and you're feeling jolly pleased with yourself, you get no credit whatsoever – but when the album's not number one you will without doubt find someone poking you in the chest and complaining about the orangeness of the logo, or the fact that the band are wearing deeply unhip Big Shoes on the posters and this was totally your lookout. Oh God.

Marketing people need to have a long-term vision for long-term acts and maintain it within financial constraints. They nearly all work in-house at major companies. Jo Power left Sony after five years to work as marketing manager at Food Records, who are owned by EMI. She thus works very closely with Food's bands, but then has to go through EMI's product-management people. At this smaller, more intimate, company she is far more involved with the A&R people than she was at Sony, and feels far less corporate pressure. As ever with marketing positions, though, she still has a creative job to perform and a lot of people to answer to. And lots of posters in the office that might fall on her head.

Peter Loraine, now head of marketing at Polydor, went from the job of editor of *Top of the Pops* magazine to the marketing department. He was head-hunted, no less. At the time Polydor wanted to sharpen their pop roster – the acts they had included the more *organic* sounds of Cast, Shed 7 and Gene. Yes, they had Boyzone, but Peter knew his pop onions and Polydor wanted to, er, cook with them.[2] Peter in turn wanted the challenge of working with artists long-term. He had a business studies A-level and suddenly it was useful.

'They gave me the job of artist development,' he says. 'They wanted me to sign some acts *and* work on the marketing side of them – after a year I found that my skills were with market-ing rather than finding bands. With pop music, it's not about hanging round the **Dublin Castle** waiting to catch the Next Big Thing. It's more about which manager is going to bring their act in to you and whether you think you can develop them.

'Some say marketing is just booking a few ads,' he goes on. 'Yes, we do the ads, make sure the fly posters go up, design and create the campaigns, but it's so much other stuff. Thinking out-side of the box. With Ronan Keating, we released his last single on Valentine's Day and we did a link-up with Interflora. It rained rose petals in the video – so they sponsored taxis in the major cities and if you got in one you would get a red rose from Ronan with his signature on the packaging. It was all over the local press and men-tioned on *CD:UK*. That was fun.'

Peter also enjoyed working with S Club 7, because it was a marketing dream. 'They were so multi media – it wasn't just about bringing out a record, they had a primetime children's TV show. The first meeting we had with management, we thought this could be *Grange Hill*! We need to make this more *Hollyoaks* and less *Byker Grove*. There were ideas about filming the show in America so it immediately had an international feel.'

As head of marketing, Peter over-sees all acts on Polydor UK. Each act – from Scissor Sisters, Girls Aloud, Ms Dynamite, Daniel Bedingfield – has a product manager who reports to him. It's a responsibility and a half. Perhaps even a three-quarters. He has both artist and management on one side and record company on the other. There can be some friction – about very Important Things. For instance, if you're a member of a girl band, you need to have a slightly different look from the others, *non*?

'Perhaps Cheryl from Girls Aloud will never forgive me,' says Peter. 'I twisted her arm to get her hair cut into a bob. I told her she needed a striking look. She regretted doing it from the moment she left the salon. But they've sold loads of records . . .'

Will Young has also stated how he needs to be involved in his 'brand' as much as his marketing team: 'I think it's essential to have creative input in the way you look and your music, the whole package. I want to control the way people see me, as much as I can. If you're not in control of it, what's the point?'

Marketing initiatives can work the other way. A band can be sold on the fact they all look very similar (All Saints) or if they're not cool, why push them that way? Make that geeky look sell, guys! Remember Weezer, anyone? Perhaps not.

Some stars have to be nudged into a certain look, others are naturals.

'Sophie Ellis Bextor will tell me what she's wearing in her video,' says

2. Again, apologies.

Peter, 'and she'll look great, she doesn't need help. At the other end of the spectrum we had Hear'say who were suddenly the most famous people in the country and really needed some outside input. There really was some grooming involved.'

Marketing is hard work. There are egos to battle with, separate creative visions (man) to contend with and budgets to stick to. But the ultimate thing is always sales, leering like a parrot on your shoulder, watching everything you do. If you can't translate your campaign into units shifted ... hop off. It's intensive work, says Peter. 'Especially at Christmas,' he groans. 'We sell around ten times more records during that period than at any other time. If we release an album on 2 January, we'll sell 30,000 compared to 500,000 mid December. We might be working eight different albums, trying to put them on the right shelf in the shops. I don't think people realise that placing a CD in HMV is such a massive part of it. People need to physically get hold of the records.'

But what of this accursed Death Of The Single business that is so often talked about? Will the charts be axed?

The singles market year on year is down drastically. It is around 50 per cent of what it was at its height in the 80s. Today a single might sell 30,000 to go to number one, whereas decades before they were selling hundreds of thousands of copies. Although online retailing has recharged the singles market, for record companies, singles are there to draw attention to an artist's album.

Every pop single is costly. It requires a photo session for the cover and a video – everyone who works on these needs paying. You may need to perform your song on TV with dancers – they need a fee, a costume *plus* you have to pay for their transport. And their lunch.

'If you're not careful you can spend £400,000 on one single,' says Peter. 'If you have three of them on one album, and so you have to sell a lot of albums to make money. Record companies are just being more cautious and more careful. No one is releasing five singles from an album any more. We're also having to be more imaginative. Rather than flinging money at things, we're thinking, "How can we do this differently?"'

One way is viral marketing. 'New Media' – digital technology such as multimedia art websites – has opened up new marketing possibilities. Imagine! When you send an e-card with a picture of Enrique Iglesias on it you are helping to do the marketing job. When you email your friend an amusing film of someone's head falling off, and the very tiny email signature says 'Buy Mr Bongo's New Album', that's the same thing. Peter is highly aware of all this.

'All those kind of things weren't everyday when I started. Now ringtones make more money than singles, which is a shocking statistic. But we do make money on compilations, and ringtones are a new way of recouping what we've spent on a single.'

There are also specific independent marketing firms who specialise in arranging for bands to sponsor commercial brands. Once Simon Fuller had orchestrated The Spice Girls' seizure of dolls, clothing, pencil cases, lunch boxes, cola cans etc., he, er, didn't stop. S Club 7 had their own diffusion clothing range in Woolworths. There have been *Pop Idol* Easter eggs, mugs, a Simon Cowell doll and even perfume. These firms liaise with the management and the marketing departments of the companies. They will also try to persuade companies to provide tour sponsorship – a growing industry.

Peter Loraine explains what he likes most about the job: 'When you're working on a group or an artist, and your parents have heard of them, that's amazing. But that only works if the household name is selling records at the same time.

'It can be tough when it goes wrong,' he continues. 'I've spent up to a year with a group before their record comes out and they become part of your life. If they don't sell any records, and they've dreamed of this all their lives, it's hard not to take it personally.'

GLOSSARY
● **Campaign**
The master plan. Every department will have a strategy, a vision. Every single element will combine, hopefully, in getting the artist to the highest chart position possible. Serious business types use this word, and it's also the name of the marketing/advertising trade magazine, too. It will do you no harm to read it.
● **Exploiting**
All music-business people refer to selling an artist's records as 'exploiting' the artist. A financial term, no doubt. A bit dubious, subtextually.
● *Music Week*
Industry rag which details charts, BPI news, industry news, sales

breakdowns, management changes, radio play, etc. It is essential to read this when you are starting out.
● **Sales executives**
The people who work with the distributors in getting the records into the shops. Very important, but not very glamorous.
● **Dublin Castle**
One of the places in London's Indie village, Camden, where bands looking for a deal will play. Barfly at the Monarch is a similar venue, and only a stumble away.

SKILLS YOU'LL NEED
Long-term vision; diplomacy; to be highly organised and not mind paperwork; keenness to spot the potential in new bands; interest in all aspects of the industry; to be simultaneously inspirational, phlegmatic and self-effacing. Not easy.

TIPS
● A marketing degree might help, but ain't essential.
● A media-studies course will include information on marketing.
● Some business courses feature music-management studies, but do not give you a qualification in music management. The BPI has updated lists of all music courses.
● Start out somewhere in the industry – anything from working at the student-union entertainments office to work experience in a record-company post room will help. 'The best way is work experience, I still stand by that,' says Peter Loraine.
● Practise on your friends by trying to 'market' them to other pals/ parents/prospective partners and seeing if it works. You could,

however, lose all of your friends
because they've gone off with the
'better proposition' of the people
you've marketed them to. This at least
means you are a success ...

USEFUL ADDRESSES

● EMI Records, EMI House, 43 Brook
Green, London, W6 7EF
TEL 020 7605 5000
FAX 020 7605 5050
WEBSITE www.emirecordedmusic.com
● Polydor Records, 72–80 Black Lion
Lane, London, W6 9BE
TEL 020 8910 4800
FAX 020 8910 4801
WEBSITE www.polydor.co.uk
● Sony BMG Music Entertainment
Ltd, Bedford House, 69–79 Fulham
High Street, London, SW6 3JW
TEL 020 7384
FAX 020 7371 9298
WEBSITE www.sonybmgmusic.co.uk
● Warner Music, The Warner
Building, 28A Kensington Church
Street, London, W8 4EP
TEL 020 7938 5500
FAX 020 7368 4903
WEBSITE www.wmg.com
● Dublin Castle, 94 Parkway, London,
NW1 7AN
TEL 020 7485 1773

MERCHANDISER

MONEY: Around £10,000 p.a. if you've just started helping out, but can rise to £50,000 for your own business.

HOURS: 9.30 a.m. to 6 p.m., with the added option of going to gigs.

HEALTH RISK: 7/10. A box of keyrings may fall on your head, or you could get smothered in promo T-shirts.

EQUIPMENT COSTS: Some companies farm out their work, such as printing, distribution etc., but the more in-house business there is going on the more money your company is going to make.

PRESSURE RATING: 7/10. If you've got a batch of T-shirts to be done in three days and no one can find the artwork, fairly high. If a band gets lured away by a better royalty deal ... hm, well, pretty high stress levels there.

GLAMOUR RATING: 6/10. Some of the wee pop stars might pop in shyly to express concern over a particular shade of blue on their garment.

TRAVEL RATING: 7/10. If you drive the T-shirt lorry, you could find yourself in Basingstoke one day and Norwich the next. If you're big pals of the band, they might let you go to Rome, for example.

A merchandiser deals with T-shirt design, printing and distribution. All other baubles – badges, bags, posters and jackets – will be the responsibility of the merchandiser as well.

Letting everyone know just who your favourite pop star happens to be is not a new pastime. The Beatles had a whole range of merchandise – tights, wigs and figurines are just three saucy items which were sold with The Beatles' name attached. Button badges were very much in vogue in those days, and you can still find little brooches with Ringo on them. (All the John Lennon ones are really rare.) Fans have always been proud of their heroes, even if that included The Bay City Rollers. Actually, come to think of it, the more loonish the band, the more lucrative the merchandising opportunity appears to be ...

Merchandising is now big business. Once you have a successful band on your books and are **licensed** to produce all their accessories, you can make a lot of money. There are a handful of major merchandising companies who deal with every stage of the process. The biggest company in the 90s was Underworld, who worked with 150 to 200 bands, including Pulp, Robbie Williams, Ash and Oasis. Emma Evans was the A&R co-ordinator. 'With most bands we did a handshake deal and there was no contract,' she says. 'We were good because we could turn stuff around in three days, whereas most other companies take between five and seven days.'

I MADE THIS T-SHIRT

signed a pop star

DON'T LET POP STARS DESIGN THEIR OWN T-SHIRT.

shops, or do it themselves. Shops will buy shirts for around £8. They then put a 100 per cent mark-up on the shirts so that punters end up paying between £15 and £20. Fan websites also sell merchandising, and so can the merchandising companies direct through the web like Backstreet. However, most companies deal with film and TV now – League Of Gentlemen T-shirts ahoy – the market is more diverse.

'Merch' companies (as they're sort of known) also have to deal with the festivals. Every festival such as Reading/Carling weekend, the V festivals, Glastonbury, T in the Park and the Fleadh sells a lot of T-shirts to eager punters who are soaked in lager. Each company produces the shirts, drives them up, sets up the stalls, handles the official merchandising for the event itself, employs sellers, and then uses its in-house accountants to add the whole thing up afterwards. They thus ensure skimpy tops for muddy people, and their own good standing with bands. It doesn't make them much cash; they just like doing it, claims Emma.

The 'profit and loss' deal given to big acts means that some companies incur *all* the costs such as manufacture and distribution as well as tour costs: travel, van hire and staff to sell the stuff. They split the profits 75–25 in favour of the band on most occasions, but it can vary. For smaller bands, the company will simply invoice the artists directly for every shirt made up.

Pop merchandising is the sort of job people get into by accident. Nobody

After a band decides to go with a merchandising company they'll work together on an eye-catching design and decide what sort of shirts they can afford. It's simply no use demanding silk and brocade – artists must have a large guaranteed audience for that kind of finery. There is, however, a very large range of styles nowadays. Fashions vary spectacularly. Trimmed edges were very popular at the height of the so-called mod revival. T-shirts were once very large; then they got very small indeed. At one stage in the early 90s, 'T-shirt band' was used as an insult.

Merchandisers either pay a distribution company to put their T-shirts into wakes up one morning and suddenly says 'I want to get into merchandising!' unless they are a bit loopy. Emma Evans just had a friend who knew that a job was going. 'I said to her, "If you think for one minute I'm making T-shirts, you're dreaming," but then I thought – what have I got to lose? I'd been locked out of my house the night before and I turned up at my interview wearing the same clothes as yesterday. The guy who interviewed me asked me who was up and coming. I'd just seen Oasis's first London gig so I told him about them. The next day he rang to say I'd got the job. I'd started working for Oasis in no time.'

There are, however, a few pitfalls. There's often **dead stock** which you can't even give away – in central London there are warehouses full of Blue tote bags and Pop Idol pencil cases. Creation band Adorable once produced a respectable range of leggings in an attempt to provide decent merchandising for women. They sold two pairs, but the upside is that the singer hasn't bought a dishcloth since.

If your merchandising company doesn't sign a contract with the band then another company might nick them by offering better **royalty agreements** or better designs. Some bands have successfully handled their own merchandising. Anthemic baggy pop stars James didn't have the cash to give to a merchandising company in the old days, and thus took T-shirt control. This kept them afloat through the grim times before they got famous, as every single person in Manchester had to have at least one James T-shirt by law. Or so it seemed.

If you're a merchandiser, glamour may occasionally walk in the door in the guise of a pop star pondering exactly what style of sleeve will adequately, if not analogously, define the intrinsic meaning of McFly. 'Some pop stars,' says Emma, candidly, 'didn't have a clue. You showed them this colour and that trim but a lot of them

TWO GREAT MERCHANDISING IDEAS: THE VAN MORRISON BAG
AND THE PAUL WELLER PINT GLASS.

weren't very adventurous. They don't understand what sells and what people will buy.'

GLOSSARY
● **Licensed**
Officially allowed by the band to sell T-shirts. Pirates are not allowed to sell, even though they do. You see them outside gigs shouting like fruit-sellers.
● **Dead stock**
Out-of-date T-shirts are common in this whirlwind industry. Tour T-shirts, album-cover designs etc. all pass their sell-by date quickly.
● **Royalty agreements**
A percentage for every T-shirt sold, rather than a flat fee. Like the record company's points system, the bigger the band, the higher the percentage.

SKILLS YOU'LL NEED
Good business sense – spotting the unit-shifters and deleting the unpopular designs before you lose money on them; a visual eye, obviously; some idea about fashion; a keen eye on the new groups coming up so that you can lure them to your company.

TIPS
● You could try talking to the people who help run the T-shirt stalls at gigs.
● Make friends with young bands.
● If you're a design type, approach companies with ideas – they're always on the lookout for exciting, yet simple, designs.

USEFUL ADDRESSES
● Nice Man Merchandising, Amsua House, 717A North Circular Road, London, NW2 7AH
TEL 020 8357 7950
FAX 020 8357 7955

MUSIC PUBLISHER

MONEY: Anything between £11,000 and £60,000+ p.a.

HOURS: 10 a.m. to 6 p.m. in the office, with evenings and weekends spent seeing gigs in hallowed nightspots up and down the country.

HEALTH RISK: 7/10. Signing bands and helping them to develop can be exhausting. Multi-vitamins, please.

EQUIPMENT COSTS: Not a lot, unless you own your own company. It helps if you can drive a car from the off.

PRESSURE RATING: 7/10. The heat isn't on and the competition is slightly less fierce than for A&R men.

GLAMOUR RATING: 7/10. Yes, the stars of today and tomorrow may well come whistling into your office, but you only get to talk to them about Schedule D tax returns on their PRS cheques. And whether they could write a chorus for Emma Bunton. Sometime. When they get a spare moment.

TRAVEL RATING: 6/10. If the Northampton Roadmender's Club is your idea of an exotic locale, then cheers to you. Otherwise, you may not be roaming very far.

Almost every signed band has a publishing contract. You don't need to have your music published in order to have a top-forty hit, but someone has to collect your songwriting royalties from all over the world, and a publisher will do all the paperwork for you while you can go and try on new shoes for your TV appearance.

So you're in a band and a few record companies have expressed an interest. One night, a man in a hairy suit comes up to you after a gig and announces that he is an A&R man from Hairy Suit Publishing, and can he buy you a Campari and soda? You're worried, as well you might be – you've never met his like before.

Publishing is the only branch of the music industry that doesn't manufacture anything. It's thus one of the hardest to comprehend. All publishing companies scout around for new acts in the same way that record companies do. Anybody who writes songs is legally entitled to be paid every time they are played on the radio, or every time someone buys a record. So artists sign a publishing deal, which is a bit like a record contract – they sign up, on average, for between three to five albums. They receive an advance payment, the same as they do with a record contract. Excitingly, they can belong to two different multinational corporations (e.g. a band can sign to Polygram Publishing but release their records on Sony).

Essentially, publishers collect **songwriter** royalties from record companies and TV and radio stations. The recipients are the people who write the music and the lyrics – tambourine players tend not to feature. When bands sign a deal, the money may be split equally but more often than not the main songwriter gets a higher percentage of publishing royalties. Noel Gallagher, for instance, is a lot better off than Liam because he wrote all those hoary pub anthems. And while pop fluffets like Britney and Blue may need songwriters to do most of the hard work for them, they're the types who'll write the 'top line' and get a publishing credit and get a percentage too. See songwriter chapter for more details.

Songwriters get royalties from the Mechanical Copyright Protection Society (MCPS) and the Performing Rights Society (PRS). MCPS makes sure that, from every CD pressed, around 8.5 per cent of the **dealer price** is given to the songwriter. PRS deal with TV and radio programmes, which have to pay money to broadcast songs. Pubs and cafés also have to pay the PRS as jukeboxes and radios in a public place count as a 'performance'. However, the PRS may well take ages to wing the 30p round to the artist's door, so as a publisher you'll chase it up for them. For overseas royalties, international publishing collection agencies need to be approached.

YOU DEAL WITH SONGWRITERS WHO MAY NOT HAVE THE RIGHT LOOK TO GET A DEAL OF THEIR OWN. ROBBIE WILLIAMS'S SONGWRITER, ABOVE.*

Tricky, isn't it? There's a lot of paperwork, and that's what publishers are there for.

You can get a publishing deal, or get help from a publisher, even before you get a record deal. Mike Smith is head of A&R at EMI UK Publishing. 'Elastica is the obvious example of this,' he says. 'Justine came to me saying she'd got an idea for a band but only she and Justin the drummer were involved at the time. A guy who worked in our studio knew Annie [who became Elastica's bassist], and Justine found Donna [guitarist] through the small ads in *Melody Maker*. We booked them some early gigs in Windsor under an assumed name to give them practice, then demoed them in our studios, and they got a record deal from that.'

Mike Smith began by managing a band then met some record company A&R people and realised that he'd discovered 'the best job in the world'. He moved to London after university, got a temp job in the post room in the office building which housed MCA Music Publishing, and he got to know the A&R people there.

'I was going out, then telling the guys at MCA what bands I'd seen and who was good,' he says. 'I made a mock card with my name on it and I'd ring venues and blag in. It did get tricky cos

* NOT REALLY.

PUBLISHER

writer, and then it's my job to help them get a manager, an agent, a drummer and bass player ... and a record deal. We have our own demo studio that bands can use. Helping artists to do everything in the early days is possibly the most rewarding part of the job. Publishers are best at launching a band's career, then developing the group until they can go to a record company with a complete package.'

Once a record company is involved they will make the final decision on releases and general strategy, but a publisher can always give advice. Publishing companies also have a soundtrack department, which is essentially involved in pitching music for films and television. Ronan Keating had his first solo single 'When You Say Nothing At All' – an ode to mousey women perhaps – placed in the film *Notting Hill.* It was number one, oh yes. This is more common than it ever was, with artists donating songs knowing they will fling them higher in the charts. Some write songs specifically, like Destiny's Child's 'Independent Women' – specially produced for the first *Charlie's Angels* film. Often the soundtrack department will work *alongside* the director and producer of a film to craft a bangin' contemporary soundtrack which will help the film achieve new levels of youth kudos and help the artists involved sell more of their own records, a classic example of this being *Trainspotting*, which got Underworld heard by thousands more people. And what criticism an artist used to receive for letting a song be used for an advert has all but evaporated. It's more of a case of who *hasn't* licensed their songs to be used (um, the only band that springs to mind is

I started to meet bands and say that I worked at MCA and they'd think "Great!". Before they were signed, the Darling Buds' manager thought it was fantastic that MCA Publishing were interested in them. He didn't know I was just the guy from the post room.'

Smith believes publishers can nurture talent in a way record companies often can't. 'The best part of being a publisher is the chance to work with a band that has no record deal. Sometimes I work with just one song-

Radiohead). It's not the revolution any more, kids, they all want the Man's dollar.

EMI Publishing also deals with individual songwriters, who sign a publishing deal and then sell their songs to singers and bands or work with them in the studio. Paul Lisberg works at Sony BMG nowadays, having come from EMI Music Publishing, and handles writer/producers. 'Some songwriters can't get deals because they're not artists. I try to marry their work to any opportunity in which it might get released. Nowadays, you can also get artists working with writer/producers. For instance, producers Stannard and Rowe wrote with The Spice Girls. 'Wannabe' was co-written with The Spice Girls in the studio – the girls came up with the words and melody and together they built the song.'

Lisberg says his job has got more difficult because nowadays most artists write their own songs and it's regarded as far less credible to work with songwriters, even if you're a pop pancake like The Spice Girls.

Richard Manners is the managing director of Warner Chappell after having been at Polygram Island Publishing. He began as an A&R scout for Island Records, then hopped over to publishing and worked his way up, with his first hit signing being 'Pump Up the Volume' by MARRS. His signings include Pulp, The Cranberries, The Lighthouse Family and Suede. How does a top bigwig keep a company successful?

'You have to work hard and make sure that when you have success you're prepared for it,' he says. 'Don't sit around celebrating that success, then wonder what went wrong. It's like

a good football team – having got to first place it actually stays there and builds on that success.'

He trusts his team to pick the good songwriters and to stick with them and encourage them when they're down in the dumps and haven't made it yet. He is still in awe of his acts because he regards them as such good tunesmiths. 'I love them all,' he mutters. 'I've never lost my passion for a good song.'

When a cover version is released, the publishing money goes to the original songwriter. Wet Wet Wet's 'Love Is All Around' may have earned them a few bob when it was number one for a billion years, but Reg Presley from The Troggs made a tidy sum as the original songwriter. He then proceeded to spend the entire fortune on investigating the cosmic mysteries behind crop circles, apparently. Ah well. There you go.

GLOSSARY
● **Songwriter**
The person, or team, who composes the melody, lyrics and chord structure of a song. Songwriter's royalties are often split between the members of a band. They may each get a different percentage of the whole, depending on how key their contribution was. Can cause friction within the band later on.

● **Dealer price**
The price at which the CD is sold to the record shop, which varies a great deal, depending on how the record company envisages the product will sell.

SKILLS YOU'LL NEED
Ability to spot a good chorus, irrespective of whether the bassist has

a beard or not; communication skills, including being tactful about a ropey verse; sociability; dedication – results aren't often as immediate as in other areas of the industry.

TIPS

● You can get into publishing from a record company; A&R scouting is good practice.
● Media studies courses are invaluable as background training, but won't guarantee a job. Experience counts.
● Take a job in the post room, if you have to, to get a foot in the door.
● Always be aware of different musical trends – whether you personally like them or not. Folk music might come back again. Well, you never know. It might.

USEFUL ADDRESSES

● EMI Music Publishing, 127 Charing Cross Road, London, WC2H 0QY
TEL 020 7434 2131
FAX 020 7434 3531
WEBSITE www.emimusicpub.co.uk
● Performing Rights Society, 29–33 Berners Street, London, W1T 3AB
TEL 020 7306 4777
FAX 020 7631 8957
WEBSITE www.prs.co.uk
● Sony BMG, 69–79 Fulham High Street, London, SW6 3JW
TEL 020 7384 7600
FAX 020 7384 8164
WEBSITE www.sonybmgmusic.co.uk
● Warner Chappell Music Group Ltd, Griffin House, 161 Hammersmith Road, London, W6 8BS
TEL 020 8563 5800
FAX 020 8563 5810
WEBSITE www.warnerchappell.co.uk

MUSIC-TV PRESENTER

MONEY: From around £16,000 p.a., as a BBC presenter starting out. Around £15,000–40,000 a show as a primetime terrestrial presenter and top whack are those million-pound yearly contracts that Ant and Dec and Graham Norton have.

HOURS: A lot of them. Getting up early, staying up late, doing whatever the programme or producer demands.

HEALTH RISK: 7/10. Stress-related: everybody laughs when you make a mistake, and you may have to maintain a crazed grin for hours on end. You will want Botox by the time you're 22. A facelift when you're 30.

PRESSURE RATING: 9/10. You have to get things right on camera, be the 'public face' of the programme, not go out and visit 'women of the night' but still remain reasonably interesting for that *Radio Times* cover feature.

GLAMOUR RATING: 8/10. You get to talk to pop stars in exotic locales, go to premieres, snog famous people, get free clothes etc. Ooh, the agony.

TRAVEL RATING: 9/10. Hopping about hither and thither, countrywide and abroad, to file on-the-spot reports with Britney in China or one of the Arctic Monkeys in chokey.

A presenter is in charge of presenting top nuggets of rare insight, hot news and philosophical interviews on the television.

Television allows bands to parade around in moonboots singing songs about snogging and doing interviews in which they harp on about the number of raisins you get in Fruitibix. The wibbly wobbly world of the pop star fits like a glove into the bright and breezy world of TV. But! The medium needs someone to translate the genius of the bands for the audience! A presenter! Someone who 'anchors' the programme, provides a beaming face which welcomes you into the magical world of the programme. No joke.

Despite its appearance, presenting isn't something you can have a go at just because you've got all your own teeth. Most people have to spend years working behind the scenes in television before they get in front of the camera. Some may appear to be novices, but even they'll have gone for trillions of auditions and screen tests and been subjected to the Great Pondering of those powerful producers and directors. You can't just ring up SquareEyes Productions and demand that you present *That's My Bassline!!* next Monday, although they may appreciate your gumption and take you on as a **runner**.

This is how many people first start out on the rocky road towards being a presenter. Runners may spend their time making cups of tea for the staff,

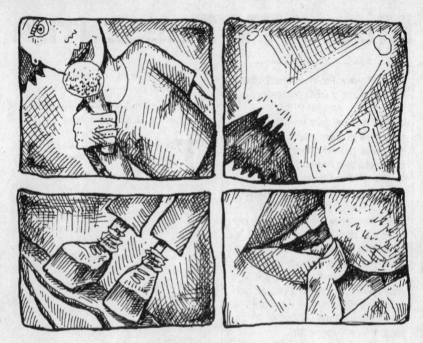

TV PRESENTER AND TV ANGLES

but just being on the inside of a production company will help you learn how television programmes are commissioned and made. Researchers, the next step up from runners, are there to liaise with promotions people to get the gen on new releases and who's around for interviews and performances. The final decision on which artists will appear on the programme rests with the producer, and the researcher then books them and gets hold of press clippings, videos and general info so the presenter can swot up on them. Most presenters will have a huge turnover of guests – but will need to know their onions all the time.

There are many routes into the job. Jonathan Ross was a researcher before he became a TV presenter. Vernon Kay was a model. Ant and Dec were actors, then pop stars. A lot of presenters on the main five British networks started through cable and satellite television.

Zoë Ball was a runner then a researcher, and she believes this is the best way to learn the ropes. Her first break was through 'a friend of a friend of a friend' starting on a kids' show in Manchester which went out on BSkyB (now Sky television). Promoted to researcher, Zoë set about attending auditions and **screen tests** for presenters because that's what she decided she wanted to do (after toying with the rival ideas of acting and journalism – no train driving for this one).

'At first I'd get so nervous that I'd bodge things up,' she remembers. 'I'd speak much too fast and I had to be a lot more controlled – but auditions and screen tests are terrifying things.' After a couple of screen tests Zoë 'began to wonder why I was bothering'. She hadn't realised how fierce competition was for this particular line of work. However, she eventually got a job as researcher for *The Big Breakfast*. She is keen to emphasise that she did it all off her own bat: her dad is ex-TV-presenter Johnny Ball, but Zoë was far too mortified to ask him for help and opted not to mention the connection to potential employers. Next up she went for a job on *Going Live!* and her screen-test tape was passed on to a bigwig at Children's BBC who rang her to ask her to join the CBBC team. She was in.

Zoë Ball says the BBC is good at training people, rather than simply chucking newcomers in front of the camera as some channels tend to. The BBC, even today, tends to be loyal, has lots of job opportunities, and is more reputable than some small independent companies who work presenters to the bone for very little cash, on a channel that no one watches. Zoë started off doing birthday links and built up confidence through this lower-profile stuff on CBBC. It's good training, and far better than being suddenly plucked from nowhere to be a pressured and high-profile new presenter – anybody remember **Huffty**?

Ms Ball had a spell on *The O Zone*, interviewing surly pop stars and chirpy rock types alike, before moving on to *Fully Booked* and then *Live and Kicking*. She quickly became the gleeful face of Saturday mornings, happy and kiddy-friendly, while also appealing to chaps who quite liked the fact she wore satiny trousers and looked like she might have had a few too many the night before.

TV presenting is a hectic job. There are invariably early starts and late finishes. Kate Thornton is used to all that. Working on *Pop Idol* she had a 5 a.m. start many mornings. That wasn't the half of it. Kate had to be alert, because she was **live on air.** Kate started as a journalist (and still writes), and knows that a print interview is a different beast from that which is on TV. If you're writing about someone who is boredom on legs, you can snip the dull bits and, in print, the person may come off a little less irksome than in real life. But if you're sitting in front of them, live on telly, you can't edit them afterwards. You have to be a rolling thundercloud of larks and distractions in order to make other people look good.

'It's like pulling teeth if someone's dull; they're hard work,' says Kate. 'It's a totally different set of skills compared with print. You can't talk over each other, you can't let things run on – you've got to be tight, to inform and be entertaining.'

After editing *Smash Hits,* Kate appeared on a show called *Straight Up* where she found, researched, scripted and presented pieces to be broadcast over a live hour slot. A producer had seen her on TV as *Smash Hits* spokesperson and liked her style. Kate then went on to do a variety of shows, many music-based which reflects her love of toons. She has interviewed them all, from Gareth Gates to Madonna.

'She's a real challenge because she's nobody's fool,' says Kate seriously. 'You really have to do your homework because she'll eat you for breakfast. And Noel Gallagher is great. A good interview is like a game of football, you're passing the ball and trying to score goals ... you just don't change ends at half time.'

Zoë Ball knows it's tough because your producer wants certain things out of the interview, as much as you'd like to ask your guest about the price of cheese. 'Sometimes I'm made to ask questions I don't want to,' she exclaims. 'I'm told, "You will ask so-and-so about his private life, you have to!" There are things I wouldn't want to be asked, so I hate doing it to other people.'

Jobs on the telly can lead to many other lines of work, DJing being an obvious example – Zoë, Kate Thornton, Sara Cox, Edith Bowman and Cat Deeley all do radio work. The state of music TV, according to Kate at time of going to press, is 'dreadful'.

'Not many new programmes are being made,' she says. 'They're expensive and they don't get the ratings. There are 24 music channels on all the time, and about three of them require presenters. It's a shrinking market, although *Pop Idol*, *Popstars* and *Fame Academy* are music-based entertainment shows ...'

Kate is adamant that a career in telly can be yours, with a bit of perseverance. Even though it looks like you can only get on TV if you've had a lot of exposure in the tabloids: Jack Osbourne, Neil and Christine Hamilton, Paris Hilton ... hm and double hm.

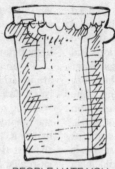

PEOPLE HATE YOU COS YOU'RE ON TELLY AND TRY TO SPILL THIS ON YOUR TROUSERS.

'It's difficult but not impossible,' says Kate, full of optimism. 'More and more people have come from a background in music journalism but there are a hundred million ways to get into TV. Just get out there and do work experience. MTV and VH1 have a lot of opportunities.'

Overall, the further career opportunities for a successful presenter are immense, even more so if you become an intrepid businessperson and start your own production company, Chris Evans or Ginger Productions-style. Obviously, you have more power within the industry, more control over what you do, and loads more cash as head of a company. Buy all the Prada rucksacks you wish! Shout at people in board meetings!

'If the face falls, you move to a medium that doesn't require visuals,' says Kate, cunning as ever. 'I'm one of the lucky ones because I can always pick up a pen and earn a living, that's why I've never stopped writing, because one day I will have to do that. But that's no punishment, it's a brilliant way to earn a living and not a proper job.'

Presenting is not something that everyone can do, even though it may seem a wheeze and an absolute doddle from the outside. Take *Big Brother* winner Kate Lawler on *RI:SE*. She was, let's face it, rubbish. Some people, however, are naturals – they get in front of a camera and make talking about Elton John's promotional pyjama competition seem like the most natural thing in the world.

'A lot of people act when they're trying to present, but you have to be yourself,' says Zoë. 'Someone told me when I first started out that I should imagine there's one small child sitting at home on their own and you have to make them feel that you're their friend. You have to be cheerful, no matter how crappy you're feeling or how crappy your life is that day.'

Naturally, appearing on television comes with its own inbuilt pressures. Everyone knows who you are. Both Zoë and Kate have had to deal with tabloid intrusion but are pragmatic enough to know it comes with the territory. One music-TV presenter used to go out, only to have people 'accidentally' spill their pint on her just because she was on telly. She says, 'I'll never do it again. I don't mind being successful, but not on television. It can screw you up if you start young.'

'People expect you to smile and be charming all the time,' says Zoë. 'Sometimes I wish people would leave me alone. The papers build you up and knock you down. You can't take it too seriously, or take yourself too seriously.'

Zoë's advice for budding presenters is to get into drama clubs, work on the school magazine, and generally put yourself about a bit. If you ring up TV and production companies and offer to do work for nothing at weekends and in the holidays, you might be lucky and they might need someone. Even if you have had no experience of telly, the fact that you've done other things, like drama, shows people you have an interest in performing. Follow the charts, watch presenters, and work out why you like the ones you do – what their special bit of magic is. As mentioned above, there are many youngsters doing work experience or working as runners in television who will eventually go on to do other, far more exciting, things – but not without a lot of determination.

Zoë is very honest about her job, which she adores. 'I love my job, I fully recommend it – but at the same time there are other sides,' she concludes. 'It's not always glamorous and you're not always up for it! But you get paid a fortune and it's a great laugh – I honestly don't know what else I'd do.'

GLOSSARY
● **Runner**
The tea boy/girl position. Runs errands, mails things out, files pieces of paper, rings up other runners when things are needed from other companies. Also, goes out to Prêt à Manger to get the presenter a nice sandwich.
● **Screen tests**
When you present a piece of news, gossip or off-the-top-of-your-head nonsense in front of a video camera. You might have to interview someone. Generally, they put you under the same pressure as a TV presenter live on air, to test you out. The director watches all of them afterwards and decides who to employ.
● **Huffty**
Ill-fated TV presenter who was roped in to present *The Word* because she was deemed 'alternative' (a lesbian in City braces). She left after one series.
● **Live on air**
Some programmes are pre-recorded; others go out as they happen. Live TV is very demanding and extremely difficult to master: you have to be

prepared for anything to happen – pop stars swearing etc.

SKILLS YOU'LL NEED

To be natural in front of a camera; to be able to get on with kids, suits and rock stars alike; to be interested not just in music but the world and people and their pets; to look reasonably cheery.

TIPS

● Get work experience – helping at weekends with independent companies or the BBC is ideal. Ring them up to find out what sort of people they require. MTV offers internships and pays £190 a week.

● Watch other presenters and see how they do it.

● Never try to copy anyone. It'll end in tears.

● It's best to realise that you won't be on *MTV* next Friday. The rungs of the ladder have to be scaled and there are no short cuts.

USEFUL ADDRESSES

● BBC, TV Centre, Wood Lane, London, W12 7RJ
TEL 020 8743 8000
FAX 020 8749 7520
WEBSITE www.bbc.co.uk
● Channel 4, 124 Horseferry Road, London, SW1P 2TX
TEL 020 7396 4444
FAX 020 7306 8630
WEBSITE www.channel4.com
● Channel 5, 22 Long Acre, London, WC2E 9LY
TEL 020 7421 7161
FAX 020 7497 5575
WEBSITE www.five.tv

● Granada, Quay Street, Manchester, M60 9EA
TEL 0161 832 7211
FAX 0161 953 0298
WEBSITE www.itvregions.com/granada
● MTV UK & Ireland, Hawley Crescent, London, NW1 8TT
TEL 020 7284 7777
FAX 020 7284 6466
WEBSITE www.mtv.co.uk
● VH-1, Hawley Crescent, London, NW1 8TT
TEL 020 7284 7777
FAX 020 7550 5575
WEBSITE www.vh1.co.uk

MUSIC-TV PRODUCER/ DIRECTOR

MONEY: From a few hundred quid per show if you're working on cable or after-dark programmes, to thousands and thousands per year on mainstream programmes, like that *Pop Idol*.

HOURS: From a couple of days to more than seventy hours a week.

HEALTH RISK: 7/10. Having to work with people 'in television' is enough to give anyone permanent heartburn, at least.

PRESSURE RATING: 9/10. It's your job to make sure the programmes are top quality and have artists that people want to hear. You never switch off.

GLAMOUR RATING: 7/10. You get to talk to the stars about how they want their close-up, then try not to hit them if they don't agree with you.

TRAVEL RATING: 6/10. Mainly working from your office, the studio, and perhaps some location work.

Music-TV producers are the people that book all the sumptuous new sounds on to their programme and are responsible for providing a good visual bed for tunes to lie down on, as it were.

You'd think getting a band on to TV would be easy. They have a hit single, you like them, they have a spare afternoon and wooh! They're playing live to an audience of several million with time for a chip supper in the canteen before they whizz off home to catch *Hollyoaks*. Not so! Putting pop stars on the box is the job of the TV producer, and it is a lot of hard work. Producers deal with the whole programme: it's their vision; they're the ones who ultimately have to come up with ideas and the feel of the series they're working on. They have to make pop stars either look a bit shiny, or a bit pasty, or ugly – whatever the remit they've invented for themselves is.

Andi Peters started out as a TV presenter when he was seventeen, after writing to the producer of a young person's programme called *Free Time*. Two years later, in 1989, he was presenting BBC music programme *The Ozone*. He's gone on to become a director and producer, for the BBC and LWT before moving to Channel 4 in March 1998 as Commissioning Editor, Children and Young People, where he created *T4*, the weekend TV slot. He is now Executive Editor, Popular Music for BBC Television. Churgh.

'When I worked for Children's BBC, we never had enough staff so I did a bit of everything,' says Andi. 'One day on *The Ozone* there was nobody who could make the film so I said, "OK, I'll have a go at making it." It went from there. It was quite an easy transition to make.

TV PRODUCER

WHAT I SAY GOES, RIGHT.

VERY IMPORTANT BUTTON

'I was filming every day of the week,' he continues. 'After six months you get used to how every director works, and having a high turnover of directors I picked up a lot of tips from different people.'

His first film was about trainers, the second, how to be a DJ. He loved working on both sides of the camera and did both presenting, producing and directing for four years at the BBC.

'You have to be very calm to be a director,' he says. 'You have to be able to visualise everything – the best directors know what the end product will look like, but also are able to change it constantly when they need to.'

As a director, you have a team of people working under you.

'You've got to be able to be the captain of the ship,' says Andi. 'Everybody around you is expected to be told what to do. I have friends who produce but they've never directed, they don't want that much responsibility. Everyone

makes mistakes at first, but you learn from them. I did a shoot where I literally forgot to check if they were recording. Now that's not my job – but I forgot to check. So we did a whole piece without the sound. We re-synced the whole thing, it took forever but it had to be done.'

The essential difference between producer and director is that the producer comes up with ideas and makes sure things stick to a budget. The director turns the ideas into reality and works within the boundaries the producer has set. 'The rest of the team are there to make the producer and director look good,' reckons one insider. These people do the boring stuff which is the same for every music programme, such as booking stars, getting them to the studio on time, writing links for the presenters and making sure they know what's going on, but these are the people that rise through the ranks and become top dogs. 'There are people who used to work for me as runners who are now commissioning editors at Channel 4,' says Mr Peters.

Andi moved to Channel 4 in 1998. He 'identified that the channel would make a killing if it increased its 16–24-year-old audience'. He was at a position where he could make executive decisions, making sure *Hollyoaks* was seen by a wider audience, overseeing *Shipwrecked* and introducing Dermot O'Leary to our screens. Are his executive decisions made sitting on high in his office? Or on the ground, so to speak, with the guys?

'I do both,' he says. 'My office used to be right next to the *Top of the Pops* team, so I always made sure I knew what they're doing. But I'm hands on – I used to do edits for *Top of the Pops*. The team were like, "Oh God, Andi's in the edit!" but I've got to keep my hand in, to make sure I always know what's going on. In any job, if you're in a position of power, you have to be able to do what you're asking someone else to do for you. If I'm asking a runner to do something, I must make sure I know how to do the job myself. That's important.'

TV people still have a reputation for being loud and arrogant, always stamping about trying to be important. They are the Gordon Ramsays of the media.

'I don't rule by fear, but I know people who do,' says Andi, who also says he hates 'doing lunch'. 'There definitely are those people, but I don't choose to run my teams that way. It does happen, but I think it's getting less and less ...'

Many people in TV think that they are the most important people in the world. Even if you tell them they are

not, they get shirty. TV is all about confidence, ego and drive. You really can't be a wallflower if you fancy going into this line of work. Oh, and people in TV have to be ruthless – it's all about ratings. You can't be sentimental or want people to like you. True.

'People either want to be pop stars or to work in TV,' reckons Peters. 'TV is hard to get into. I'd rather hire someone with common sense than someone who has a degree; it counts for a lot. It really does.

'I did a seminar once with 2,000 people,' he continues. 'This one girl stood up and said, "I have tried everything to get into television, how do I get in?" I said, "Fine, be at Channel 4 tomorrow morning at 9 o'clock and I will give you a job." She turned up, I gave her a job as a runner and she's now a producer. I feel really passionate that people should be given a chance; she was cheeky enough to stand up in front of all those people.'

Another keen type sent his CV in to Andi while he was stuffing CDs in envelopes for a record company. Andi 'loved it ... the tenacity, the drive, he used his head. To get into TV you've got to be yourself and don't give up – there are a lot of people fighting for jobs so do what you can do to be different.'

Do you have to be young?

'Just today I've taken on a 28-year-old runner. At the same time, he's working with a 19-year-old, so it will be interesting to see the dynamic between the two. I often take on young people because it gives them opportunity, they generally have a lot more ideas and I can teach them to work in a certain way without too much baggage.'

People think TV is a black art. The fact that it's so difficult to get a foot in the door enhances this. Some disagree.

'There is a huge amount of mythology surrounding television,' say Chris Cowey, former *Top of the Pops* producer. 'People say it's really competitive, pressurised or hard work. Well, from the first time I walked into a TV studio I've been trying to find the hard bit. I'm from a mining family in Sunderland, and true pressure is working a mile underground in a three-foot-high coal seam with six inches of water around you. No, TV is sheer fun.'

Ideas are the solid-gold currency of TV production, and sometimes they can prove vulnerable to exploitation from cynical people – people may nick your format or pass it off as their own. New TV shows have to go through the pilot stage, and deregulation means you have to employ a production company to pay for the **pilot**. Now, if they pay you to produce the programme, some production companies can assume they've also paid for the original idea. Many people get ripped off in this game and a lot of people are utterly ruthless. Everyone on every rung of the so-called ladder has to deal with pressure. Andi Peters was in charge of making *Top of the Pops* better. A difficult job.

'I didn't run the show day to day, but it was still a huge thing to handle,' he says. 'It was the only music show in primetime. It was never my ambition to work on it, but to be given such a big brand to suddenly look after was a huge accolade. I worked on new programmes too; the trouble with the job is that you never stop, but it comes with the territory. I'm used to it. The perks are that you work in TV, make live TV shows and work with some really fun people.'

GLOSSARY
● **Pilot**
Every show on telly has had a pilot made: a practice show to give the TV station an idea of the content, tone and design of the programme. Nothing to do with aeroplanes.

SKILLS YOU'LL NEED
You must be calm, organised and adaptable, have a sense of humour and be a born optimist.

TIPS
● Start by getting your foot in the door: do work experience, write lots of letters to TV stations.
● Learning camera technique isn't really necessary. Few people come from the technical side; most come from researching and presenting.
● Journalism courses are good training for researching. A media-studies background is also a good starting point.
● Simply, if you have a brilliant idea and some knowledge of the media, you can approach an independent TV company with a view to producing a pilot. They're desperate for great formats.
● Practise on your friends by inviting local bands to their houses and seeing if they want to hear their tunes or not.
   Well, it's a start.

USEFUL ADDRESSES
● BBC, TV Centre, Wood Lane, London, W12 7RJ
TEL 020 8743 8000
FAX 020 8749 7520
WEBSITE www.bbc.co.uk

● Channel 4, 124 Horseferry Road,
London, SW1P 2TX
TEL 020 7396 4444
FAX 020 7306 8630
WEBSITE www.channel4.com
● Channel 5, 22 Long Acre, London,
WC2E 9LY
TEL 020 7421 7161
FAX 020 7497 5575
WEBSITE www.five.tv
● Granada, Quay Street, Manchester,
M60 9EA
TEL 0161 832 7211
FAX 0161 953 0298
WEBSITE www.itvregions.com/granada
● MTV UK & Ireland, Hawley
Crescent, London, NW1 8TT
TEL 020 7284 7777
FAX 020 7284 6466
WEBSITE www.mtv.co.uk

PERSONAL TRAINER

💰 **MONEY:** From £15,000 to £60,000 p.a. – or freelance, paid by the hour, if you're just starting out.

🕐 **HOURS:** Starting early in the morning (you know how people like to jog) to evening time.

➕ **HEALTH RISK:** 7/10. You may drop a barbell on your foot, or trouble yourself going for that all-important last bench press.

🧰 **EQUIPMENT COSTS:** If you own your own gym, you'll have to pay for the machines. However, freelance trainers use public gym facilities.

✊ **PRESSURE RATING:** 5/10. Getting the stars to find some motivation isn't always the easiest thing.

🍸 **GLAMOUR RATING:** 5/10. You see famous people sweat. Not so glitzy.

✈ **TRAVEL RATING:** 3/10. To the gym. Around the park. Only if you work for someone like Madonna will she ship you around the world with her curling tongs.

Fitness instructors help many pop stars keep lookin' good and feelin' great. There are so many opportunities to eat badly and sit around a lot that many artists are gagging to get on a rowing machine for twenty minutes every day, unbelievably enough.

Pop stars sometimes get lardy around the middle. One day they'll look in the mirror, or espy a particularly ropey picture of themselves, and realise it's time to slim down. Personal trainers are the people to give them motivation to jog around. Where would Peter Andre be today without his sparkling **chest teeth** (and, er, without the blessing of Jordan's own ample chest as she struts beside him in publicity photos)? What price Misteeq if they didn't go to the gym for their **butts'** sake? And Robbie Williams? Exactly. He didn't shrink because he got left out in the rain, you know.

John Plum has his own company, the London Fitness Consultancy Ltd, and trains pop stars so they can get fit and slinky. He started out by getting a sports science degree – concentrating on biomechanical analysis(!). No rugby was played; it was strictly theoretical stuff: how muscle strength affects movement, for instance. The degree course is combined with chemistry and maths, psychology and sociology, and more stuff about exercise.

A lot of trainers aren't all that qualified, and so if you do a tough university course like the one above it should help you to get a good job ... eventually. Most trainers start out being fairly badly paid but working in the leisure industry is attractive and you get free turns on the stair-o-lator, which means that a lot of people want to do the job.

John started at the Champneys Health Club below the Meridian Hotel in Piccadilly, London, as a fitness

PERSONAL TRAINER

instructor assessing people and devising exercise programmes. 'The pay was atrocious,' he remembers.

The next step for a muscly type is to go into management – but, again, it's not that well paid and there's lots of paperwork to do. John therefore decided to go travelling and looked around Australia and North America to see how the fitness industry worked there. This turned him into a man with a mission – to become a personal trainer.

Being a personal trainer involves dealing directly with individual keep-fitters and being with them at every session or alternate session in order to monitor their progress and keep their motivation levels up. A personal trainer is neither a nutritionist nor a doctor, but you should certainly know the basic ins and outs of healthy eating and first aid.

Some experts train people in their homes if they have enough room to fit in a rowing machine and treadmill. Other trainers take them out to the park to jog around the ponds. John started a gym in west London with two other trainers by converting an old industrial unit. It's all by appointment only. So what are these stars like to work with?

'Mostly they're nice people,' says Mr Plum. 'I wouldn't treat them any differently from anybody else. I've met some trainers who think it's important to get a few stars so they can then raise their prices. I'm into this to improve people's health. Celebrities are all well and good but we can never view them as long-term clients. They're not easy clients, through no fault of their own. They travel a lot and you don't see them for months.'

John says he never gets free T-shirts or gold discs. He charges per hour but admits it's hard to take holidays and the levels of work are inconsistent. However, seeing plumpies develop glistening pecs and thighs of steel is recompense enough. He also thanks his lucky stars he's never got into too much bother with clients.

'My friend is a trainer in LA. He was hired by a film studio to help a star lose a few pounds. He was going to get $20,000 to work two hours per day for three months. The trainer was pleased

WARNING. SOME CLIENTS MAY
HAVE SHOES THAT ARE PRICIER
THAN YOUR EQUIPMENT.

to do it because it was good for his
kudos and it was good money – he got
half the money up front. The star took
a fancy to the trainer and told him, "If
you don't do exactly what I say you
ain't gonna get the money." He didn't
continue with the job. There are some
unscrupulous people out there.'

GLOSSARY
● **Chest teeth**
Or 'abs', as they are also known.
Abdominal muscles are cubey and
bobbly and spring out if you do about
a hundred sit-ups a day. They look
like teeth, a bit, if you hold your head
at a ninety-degree angle. Watch out
for them.
● **Butt**
Bottom.
● **Kudos**
Very important in the world of
entertainment. Kudos is the glory that
you'll garner from being involved in
something trendy or well respected. It
usually does not last, unless you've

discovered a cure for a disease, or
something.

SKILLS YOU'LL NEED
Ability to get on with people, being
fit, knowing about the human body
and fitness, knowing about how the
expensive weight-trainers work, being
muscly so people think that you know
what you're talking about. Looking
like Charles Hawtrey won't help.

TIPS
● The better qualified you are, the
better the job you will get – and the
better job you will do. A degree in
sports science is a good way to start.
● You have to be interested in
exercise and have at least played a bit
of lacrosse in your time. It's no use
explaining how the abs develop if you
don't possess any yourself.
● Gain experience in a health club.
● At least you'll have access to the
abs machine. Some people start as
members and become instructors.

PHOTOGRAPHER

MONEY: Varies. Photographer's assistants often work for nothing when they start, and yet top photographers get paid by the thousands for shooting album campaigns and tour programmes.

HOURS: 'About 24 hours a day, every day,' many of them say. You can start a shoot at five in the morning and it can go on until well past midnight.

HEALTH RISK: 6/10. Those developing fluids aren't kind to the system, especially if you start drinking them, hur hur.

EQUIPMENT COSTS: Fairly high. Camera equipment is being constantly updated and a new lens alone can set you back £1,000. You may have to pay your own film and developing costs for magazines, and these can easily be at least a couple of hundred quid. Unless you're digital.

PRESSURE RATING: 8/10. If you have two minutes to take a picture for the cover of *Smash Hits*, which is often the case, then the pressure is high. However, most photographers survive on the adrenalin. Man.

GLAMOUR RATING: 9/10. You get to meet top celebrities and have to ask them to 'Please stop doing that with your nose' and so forth. You may go on tour with a band and be mistaken for the bassist's aunt in Ohio.

TRAVEL RATING: 9/10. You go all over the ruddy place. However, you must always remember to complain about how heavy your equipment is and how you don't want customs to scan your bag containing sensitive film.

Every band needs their picture taken, and they have to rely on someone who won't put their finger over the lens.

There has never been, in the sizzling history of rock 'n' roll, a band who didn't have their picture taken at some point. Never. And rock artists are not happy with one little snap. They want rolls and rolls of film: different ones for every magazine article, single release and tour. Hair up, hair down, with a new moustache, dressed as a prawn ... Bands and artists always need someone to press the shutter in new and dynamic eye-startling ways.

There are many courses in photography from GCSE and HND right up to degree level. Some budding snappers start with a course – although many more don't – then graduate and help out already established photographers in the studio and on location shoots – 'assisting'. John Spinks, who has worked for *The Face* and various other magazines, rang around the photographic studios he found in Yellow Pages.

'Eventually I phoned Metro studios,' he says. 'I spoke to someone there and explained who I was, and he said, "What are you doing next Friday?" So I borrowed money from my mum to go down from Manchester to London for a couple of days. In the end they gave me a job but it didn't pay.

'When you are an assistant, you are basically a skivvy,' reckons Spinks. 'You do menial things such as sweeping up, painting **the infinity cove** and doing the washing-up. You're below even the bottom rung of the ladder.' John soon became the assistant to swanky fashion photographer Jurgen Teller, and then started a photography collective called Sixsixfour.

Tom Howard, a top *Smash Hits* snapper, started out as a freelance assistant then worked full time for lensperson Simon Fowler, who created his own distinctive style of brightly coloured bouncy pop images which every pop band of the late 80s and early 90s wanted – yer Kylies, Bros and, um, Big Fun.

'I gained confidence from that experience because I felt I had plenty of creative input,' says Tom. 'I reached a stage when I would be standing beside him, thinking: I can do this. After two years I decided to move on and do my own thing, and then I realised how difficult it actually is. Suddenly you are the photographer and the buck stops at you.'

Valerie Phillips also began working at *Smash Hits*, and now has sessions with Tricky and PJ Harvey and swanky fashion shoots in her portfolio. However, she has never even studied photography or assisted anyone.

'I was completely unqualified,' she says. 'I did a foundation course at art school in New York. It was a four-year course, of which I did one year. Then

I moved to London and started going to concerts and taking live photos of bands and showing them to people who might know someone who wanted some pictures done on the cheap. I was rubbish, but I had a lot of enthusiasm and did whatever it took to do a job.'

Valerie persuaded the then manager of the Manic Street Preachers to let her take pictures of the band live. He liked the photos, and she was consequently commissioned by the band to do a couple of record sleeves. This led to work for *Smash Hits* taking pictures of New Kids On The Block, Take That and all the other young nippers on the scene. She was such a novice when she started, having blagged her way in, that before her first studio session – with Van Morrison – she had never even used **lights** before. For another session, she put the film through the wrong process and completely melted it. Luckily she had another few rolls which she processed very carefully and correctly. 'I was mortified, but I never owned up,' she recalls.

Magazines employ a picture editor (see 'Picture Editor' chapter) to commission photo shoots for features and other items. And once you work regularly for a magazine such as *NME* you're strongly discouraged from working also for rival titles such as *Q* magazine. The *NME* still pays photographers according to the size of the picture used on the page, but all other magazines pay a day rate to cover the shoot, cost of film, developing and the pictures.

A few months after the publication that commissioned you has used your pictures, you can sell them on to a

picture agency who may syndicate them worldwide, mainly to foreign magazines who can't get an exclusive shoot with a band. There is a lot of money to be made in syndication, but top pop persons such as Justin Timberlake or Beyoncé will nowadays make you sign a form which promises that you won't syndicate the shots, as this inevitably means that the act loses revenue from their own merchandising sales. Tough, isn't it?

Record companies commission their own photos to send out to the press (for use alongside news stories, small articles or simply for their files) or for album and single sleeves. After a certain amount of time working for magazines, record company types will get to know your name and ask you to take a picture for new, entirely made-up, band Boyzerk's single sleeve, for example. If they get to really like your work, you may be sent on Boyzerk's round-the-world tour to shoot sizzlin' snaps for a tour programme, for worldwide press pictures for the record company to use, or perhaps even eventually for a book of Boyzerk's currazy exploits. This, as they say, rakes in the cash. You'll also see the world's hotel bars, from Bahrain to Bournemouth.

For each job you will be given a brief by the commissioning editor or record company – you are told exactly what sort of shots are wanted. This can get a little complicated, says Tom Howard. 'The worst brief is where there are four or five people involved in a job and they all have different ideas as to what should be happening as far as pictures are concerned,' he says. 'My job is to please all of them and the people in front of the camera. The easiest part of being a photographer is taking the pictures; dealing with the egos that are inevitably involved is the hardest part. You can't please everyone the whole time.'

A lot of the photographer's skill lies in bringing out something special in the person in front of the lens, which may well prove tricky if the star thinks he is such a cool hunkin' dude that all he has to do is sit there with his shades and muffler on.

aww...

YOU MIGHT SPEND MOST OF YOUR TIME PERSUADING YOUR POP STARS NOT TO WEAR SHADES.

'When I've got someone really difficult and arrogant,' says Tom, 'I take whatever quality is there in them and try to exaggerate it. If someone is really self-satisfied then I play on that and encourage them to be even more so. They should feel relaxed in front of the camera, so sometimes I end up making a fool of myself. I just go twittering on – sometimes it works and sometimes it doesn't.

'You have to gauge each situation as it arises,' he continues. 'You may have only five minutes, so you have to just steam in and see what happens. I always like to create an atmosphere where a) people are relaxed and b) you allow space for sponta- neous things to happen and are ready for them when they occur. One of my favourite people, who I think has complete charisma, is Robbie Williams.'

When photo- graphing super- top stars for a magazine, time is very much of the essence. You may well have taken three months at col- lege to complete one project, but some stars rarely allow a photogra- pher to take more than a few frames, and Spike Milligan (although not a pop star) once famously

PHOTOGRAPHER

let a hapless photographer take just one solitary picture before booting him out. Mariah Carey would only be snapped from one angle, showing her 'best side'. Very irritating. This writer once worked on an All Saints book. They looked a bit 'tired' when it came to interviews, but soon perked up when the photographer got the Polaroid out and they could instantly get a visual take on the whole concept. They got so excited they started pulling up their tops and 'revealing' them- selves! Goodness moi.

Many music photographers diver- sify into fashion, although this is noto- riously badly paid when it comes to

magazine work but can effectively act as an advert to get you into the high- cash world of fashion advertising, where a single campaign can net you tens of thousands of pounds. The downside to music photogra- phy is that you're too often working with someone else's ideas, or else with people who may not even want their picture taken in the first place and are hell-bent on keeping on the windcheater which sure as anything will ruin your **chiaroscuro**.

Valerie Phillips soon found that fashion pho- tography could be more creative than working for pop magazines. 'I realised how unbelievably *simple* a lot of people were when I worked with bands,' she says, in outspoken style. 'I found it frustrating trying to communicate the things that I wanted to do. I also kept having to go on tours with people I wouldn't voluntarily have spent time with. In the end I simply thought: I cannot suffer another **Menswear** ses- sion. I didn't want to get stuck with the inevitable, never-ending look-it's-a- pop-star-wheel-them-in-wheel-them- out thing.'

Contrary to what you may instinc- tively believe, many pop stars absolutely hate having their picture taken. Sheryl Crow has been known to cry after some photo sessions, even if they've gone well. Sarah Cracknell from St Etienne has been quoted as saying, 'They say the camera never lies. Well, it does. It's a lying bastard.' Singers are often so vain that they fear the camera will make them look too ugly. They will often only let photographers shoot the first three songs of a live set, before they start looking sweaty. What an odd bunch these people are.

Once you have a body of work in a portfolio, you can approach magazines that you like and show them your stuff. Hopefully they'll think that David Bailey's got nothing on you, and generously allow you to go and take pictures of some nonentity playing in a portaloo in Coventry – you will almost certainly have to start this way before you start snapping glamorous front covers. A lot of photographers eventually get agents who show their portfolio around for them, liaise with the bigwig editors, and take a percentage fee accordingly.

Photography is often seen as a loner's trade – but it doesn't have to be that way. John Spinks and his mates started their Sixsixfour company in order to boost each other's morale. 'We pooled our experience, money and equipment,' he says. 'We only ever had our photos credited to Sixsixfour, rather than our individual names.' They all fell out in the end. Oh well.

Photographic equipment is expensive but it's not an absolute given that in order to be a good photographer you need bucketfuls of flashlights and twenty super-snoot lenses. Anton Corbijn – ground-breaking and much revered stylish Dutch music photographer who is first port of call for U2, REM and Depeche Mode – apparently has two lenses and one 35mm camera.

Tom Howard reckons he has a bag that has £12,000-worth of camera malarkey in it: a lens, a camera, a flashlight and little else. Insurance bills are naturally very high and, if you drive, your car insurance is higher because insurers automatically expect that rock photographers will be taking Jon Bon Jovi to his favourite Chinese restaurant every evening, whether that's actually the case or not. Digital photography has made the process a little cheaper – no rolls of film or developing costs. Certainly it's faster, magazine and newspaper news desks rely on snappers downloading photos they've just taken onto a laptop, then emailing them in to be designed around the copy immediately.

Valerie Phillips says of being a rock photographer: 'Never take no for an answer and don't start compromising.' John Spinks disagrees. 'There are loads of arseholes out there, so try to be nice,' he advises. 'I once spent seven hours painting the infinity cove red, yellow and green, then when the photographer arrived he just screamed and swore at me in front of the whole crew of models, clients and assistants.'

Tom Howard says he would never have considered becoming a photographer had he known what it was really like to do the job. 'I was blessed with ignorance,' he reflects. 'If I'd known what the competition was going to be like, I would have had second thoughts. But you have started: your enthusiasm carries you through. The only other thing I have to say about the job is ...'

What?

'It's not a good way to sleep with

pop stars. I wouldn't recommend it for that.'

There you have it.

A bit about paparazzi photographers:

Liam Gallagher describes them as a 'pain in the arse'. Chris Martin from Coldplay sometimes loses his temper with them. Catherine Zeta-Jones got in a huff when one of them took a picture of her eating a tiny morsel of grub at her wedding. Even The Chemical Brothers have been had by the paparazzi. Honest. *The Chemical Brothers.*

The word 'paparazzi' literally means 'buzzing insects', but these insects help sell newspapers – would anyone buy the tabloids or *Heat* magazine if they were just filled with words?

Jack Ludlam from London Paparazzi has been doing the job for around fourteen years. Formerly a cameraman, he got fed up 'waiting for the phone to ring' and decided the snapper's flexible hours were much more suitable.

The first picture he had printed was David Bowie coming out of a Japanese restaurant. Next picture was Kim Wilde and Chris Evans, when they were going out. 'I thought, "This works!" I was hooked from that point.

'I've done some pictures that were good, but weren't newsworthy,' continues Jack on the nature of his craft. 'I've taken some absolute crap by contrast, but it was in demand. *Sometimes* you take a good picture, it sells and you get both.'

Jack is keen to stress that he doesn't doorstep celebrities and says the good lensman will 'pull back' if he senses his subject is uncomfortable. The pics are mostly of stars walking along, shopping or getting out of taxis. No perv-shots of naked celebs on beach holidays, thanks.

'You know what you can and can't do,' he says. 'I don't betray anyone's confidence. The pictures I take are generally not used detrimentally. People link the term *paparazzi* with the *News of the World*, or undercover journalism.'

Ludlam has snapped Robbie Williams kissing Nicole Appleton when they started going out – 'they just started snogging in front of me'. He's taken pictures of Sophie Ellis Bextor surreptitiously at the West End club G-A-Y. ('Although I had a moment of angst about that one.') He's never had anyone threaten to punch his lights out.

'Most of that is horse play,' he says. 'Sometimes people do get a bit funny, but if you're taking pictures outside a club at three in the morning, and they're out of their box, it tends to happen.'

Ludlam, who sounds a bit like a London cab driver, says his fellow paps come from 'every walk of life ... Some are proper photographers, others are snap happy. There are a few autograph hunters who go out with a camera ...' Most paps go through agencies, but some go it alone and deal with the newspapers direct. Whatever, you don't have to be an intrusive moron and it can be a lucrative job. As Jack says, 'There's no ceiling limit to what you can earn.'

GLOSSARY
● **The infinity cove**
Where the wall meets the floor in a studio. It's all smoothed around so you can't see the line when Mr or Ms

Pop Star stands in front of it. It has to be painted (mainly white) every time it's used – which is many times a week. What a job!

● **Lights**

The big tungsten things that burn holes into your brain if you look at them when they flash. A lot of photography is about getting these 'right', i.e. making people look like they're among the golden sands of Tahiti rather than dossing around in a shed. Unless you want them looking like they're in a particularly artistic shed, that is. Very difficult, that one, as it happens.

● **Picture agency**

These represent individual photographers, from *NME* lenspeople to paparazzi, and sell their work around the world. Shots of Axl Rose coming out of Mr Byrite, for instance, will be bought for a price by a magazine to print in a future issue. Studio sessions already printed in Britain will be sold overseas by the company, who take a percentage for every picture used.

● **Chiaroscuro**

The treatment of light and shade which make up the composition of the visual image. Very Anton Corbijn.

● **Menswear**

A band of the 90s, who were hyped for about four minutes but were not necessarily … um, you know, *with it*.

SKILLS YOU'LL NEED

A good 'eye' for a picture, communication skills (to wake up bleary pop stars who've not been long out of bed), friendliness, organisational skills, a good memory, enthusiasm. Lots of photographers turn into video directors, so it may be an advantage in the long run if you are interested in cinema.

TIPS

● Look at photographic books to see which styles you like.
● The London College of Communication provides good photography courses, as do art schools. You'll need to do a foundation course first.
● Try to assist either at a photographic studio or with a specific photographer to learn the trade – ring them up and sound friendly and confident. Don't try too hard: be honest about your experience, and don't crack any bad jokes.
● Realise that you'll be making cups of tea for people who probably have several grands' worth of hangover.
● You can't make too many blunders. If you forget to put the film in a camera during an average session, you can just shoot another roll – but don't do it too often.
● Take pictures of friends. It's good practice and they never insist on wearing sunglasses.

USEFUL ADDRESSES

● www.londonpaparazzi.com
Jack Ludlam's website.
● London College of Communication, Elephant and Castle, London, SE1 6SB
TEL 020 7514 6562
FAX 020 7514 6535

PICTURE EDITOR

MONEY: From £17,000 to £30,000+ p.a. if you're on a magazine's staff. Between £75 and £150 per day for a freelancer.

HOURS: 10 a.m. to 6 p.m. Pretty regular, really.

HEALTH RISK: 4/10. You may die laughing at early photos of Peter Gabriel.

PRESSURE RATING: 7/10. Because getting that snap at the last minute of Mick Hucknall walking out of Woolworths can be a bit irksome.

GLAMOUR RATING: 6/10. You might get to meet some top pop people at photo shoots, but you're likely to be suggesting that they might 'not wear that hat' rather than downing a couple of bottles of Moët with them.

TRAVEL RATING: 7/10. Sometimes you might go on location to do some shots, but budgets don't often stretch to taking the picture editor abroad. Bah.

For magazines, the picture editor ensures that shoots are commissioned for most features and, when this is not possible, that there is a photograph for every piece of editorial copy that demands one. S/he also files pictures in alphabetical order a lot.

Picture editors are at the core of magazine production, and will invariably claim that every reader looks at the pictures first in a magazine. They like to get statistics out to prove this, as they are often much neglected and don't get many of the glamorous bits of being in the music industry.

Almost every music magazine commissions **studio shoots** with a regular team of photographers for the main features. The picture editor will ring up Snotty Snapper and ask him if he is free the next Friday to photograph a particular band. S/he will then have to haggle with the photographer about payment, as there will be a very strict budget for every issue of the magazine. The picture editor's job is to give the photographer a brief: explain what different kinds of shot they might want, whether they need colour photos, black and white, or both, and when the shots need to be delivered. Teen magazines like *Smash Hits* often want to do more than one session, especially with a band they may not get access to again in the next year. One shot will be used for a feature, another for a poster, another for a different feature etc.

Kate Suiter, picture editor on *Sunday Times Style* magazine, started as editorial assistant on *Premiere*, the film magazine. 'I left college and had a few jobs then did a night-school course in learning to type,' she says. 'Then I became a temp and got the job at *Premiere*. I really wanted to work in music, and preferred magazines to television because TV people didn't seem

PICTURE EDITOR/AGENCY

After becoming editorial assistant for *Smash Hits* when it first started, she went over to *Just 17* when it launched, as picture editor. Then she returned to *Smash Hits*.

'*Just 17* was the first magazine of its kind when it launched, just as *Smash Hits* had been,' she recalls. 'We didn't have a proper budget and were making it up as we went along. Now there are a lot of rival magazines and I think jobs like that are a lot harder to get.'

Picture editing requires a great deal of organisation. Editors have to schedule shoots, file pictures in big cabinets in such a way that any member of the editorial staff can find them easily, and return pictures to photo agencies when they've finished with them. They are charged a whole heap of cash if they lose **transparencies**, and it is thus essential that they stay firmly on top of the job.

Picture editors need to be stern with photographers who may try to up their day-rate pay, or claim ludicrously high expenses which the magazine simply does not have the budget for: some top photographers are notorious for charging expenses which are four times higher than their agreed fee for the job. You also have to persuade picture agencies to give you exclusive shots, and bargain with them for the best rate. And, absurdly simple as this may sound, you need to choose a photo which is in focus. Transparencies are so small, even on a **lightbox** with a magnifier, that it's also essential that you have good eyesight.

'Sometimes the best picture from a

very nice. I was so happy to be in an office where you could listen to music when you worked. It was a beautiful job compared with the real world, even if you did have to do filing.'

Kate then became editorial assistant on now defunct music mag *Select*, working with the picture department when they needed extra help or the picture editor was on holiday. She was given a contact book full of the numbers of picture agencies and photographers, and told to get on with it.

Sue Miles, former picture editor at *Smash Hits* and now freelance, did work experience at Polydor Records when she was sixteen, which she found through a friend's sister who worked at their sister company, London Records.

session may not be the one that's used,' says Kate. 'You have to pick a picture that goes with the text, not just a great picture. You really have to check everything – whether the bass player's got his eyes closed, or the singer's not lit properly.' No magazine likes putting a singer on their cover if he or she is wearing shades.

Different magazines require different skills. An old toad's magazine for ancient music lovers like *Mojo* needs somebody who is good at research – very few photographs are especially commissioned. You will be asked to find a picture of The Greats as they have never been seen before, which can sometimes be a tad tricky. *Heat* magazine publishes lots of news stories which are picture-led and thus deals with a lot of picture agencies (which the tabloid newspapers also use), which are the only places you can get pictures of Justin Timberlake romancing ladies.

If the shoot has a curious angle to it, it is the picture editor who will have to find comedy props such as a bunny suit, a large hedgerow or twenty old people for the background. The picture editor works with the **designer** on the magazine, gauging exactly what's required. 'You have to think quickly and get props even quicker,' says Sue. 'There's always something that's been forgotten. You have to keep coming up with good ideas for shoots to make them different.' There was a great ses-

aww...

YOU MIGHT ALSO SPEND MOST OF YOUR TIME PERSUADING YOUR POP STARS NOT TO WEAR SHADES. HMPH.

sion *Select* did where The Chemical Brothers were seated at a children's party. All around were four-year-olds hurling things at each other, while the Chems looked on, slightly appalled. Needless to say, the Chems needed a lot of persuading to embrace such a concept, and one would imagine they would not like to see those shots – which *someone* must have – resurface now.

Newspapers rely on agency shots, or pictures which they gather through their team of paparazzi-style photographers. They only do studio sessions if it's with a buxom 'lovely' who's doing an interview about snogging David Beckham. Picture editors are generally regarded as more important than the journalists on the tabloids. Fancy that.

Being a picture editor is very much an office job, but because the agencies shut, at the very latest, by 6 p.m., you can leave work at a reasonable time. And you're still part of the rollercoaster world of pop.

A bit about picture agents:

The picture editor liaises closely with picture agents. Sometimes photos from previous sessions are needed, or press shots which the editor won't have on file at the magazine. A band may be out of the country or too busy to do an exclusive session, and no one wants to see old pictures when the bassist had long hair and the wrong trainers on. However, band promotion is a worldwide business, so you can always get something from an agency in an emergency.

Idols is a picture agency which specialises in entertainment. Some agencies deal in anything from pictures of livestock to ham sandwiches, but Idols is on the button for pop stars, film stars and the like. 'We look after the interests of photographers while protecting the rights of the artists,' says Simon Kenton, director of the agency. Bands today are, more than ever before, involved in controlling their image. New photographs are absolutely imperative if you're in a band. You have to feed the press constantly with updated images as they clamour on your proverbial door night and day. An agency like Idols deals with established artists so that the impossible can be done and the press can get the pictures they want but would never normally have access to. For instance, a photographer might take a picture of Davey from Boyzerk, and sell it to Germany, a place that Davey hasn't had time to go to recently, through the agency. Likewise, Shula from Girlzoink! in Germany can get top photographs seen in South Korea. Magazines and newspapers round the globe commission work through Idols. Nowadays, artists and their management work with the agency so the whole process is very official – no coming-out-of-a-chip-shop-with-no-make-up-on shots. Idols functions virtually as part of the band's PR team. Nothing is given to magazines or newspapers without the band's prior knowledge or consent.

Some artists choose to take a photographer with them on a round-the-world tour. This always comes in handy for tour brochures, merchandising, CD and video packaging, inclusion in the fan club newsletter, band annuals, and myriad other uses. Other, high-profile, artists need photographers to hang around at video shoots or at special events like turning on Christmas lights. All artists have the right to give their approval, so the chip-shop pictures won't get circulated. Everyone's interests, as they say, are served.

Each magazine has its own rates of payment for shots, and will haggle with agencies. Sometimes publications will ring to tell the agency what they're looking for: e.g., a shot of Davey in Australia. Or the agency may have some good shots of Shula, and will ring magazines who they think might have an interest – many magazines rely on agencies to give them shots for news and gossip pages. A lot of Idols' work is scheduled in advance, while press and promotions dates are being confirmed by the management. This way the bands have full picture control – it's all very regulated.

Idols and similar agencies have a **roster** of photographers who work for them round the globe. The demand is always met. How much you are paid as an agency photographer depends on the type of photograph, the shoot, and the artist concerned, but agencies will always take a commission on every shot they license.

It's also important to note that sometimes a band feels there's been too much exposure, and a need to hold back pictures, so the **market isn't saturated**. Idols, like all agencies, is well versed in strategically refusing to supply photos.

'We're quite an established company,' says Kenton. 'People see our credits in magazines and know we can get material into a long list of publications on an international basis. Also, we can control picture release very carefully. We can do as much or as little as people want.'

GLOSSARY
● Studio shoots
A photographic session lasting a few hours in a photo studio. Most magazine features include new studio shots.

● Transparencies
These are processed films, a bit like mini-slides, and are used to check all pictures before they are scanned onto the page. They come in big sheets from the photographer or from the processing company.

● Lightbox
A small table which lights up from within so that designers, picture editors etc. can look at transparencies properly through a special magnifying glass.

● Designer
Designs the pages of magazines, using computers to plan layouts and scan pictures onto the screen digitally. In the old days they used felt-tip pens, you know.

● Roster
Group of regular employees: freelance photographers in this case. Record companies have rosters of acts, as do independent press officers.

● Market isn't saturated
The one hope of everyone involved in a successful band. The Spice Girls' extensive promotion of numerous products did lead some to believe that 'saturated' was indeed what the market was.

SKILLS YOU'LL NEED
Organisation, ability to communicate well, responsibility, good eyesight, the ability to haggle and to think on your feet.

TIPS
● You can start at a magazine doing work experience. Ask to go in and help during the holidays.
● Many editorial secretaries help with pictures and become picture editors. Secretarial skills are good. Evening classes and holiday courses teach basics.
● Media-studies courses focus on picture use, and provide good background knowledge.

USEFUL ADDRESSES
● Idols, Time Place, 593–599 Fulham Road, London, SW6 5UA
TEL 020 7385 5121
FAX 020 7385 5110
WEBSITE www.idols.co.uk
● The Kobal Collection, 4th Floor, 184 Drummond Street, London, NW1 3HP
TEL 020 7383 0011
FAX 020 7383 0044
● London College of Communication, Elephant & Castle, London, SE1 6SB
TEL 020 7514 6569
FAX 020 7514 6535
WEBSITE www.lcp.linst.ac.uk
● London Features International, 3 Boscobel Street, London, NW8 8PS
TEL 020 7723 4204
FAX 020 7723 9201
● Redferns Music Picture Library, 7 Bramley Road, London, W10 6SZ
TEL 020 7792 9914
FAX 020 7792 0921
WEBSITE www.redferns.com

POP STAR

MONEY: From owing the record company lots of money to suddenly making thousands for yourself, owning a small record label, publishing company, many golf courses in Surrey etc.

HOURS: 24 per day, seven days per week.

HEALTH RISK: 10/10. You work all the time and never eat. You stay up late and forget to floss. It is very bad for you indeed. Look at the Cheeky Girls.

PRESSURE RATING: 10/10. You can always blame someone else, but ultimately you feel it's your responsibility if it all goes wrong. As it probably is.

GLAMOUR RATING: 10/10. You get to meet other famous people who have heard of you, get snapped leaving CostCutter by paparazzi, see your love life splattered all over the tabloids. Glamorous. Yes.

TRAVEL RATING: 10/10. You're always whizzing about somewhere. Trouble is, you forget you have a home and find yourself in hedges of an evening, or trying to order room service in your bedsit.

Pop stars are the people who wear dubious trousers on telly and appear in the papers coming out of nightclubs. And some of them really do sing on their records.

Glamour! Excitement! Swanky high-rise living! These are just some of the things that people associate with being a pop star. Just think! To be part of an industry which revolves solely around the product that you make, the tweakings of your mind in melody form. To be pampered and preened, lauded and applauded, ridiculed and ripped off, and the ignominy of doing it all in public. It's a rotten job, but lots of people want to do it.

Are pop stars born or are they made? The Darwinians will never provide conclusive evidence, but most people decide they have pop-star potential from an early stage. Once someone decides to be a pop star, and is really rather determined, there are a variety of routes to take. Some of our most shimmering lovelies on the pop scene spent their adolescence at stage school. Stage school is an evil place where four-year-olds who think they can survive on one packet of TicTacs a day chill out with people who shout a lot. Stage training can produce cracking pop stars though: the phwortastic Louise, the Appletons, Emma Bunton, some of Busted and Damon Albarn. However, it also gave us the horrors of John Alford (from *London's Burning*), Chesney Hawkes and Darren Day.

Former pop star and actress Billie went to the Sylvia Young stage school and survived.

Says Billie: 'I suppose there was quite a lot of bitching, but that's a general thing in every school now. I loved it there. There was a lot of competition but that was the fun of it. I suppose I could say there was a lot of favouritism, but I wasn't a favourite.'

Other types – who want to make 'genuine' music for people who don't like homework – play guitar in their bedrooms and hang around shopping centres trying to look pale and interesting (e.g. Starsailor). Either way, the ambition is the same and, eventually, if you try hard enough and long enough, you'll at least get to number 68 in the charts and have the local paper coming down to interview you.

So, you have to be ambitious. You have to have a whole bucketful of self-belief and a bit of spare time to practise in front of the mirror. The next thing – do you have to be good-looking?

The answer, oddly enough, is no. Some pop stars are good-looking and some have the advantage of fancy make-up and nice lighting. Some have the full complement of features but in no way, shape

POP STAR

or form could ever be said to have anything approaching looks. However, this has nothing to do with attractiveness. Noel Gallagher is arguably not beautiful, but his thick Northern nose and brutal features have charmed ladies since he became a millionaire songwriter. Jimmy Nail, Bono, Elton John, and even the lovely Celine Dion aren't exactly God's gift in the forehead department.

It's not necessary to be pretty at all, but you do have to have a certain spark which shows up behind your eyes: a magic glow that tells everyone you've just smelt the greatest flower, just eaten the nicest pie, just talked to God and He says your next single has a ripping good chorus. This is what people like Simon Cowell call Star Quality. And, if you ain't got that, you ain't got much (or you're a bassist, so that's OK).

As a wannabe rock star you can go one of two ways. You can decide you're a **pop** act, and therefore need a whole team of people to write songs, cut your hair, buy your socks and laugh at your jokes. In this case, you need to get yourself a manager, or find someone who can get one for you – a friendly publisher, a chum who's in a band, any sort of person connected with the music biz who knows a few names. You can also enter a TV talent competition, and hope to get through.

You can answer adverts in the press (the drama-industry rag *The Stage* and industry weekly *Music Week* have adverts all the time for singers) which are placed by managers looking for top acts.

At this point, however, be very wary. Some such managers are sharks. If you take this route, make sure the people you contact are not asking you to put up any recording costs, and find out whether they have contacts and a music-business history. If you meet them at their office and it turns out to be above Toys Я Us and one of them's never heard of Jon Bon Jovi, then beware. However, don't despair: Take That, The Spice Girls, Atomic Kitten (!) and En Vogue were all discovered by this method, so it can work. In each case, management companies took some nippers who looked nice, could sing, and had a bit of spark and made them into the lovable superstars they are today.

So how do you go about succeeding by this method? Well, make a tape of your singing, hawk it around, and see what people think of it. Perhaps invest in some singing lessons – there are always local teachers who can help. If you've formed a pop band, try to find out the names of producers, or producers' agents who might be able to help. If a producer likes something, they might help you record a cheap demo, because it means they're getting in on something first and can reap the rewards later. You don't need a manager from day one.

The other way to achieve rock stardom is via **indie** – and indie works a little bit differently. Indie is from the heart, man, and indie bands start when friends start to **jam** together, or else some young pup with a handful of tunes and a

head full of a load of rubbish advertises for like-minded cheekboned vibers to jam in a rehearsal space for fifteen minutes then listen to her/him rant on about The Velvet Underground in the pub for three hours.

Elastica were formed through the *Melody Maker* classifieds, as were Suede, and a local paper was the birthplace of American indie icons The Pixies. Yer average indie band forms, rehearses some top tunes, argues about who had the nicest hair in The Beatles, and gets a few live dates by ringing up local venues and sending them a demo tape. Around this point, the band also makes demos and flings them out to local journos, potential managers and record companies. The latter can prove fairly fruitless, as A&R departments tend to go to see bands there's already a 'buzz' about – word of mouth counts for a lot. They don't have much time to listen to tapes, although they get sent hundreds every week. A friendly manager might get meetings with different A&R people to play tapes, but it's not easy. Live music is most often the key. And, if you're good, someone will start gabbing about how 'hot' you are.

Generally speaking, once any artist is considered to be slightly warmer than average, the record companies will pounce like a pack of wolves on a hen. You get invited out to dinner, to lunch, even to breakfast sometimes. You will be invited to make more demos of your songs at the

POP STARS LIKE LIVING IN CASTLES.

record company's expense. People will listen to you talking about middle eights and even try to stifle their yawns. Suddenly, you may be bumping into Peter Andre on the streets of Soho, where all the media people hang out in London, and he will be looking less happy than you are.

This will be a magic time, but it will not last for long. If the buzz is great you will get a bidding war, when different record companies (a lot of them just copy each other in these matters) will put in assorted bids to sign you up for five or six albums. You can simply accept the largest offer, but this

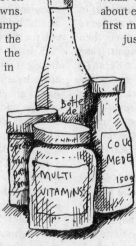

YOU'LL NEED VITAMINS TO REPLENISH YOUR FRAIL JET-LAGGED SYSTEM.

amount is recoupable (you have to pay it back eventually), so this may prove a very short-sighted move. You have to tread very, very carefully. Sometimes, the smaller record labels can prove to be the most restrictive.

At this point, when you are being offered deals by record companies, you will need to have found yourself a lawyer and accountant to assist you. Your manager should be able to help you to obtain these, and the number of meetings with men in suits will increase. However, all companies know what pop stars are like and could even offer you a beer even though it is only 10.30 a.m. They are probably surprised a) that you got out of bed that early and b) that you aren't already drunk. (They will expect you to be the cliché – so why should you disappoint them? Cheers.)

'I never set out for a career in the music industry,' says piano whizz Jamie Cullum. 'I was in about eight different bands when I first moved to London and I was just making my jazz records to make money. I was doing hotel gigs and people were always asking for CDs. *Pointless Nostalgic*, my second CD, was made to sell at gigs. I made it with my own money, printed it up myself and did my own artwork and everything – that was the one that got picked up by a small record label. I got on really well with the guy that was doing the PR for that. Although he's only from a small label background, he remained my manager because I trust him, and to be honest that's the most important thing.'

Once you have secured your record-company deal, you'll have to record some tunes, release them, see how they do, go on tour, do press, telly and radio promotion, see that the business side of things is dealt with by your lawyer etc. There'll be meetings, meetings about meetings, you'll hear people waffle on about cross-collateralisation and talk about you as if you're not there or the band you're in is a brand of peas.

Shaznay Lewis, a solo artist and also in the reformed All Saints, got a shock when she first became a pop star. 'It wasn't what I expected it to be,' she says. 'I only ever expected to write songs, make records, perform on stage, and be on TV a couple of times. I didn't imagine all the rest of it – the politics and the serious business side. You find you're not performing as much as you're caught up in the other stuff.'

'I've always worked pretty hard,' adds Jamie C. 'It's just the work is different. Before I got signed I was driving the van, carrying the amps, booking the gigs, selling the T-shirts, printing the T-shirts – now

THE VERITABLE 'BULGING' POST BAG. FANS, EH?

although I've got other people doing that stuff, I'm travelling a lot more, doing more interviews, photo shoots ... Working in the music industry is so close to the thing you love, it means your raw nerve is right out there ready to be chopped up. When you're up you're up, when you're down you're down. So you have to love it. I think it is harder work than everything else, but it's also the most rewarding.'

In reality, the ratio is probably 10 per cent singing and playing songs, and 90 per cent 'the other stuff'. You appear on radio shows and have to record horrible commercial idents for the station: 'Hi! I'm Cliff Richard and you're listening to Radio Popsnot 86–88 FM. Weeurgh!!' You have to battle with foreign telly producers who insist their pop stars wear chicken costumes while playing. They may also have go-go dancers in the background. Boyzone were sponsored by a cigarette company for part of their Asian tour, which they didn't know about until they got to

the first venue, then went suitably nuts. It's a battle, it honestly is. As much as it is with your own soul, as Kylie points out:

'There are definitely days when I think "I feel like I'm a hamster on a treadmill ..." If I calculate the amount of time I spend talking about myself, I could've learned three languages!'

Pop stars, of course, throw epic sulks all the time, which is little wonder when the whole thing can appear to be so little about the music and so much about plugging, playlists, marketing, and corporate politics. Or rather, it is until the pop star becomes extravagantly famous and successful and suddenly finds that s/he holds all the power – which can lead to epic legal battles such as those between George Michael and Sony, and The Artist Formerly Known As Prince and Warners.

Pop stars haven't, as a rule of thumb, got any money – not until a couple of years or more after they've had their first hit, anyway. Pop stars live off their advance, **free taxis**, clothes and meals paid for by record-industry sorts. It takes a long time for royalties to come through, and your first few years are spent paying back your record-company advance until you've sold enough albums to cover yourself.

Artists are paid a percentage (known as points) of the money received by the record company for albums sold. It generally varies between 12 and 25 points: the lower figure is poor; the high one fantastic. If you are confident of success, you should negotiate a deal wherein the advance may be small but you receive high royalties (i.e. loads of points). Then, the more albums you sell, the more money you make.

Deals are constantly being renegotiated in the light of your success (or otherwise). If you have had two high-selling albums, on the third one you should be able to negotiate an increase in points and maybe also argue for swifter payment of royalties. Now you are holding the power – but don't forget that your manager is taking 15–20 per cent of your earnings and there is still a load of lawyers, accountants and other employees to pay.

The typical day for the pop star is a bit gruelling and can start as early as 5 a.m. for photo and video shoots. Photo shoots can involve as many as five costume changes as the photographer will invariably want different 'looks'. Promotion can also stretch from playing your record on a TV show, to doing radio interviews, magazine interviews, appearing at award ceremonies (oh the misery), record signings, PAs at festivals and roadshows – all in the UK and abroad. It can get repetitive.

'When you go on that TV show and you're playing your single for the eightieth time,' says Jamie Cullum, 'you still have to try and enjoy it. You can't think, "Oh my God, I'm playing this stupid song again." If it's a song that you wrote and you're proud of, you should love playing it every time; reinvent it every time.'

Then there's the gritty other side. There could be a dinner-date meeting afterwards with a lawyer, an accountant, your manager, your A&R person. You'll have to think numbers, percentages, net and gross. You may go weeks, or even months, without singing or strumming at all. Hell.

'Our first year was so hard,' says Richie Neville who was in top boyband Five. 'We'd flown all over the world because the record company decided they wanted us to conquer Europe, America, Asia and South America. When we got to Japan, we were so tired we were arguing all the time. We sat down and said, "Look, this is stupid. We're fighting with each other, the job we're doing is rubbish cos we can't concentrate more than two seconds." We had two weeks off, went back and said, "You can't work us like this."'

Jamie Cullum feels fear when he looks at next year's schedule.

'I looked at it yesterday and my stomach dropped,' he gurgles. 'It was the most frightening thing I've ever seen. I've got one day off in September, literally.'

One thing you may not be prepared for is the press. The media is an unruly beast – nice one minute and nasty the next. It can eat you up and spit you right out again. And all those other clichés.

POP STARS OFTEN SIT BY A BOWL OF FRUIT DURING INTERVIEWS.

The biggest surprise about the industry, according to Cullum, was the way which people turn so quickly.

'When you're starting out, you get everyone on your side, they think you're great, but so quickly people are out to kick your arse. I used to read stuff about other people and think: Ha ha ha! That's hilarious! Of course when you're the person in the driver's seat, it's hard to disregard it. You have to rely on the fact you love music, and you do it because you love it. You have to concentrate on getting better, that's the only way you deal with it.'

Kimberley Walsh from Girls Aloud admits one of the most difficult things to deal with is the constant presence of the paparazzi.

'Sometimes it's fine, they want to take a few pictures and they've got a job to do, a living to make,' she says. 'Sometimes they can take it a bit too far. We were chased in a car a few weeks ago. We were in our normal clothes, we'd just been to the hairdresser's and we were going home. We were chased to the point it was becoming quite dangerous for us and the other people on the road. The driver we had, he wasn't prepared for that kind of thing. You think, that's when you should draw the line, you should take a few pictures, just leave us. There was no big picture for them to get.

'I've also met some nice paparazzi people,' she continues, 'who have been kind and not taken pictures when I've not wanted them to. I once fell over in the street – not drunkenly, I got my heel caught in a drain. A photographer was there and I thought, "Oh great, it's going to look like I'm in a right state." The man knew that I wasn't so he didn't take any. He said, "No no, you get chased bad enough as it is because of us, so it's fine." I thought, "At least there are some decent people out there."'

Like Will Young, Gareth Gates, Liberty X and Darius Danesh, Kimberley found top pop success through a TV talent show – *Popstars: The Rivals*. This route isn't always so sweet – think Hear'say, One True Voice and Michelle McManus. It's still fair to say that Girls Aloud were blessed with a certain amount of luck. For some it can remain a stigma, or expectations are simply too high.

'I wouldn't change the *Popstars* experience for the world,' says Kimberley. 'It got us where we are. We've come a long way in a short space of time and we're not labelled so much any more, we are a band in our own right now.'

When you do get round to making a record, you have to keep within the budget the A&R department has set you, so the pressure is on not to go overtime or hire too many bassoons. You're under pressure to record a masterpiece even if the drummer's dog has

YOU MAY FIND YOU NEED TO GO TO THE GYM.

just died, you don't get on with the producer, and your manager is asking you to do interviews while you're concentrating on the hi-hat sounds. You spend six weeks or so recording something which you're not sure is any good – some of the time it sounds great; sometimes dreadful. Then you have to wait at least four months till the bloody thing's released.

Overseas promotion will mean talking to strangers on the phone who're still asking you why you called the band The Corrs, even when it's your surname and it's quite obvious why, thank you very much. Or there's flying about Europe on rattling aeroplanes, being served inedible slices of ham.

'It can be crazy when you're flying around the place and you're not eating at the right times,' says Ronan Keating. 'Your body is not used to eating at different times and you're not getting enough sleep because you're working so hard. Glamour factor? Zero. No, I'll give it a two. Out of twenty.'

Ronan has just turned thirty, but says he feels 'like forty'. As a pop star, the pressure is on you, but the responsibility is not always yours – you can at least farm it out to other people.

Really, being a pop star is a most peculiar state to be in, and one most akin to being a big kid. People are there to do everything for you. You get cars to pick you up and deliver you to where you're meant to be, your manager and record company sort out your diary for up to twelve months in advance: which countries you'll be in, when you tour, when you record, when your mum's birthday is, in case you forget. You are respected for things you didn't do – in the case of singles recorded then remixed by DJs – or things you do by

accident. You have to be strong, because pop stardom can drive people to insanity. They go around saying, 'We're the best band in the world, and I can do everything,' when quite clearly no one is the best band in the world and no one can do everything. Like flying, for instance. No one can do that. Not even Robbie Williams.

'You've got to believe in yourself and be confident,' says Ronan. 'You've got to have a good head on your shoulders and not let people walk all over you because it's a horrible business if they do. You've got to be happy and enjoy it very much, because that's the most important thing, to enjoy it. If you don't, it will turn into hell.'

Scary stuff – but The Truth, as the number of pop-star suicides, breakdowns, and plunges into drug addiction confirm. The only way to keep your sanity is to resist the temptation to take off on an extraordinary ego trip from which there may be no return. You have to laugh(!) when they make up lies about you in the tabloids. Giggle(!) when they slag off your trainers in *Heat* magazine. Smirk(!) when you fall over because your shoes are too big. You must learn to love Jools Holland, even though he doesn't want you on his adult-orientated show because your new single is about lollipops. You mustn't mind getting recognised in the street, or having fans that are, frankly, embarrassing. They will camp outside your house, send you teddies and try and get married to you when you're not looking. (One girl turned up at a Westlife album signing in a wedding dress, hoping to get wed to Mark. It, er, didn't happen.)

However, Kimberley denies she has any more male attention.

'Personally – and I think the other girls agree – I used to get more before I was in the band,' she says, slightly disappointed. 'I don't know whether it's cos people are a bit shy and intimidated – or whether I've just become more unattractive as years have gone by! Boys do come up to us now and then but they're the ones that tend to *dare* to come up, they're not realistically going to be someone you're interested in.'

Nobody is denying pop stardom has millions of perks. You get into clubs for free and never have to queue. You can get a table in a restaurant, no problem. You get free clothes, because you wear them and are thus advertising them. If you make money on tours and personal appearances it's usually not part of the sum you have to recoup against your record company advance if you are still in the red (and many pop stars are, owing their label hundreds of thousands of pounds) – you get to keep it. Tony Lundun from Liberty X expands:

YOUR PET MIGHT GET GRAND IDEAS.

'Corporate parties are a private arrangement between you and whatever company is putting on their party,' he says. 'One mobile phone company spent up to £4 million on their Christmas party the year before last. We were performing at it and the headliner was Robbie Williams. You can imagine how much he got.'

Alex James from Blur was once 'sponsored' by Camel, and thus could smoke as many free tabs as he wanted as part of his own, ahem, lifestyle choice. Bryan McFadden was reportedly awarded free kebabs for ever from Irish fast food chain Abrakebabra. Tony has done a nice little deal with Jaguar – who heard he loved their cars and offered him its swanky VIP lease scheme (if you're reading this, Jaguar, this writer loves your cars too).

Tony and his band mates had to work extra hard to become pop stars. They didn't win *Popstars* – Hear'say did. So they had to go out, in yer so-called marketplace, and prove themselves. Once the competition was over they set about writing songs.

'We did most of our writing in **bedroom studios**,' says Tony. 'So we had room to make mistakes. For every good song we wrote we might write nine bad ones. When you go into any studio, it's important to have a strong sense of what you want to do that day. If you don't have an idea then the producer will ring the record company and ask, "What do you want us to do?" Something I keep hearing in relation to another artist I know is she keeps being told she should do a "Justin Timberlake-type backing track with a Lauren Hill-type vocal". That's totally not what she wants to do, but that's the brief her producers get from her record company, because sometimes they're not too sure what they should be doing themselves.'

Tony, who talks a lot about 'respect' – from other professionals and other artists – thinks the pressures can be great. 'For a pop band you're only as good as your next single,' he says. 'Especially now.'

This is why working with top producers/songwriters is imperative. Pop bands snap at the heels of every young (or old) tunesmith, grappling against each other for the best songs. What some discard, others pick up – apparently Sophie Ellis Bextor rejected 'Can't Get You Out Of My Head' which Kylie made f-f-famous.

Ooh, being a pop star, eh? You get to meet other exciting people. And, once you do make a bit of cash, you can treat your mum to a bungalow by the sea or buy your sister a horse ... or even spend some on yourself. Jamiroquai likes fancy cars. Madonna buys fancy art. Others blow it on fancy shoes, fancy houses, or just about fancy anything really. 'It's all bikes and cars and houses,' says Ronan of male pop stars, he who has a fast motorbike. 'But there's a big gap between me and George Michael – he's on a different level. He's got millions.'

Shaznay likes the job, but admits she does get concerned that she's not in control of everything that she does and the band could be ripped off. 'You shouldn't worry obsessively, but do bear the dangers in mind,' she reasons. 'It's down to you to be smart and query everything. I am happy. You have your good days and bad days, but overall the job is cool.'

'I don't think I'd advise any of my children to get into this business, but if they really wanted to I wouldn't stop them,' says Ronan. 'It is a crazy business and it's changed my life totally. I've been round the world, I love what I do, I wouldn't know how to do anything else. I eat, sleep and breathe the

business and it's fantastic. But I can't say I'd go and rush out and tell anybody to do it.'

Jamie Cullum ponders.

'Do it because you love it, and for no other reason,' he says. 'The money isn't immediate and may never happen. The admiration – if you do get it – can disappear. The knocks you have to take are big, whether you're making your own records and you sell them at gigs or whether you're selling loads of records. I play jazz, but I was in loads of other bands so it could have taken off in other ways. A lot of people want to be a musician because they want to hang out with certain people. I'm not saying there's anything wrong with that, if you can handle it in that way. But if you're in it for the fast cars and the mag shoots and the models ...'

And Jordan knocking on your door ...?

'It wouldn't be knocking, it would be more like *doooff doooff*! A stampede.'

GLOSSARY

● Pop
The world of chirpy, high-quality, radio-friendly tunes. Often described as 'shallow'. It is not.

● Indie
The world of meaningful, genuine, serious tunes by boys with guitars (mostly). Often described as 'dirgey'.

● Jam
Spontaneous music making. Like improvisation but with the key and time signature decided in advance. Jazz jamming needs neither key nor set signature. And can sound awful.

● Free taxis
The greatest mystery of the modern world is why pop stars spend millions of their record company's money

using their taxi account. Why don't they use the bus? Some of them can drive, too.

● **Bedroom studios**

Not always in a bedroom, but the common term for a home studio with a small set-up.

SKILLS YOU'LL NEED

An ounce of talent, a bit of spark, look reasonably interesting, have something to say in songs and interviews, persistence, tolerance, being thick-skinned, humbleness, willingness to wait around a lot, willingness to lug clothes around a lot. All for your mum to tell the neighbours about your hair.

TIPS

● 'To be a musician I think you have to be honest and be yourself: rude or polite, articulate or otherwise,' says Jamie Cullum. 'It's not easy to be nice, especially in this world when a lot of people are fake. With as many people on your side, there are a lot of people out to get you as well.'

● Ronan: 'Believe in yourself. Get some tracks together, from your own pocket, to make a recording. Go to a record company, maybe get a manager along the way that you can trust, get some sort of a deal.'

● Don't worry, if you get dropped by a record company you don't have to pay them their advance back.

● Vocal coaches can be found through the local library or newspaper. Ask who they teach and whether they have any qualifications. Recommendation is the best way.

● And for those of you who worry that poor Jamie Cullum might hurt himself as he hits his hands and feet on his piano in that startling jazz way, fear not. 'It's something I don't take very lightly, I've developed a way of doing it,' he says. 'I was a percussion player for a while, and you learn how to hit percussion instruments in a certain way so you don't hurt yourself, so I use the same techniques.' Phew.

USEFUL NUMBERS

Samaritans: **TEL** 08457 909090

PRESS OFFICER

The press officer manages press campaigns and tries to maximise exposure and attention for the bands they are working with.

The job of a press officer is one of the most frustrating and rewarding in the music industry. A job in press means that you will spend weeks planning and implementing a carefully thought-out print campaign in which you will try to get as many magazine or newspaper column inches as possible.

When you join a major record company's press department (each company has an in-house department which represents most of the artists on its **roster**) you'll most likely start off as a press assistant, with a view in due course to becoming a regional press officer or junior press officer.

'You just need to get your foot in the door,' says Gillian Porter, former press officer with EMI Records, now back to independent press at Hall or Nothing who deal with Emma Bunton, Manic Street Preachers, Stereophonics and Muse among strillions more. Gillian did a music management course at Bathgate College in Scotland. She got a work-experience placement with distributors Pinnacle and never went back to her college again.

'It doesn't really matter what you do at first,' she says. 'Just get into the business somehow and apply for all the press jobs you hear about. You've just got to love magazines and want to do anything you're asked to. Every day I go through every newspaper and new magazine. You've got to be very interested in all that.'

'I never wanted to be a press officer, but I really enjoy it,' says John Best, who started as a PR for Virgin Records, then formed his own company in the 90s with ace face Phill Savidge – which did more for Brit Pop than, er, anyone else (clients included Pulp, Suede and Elastica). 'I loved music and liked going to gigs,' he continues. 'When you start there's no substitute for knowing what you're talking about. Some people start answering phones on reception and are press officers a couple of years later. Be dogged and tenacious, then you'll get somewhere.'

When you start as a regional press officer, you'll deal with the major **fanzines**, student magazines, and local newspapers countrywide. This shouldn't be too daunting. 'Everyone is generally really enthusiastic,' says Gillian Porter. 'They're pleased you've taken the time to call them. And they often move with you, becoming national music journalists at the same time as you're promoted to a press officer with acts everyone wants to write about.

'As a press officer proper,' she goes on. 'You will be given a couple of new artists to work on who may never have even had a record out. Your task will be to get them heard by as many journalists as possible, and to write a press release every time your artist has a single, a tour, or breaks an ankle. You may even have to commission a photographer to take some nice pictures of them to send out with your **press pack**. You'll inherit a long list of names, addresses and telephone numbers which will look completely daunting, but in a year's time you'll know who everybody is.'

'I thought the job was embarrassing at first and had no idea how to get stories in the press,' says Eugene Manzi, former head of press at London Records and now director of his own press company. A friend suggested he go into PR in 1984. 'I said, "What the hell's a PR?" The first act I had, I was told to go to *Record Mirror* and get a cover story. I bought the album at HMV, because we hadn't got stocks in, and took it in to the editor. I made him listen to it track by track. He should have said, "Just piss off," because you never make anyone listen to that much but he didn't. I didn't get a cover, but he did do a little piece on them.'

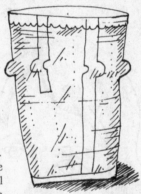

YOU HAVE TO BUY PEOPLE A FEW OF THESE, BUT YOU GET THEM ON EXPENSES.

For editorial, the usual press **strategy** for an album is this: you receive a couple of hundred **advance CDs** to send out to the journalists on your carefully compiled list. Sometimes the full album, often just a selection of tracks including the single. You need to decide which magazines would be interested. You don't ring up *Kerrang!* and ask them to do a feature on S Club 8. A week later, you may have to phone and check if any have listened to it. A week later, you have to remind them again.

For reviews, you need to send material to the reviews editor. If the artist or band are playing, you need to alert the live editor. If someone has accidentally stabbed their nose off with a plectrum, you ring the news editor.

Sometimes your act has yet to make an album and is only promoting a single – but this only really happens now with DJs and urban artists. Most musicians are signed up for at least five albums, it's a way record companies ensure the money (generally hundreds of thousands) they invest is not lost. If the act is contractually free to leave and join another company after making their name, the first company loses out. However, the contracts for pure pop acts will be more complicated, as flop singles mean no album at all. But see more in the glamorous pop star chapter.

Most music magazines, when they get excited about a new artist, will run a small piece, and wait to see what the record sales are before committing to a feature. If the single sells reasonably, or they know their readership is already interested in an established artist, they run a feature (from half a page to three pages), and usually someone who adores the band will interview them and slobber through a series of tough questions. Some artists have success with less financial and press backing. It might take Terry Wogan on Radio Two championing a little-known

PRESS OFFICER

artist and they're off. Katie Melua was turned down by every single record company (although there are now about two) but Old Tel loved her tunes and she's sold frillions of albums. The press will now be clamouring at your door, and will instantly elevate Katie into a zeitgeist parable for modern day listening – i.e. the writer will try to come over a little **intellectual**. Your first feature will almost never be negative, it will plump up the pop cushion for the artist to sit on, and shower him or her with praise about being 'fresh' and 'exciting' and perhaps 'swoony'. You have to wait for the bubble to burst.

It could be the case that no one sees the potential of your band or singer – they might be well be ahead of their time. Or they could sell loads but they're naff – take all those summer records about Ketchup and the Macarena, for example. All journalists reckon they are the font of cool, the very nub of good taste. Press officers must not get upset and shout at journalists for not liking their artists. This is futile: cynics – and musicians – claim that journalists have very little clue as to what is good or not. Feel superior: all the column inches in the world doth not a hit record make – that's down to sales, which is often down to TV exposure. Oh, and of course the record-buying public's free will.

With a gigging band, whose success grows through the **fanbase**, your job will start when you invite journalists to hear them play live. That way you hope to get interest, and a live review before or just at the time they release a single. 'You do get an expenses account,' says Eugene. 'It's a legitimate expense to pay for a couple of drinks

for the journalists who turn up for gigs.' Lunch is also a viable expense, if you're inviting people out. Press officers take journalists to lunch (the record company pays, rarely the magazine) to either discuss acts or sometimes just to link up, man.

'You don't get to know that many writers: you speak to them on the phone and they write reviews, but doing lunch gives you the opportunity to match the voice with a face,' Eugene Manzi explains. 'Needless to say, you do need a credit card as part of your job. I used to take loads of cash out with me and I didn't know how expenses worked so I became massively overdrawn. Some press officers get a company car, too.'

Once your act is successful, you'll have to beat off the hordes of magazines ringing up for a quote about anything from your artist's favourite biscuits to their secret love child. You'll also have to attempt to get on the right side of the tabloid press, the most notorious of the media.

'I was working at an office which dealt with Dogs D'Amour's press when they broke through,' recalls Manzi. 'They were a great tabloid band – real rock 'n' roll, drank, trashed hotels, had model girlfriends ... clichéd, basically. The band came into the office, looking ridiculous in full-length leather coats, cowboy boots, Stetsons. The lead showbiz story in a tabloid paper that day revealed the singer, Tyler, was in a heroin scare. They came in, saw the paper – they were all drinking – and they were fine about it. Tyler phoned his sister to say he'd be on *Top of the Pops* the next day. She said, "You'd better not show your face around here, Mum's furious!" This had never occurred to Tyler, who immediately started shouting, "This fucking paper writes lies!" He smashed his bottle on the desk and chucked a table across the room, which knocked a gold disc off the wall. "My family are being affected!" he screamed, and stormed out. I was sitting in the corner thinking: So this is press . . .'

Barbara Charone was head of press at WEA Records for thirteen years then formed her own independent press company in 2000. She represents artists including Madonna, Christina Aguilera, Anastacia, Robert Plant, Lenny Kravitz and Cher. These are not people with poor self-confidence; they can make their demands. Some of them may love talking to journalists, others may hate it.

'If an artist doesn't want to do press I don't think they should,' says Barbara. 'I think it's a waste of everyone's time. I'm sure you know how horrible it is to sit in a room with someone who doesn't want to be there. It doesn't do anyone any favours.'

One of Barbara's first artists in 1984 was an unknown singer from New York, Madonna.

'I used to call people up and say, "This artist is going to be really big!" and she was, ha! She played the Camden Palace early on and we kept the guest list for years. Lots of people said they'd come and loads didn't. I'm sure they regret it now . . .'

According to Barbara, a press officer needs to be 'diplomatic . . . And as much as you need enthusiasm you need loads of confidence. You've gotta believe that what you think is correct. You have to have an opinion – you'd be surprised at how many people don't have one.'

Has she ever exerted her press officer weight and berated a magazine editor, after a less enthusiastic piece was published?

'Erm, yeah, I've been cross,' she says. 'But mostly when I think the artist has been wronged. If you choose the writer and the paper, ultimately you can't complain, unless they've done something that is underhand. So yeah, sometimes, I have. Examples? *Nahhhhhh.* Ha ha hah! I'm too diplomatic to tell you that.'

However, a fellow journalist tells me that when she interviewed Madonna, Barbara rang the editor *the next day* to complain about a certain question. Madonna had recently given birth to her first child, Lourdes. She didn't much like being asked if she 'ate her own placenta'. Ahem.

This is a clear example that artists will commonly shout at *you* for their mistakes – if a bad picture is printed, or they're misquoted. (And no, Barbara's not constantly showered with gifts from the rich and famous. 'You don't get to be rich by giving people Ming vases!')

The press officer's life is '24/7', according to Charone. 'People ring you at home on the weekend, especially the tabloids. No, it's not that irritating; I'd rather they ring and tell you something horrible is going to run or ask you if something's true than pick up the papers the next day and see it.'

Barbara says she doesn't 'feed' the tabloids with crappy stories. 'We don't make up a lot of rubbish. I'm not into all that. I hate it when they call **Max Clifford** a PR, I don't think what he does is PR . . . I don't know what it's called.'

Barbara started out originally as a

journalist – she wrote an authorised biography of Keith Richards in 1979. 'I needed to have a little routine in my life, having spent three years with the Rolling Stones,' she says now. 'My friend offered me a press job in Warners and for two years I wrote all the press releases.'

This journalistic background, she says, 'was a really good advantage, it still is. I think a lot of people think when you do press you just ring someone up and go "Do you wanna interview blah blah?" without knowing why, or what the angle is. I've always been a newspaper/magazine-aholic. You'd be shocked how many people call up a magazine and ask them to do a live review when they don't do live reviews.'

Independent press is different from in-house press in that the former choose their artist, and thus are more involved in the development of the act. Acts choose independent press – and pay more for it – because in most cases the company will be more enthusiastic. 'I'm much happier employing people who love the bands they're working with rather than being in it for the money and the lifestyle,' says John Best, who currently does Morrissey's press.

Independent press can also give a flagging established artist some amount of credibility – dare we mention Emma 'Emma' Bunton's move from in-house to independent PR? And where independence meant indie, Barbara Charone has formed her own company with colleague Moira Bellis who represents the very pinnacle of top-selling, and thus mainstream, acts.

Some of the jobs previously held by press officers currently working in the music business are: forklift-truck driver, ballerina, pop star, artist, receptionist and model.

'I really think it doesn't matter what you did before you did press,' says Barbara. 'That's the great thing about the music biz, I don't think there are any rules.'

GLOSSARY

● **Roster**
The full list of artists currently signed to one record label. Can range from one (on independent labels) to thirty plus – not all bands will be active, but they are still signed in case the muse arrives.

● **Fanzine**
Mini-magazine privately produced by ardent music fans who don't mind wasting all their time sticking bits of paper to other bits of paper then photocopying them. Mostly non-profit-making.

● **Press pack**
Collection of recent cuttings about a particular artist, plus glossy picture, new press release, and sometimes video. Sent to journalists who want information on a band they plan to interview, or used to persuade them that the band are ace and will increase their magazine's circulation a lot.

● **Strategy**
The plan to get your band in every single magazine and newspaper, sometimes highlighting their sexy side, or their cheeky side, or their mad rock pig-death side. It's your job to make them appear new and exciting to the press, even if they've made albums which all sound the same.

● **Advance CD**
Freshly burned CD which features tracks, before the finished copy is completed and released. Other CDs sent out contain a few tracks from a forthcoming album, or the album itself. Used to be cassettes, if anyone remembers what they were.

● **Intellectual**
Don't worry if, in some articles, you don't understand bits. They are made up by the writer who has been told to portray the artist as socially relevant, and who was probably in the pub when he/she wrote them.

● **Fanbase**
Loyal fans who keep the band afloat when Radio One won't play them, thus ensuring top-forty placings for singles before the eight-year-olds think it sounds cool. Indie bands survive on 'fanbase' before they get famous, or when their records go crap.

● **Max Clifford**
Man who helps celebs maintain their public image (e.g. Simon Cowell being pictured accompanied by foxy-looking laydees), and represents certain foxtrels who want to tell the world that they have had a big extra-marital snog-up with David Beckham.

SKILLS YOU'LL NEED
Communication skills, perseverance, enthusiasm, literacy, diplomacy, organisational skills.

TIPS
● If you show enthusiasm and are willing to work long hours, work-experience jobs often turn into real ones. Ring record companies to ask if there is anything you can do in any departments during your allotted work period.

● The more you know about magazines and the more gigs you go to, the better chance you'll have. An obvious truth, but one to keep in mind.
● When you get your job, don't bribe anyone. It shows lack of professionalism and is also awfully old-fashioned.

USEFUL ADDRESSES
● Bad Moon Publicity, 19B All Saints Road, London, W11 1HE
TEL 020 7221 0499
FAX 020 7792 0405
● EMI Records, EMI House, 43 Brook Green, London, W6 7EF
TEL 020 7605 5000
FAX 020 7605 5050
WEBSITE www.emirecordedmusic.com
● Hall or Nothing, 11 Poplar Mews, Uxbridge Road, London, W12 7JS
TEL 020 8740 6288
FAX 020 8749 5982
● Polydor Records, 72–80 Black Lion Lane, London, W6 9BE
TEL 020 8910 4800
FAX 020 8910 4801
WEBSITE www.polydor.co.uk
● Sainted PR, Unit 17 Shaftesbury Centre, 85 Barlby Road, London W10 6AZ
TEL 020 8962 5700
FAX 020 8962 5701
● Sony BMG, Bedford House, 69–79 Fulham High Street, London, SW6 3JW
TEL 020 7384 7500
FAX 020 7371 9298
WEBSITE www.sonybmgmusic.co.uk
● Virgin Records, Kensal House, 553–579 Harrow Road, London, W10 4RH
TEL 020 8964 6000
FAX 020 8968 6533
WEBSITE www.vmg.co.uk

● Warner Music, The Warner
Building, 28A Kensington Church
Street, London, W8 4EP
TEL 020 7938 5500
FAX 020 7368 4903
WEBSITE www.wmg.com

RADIO DJ

Broadcasting your favourite records for a couple of hours to a rapt audience, interviewing the stars and reviewing gigs etc. is all part of the DJ life. Not bad, really, is it?

Radio DJs are some of the most influential people, in terms of record sales, in the whole of the universe. You can put a new band in a fluffy jumper and call them Free Beer, but if the radio doesn't like their record you'll have a hard time making it a hit. Even television follows the lead of radio in music broadcasting.

The radio producer will work together with the DJ, sorting out a list of records for each show. Most radio stations work on a playlist system: the station chooses a bunch of records to play each week, which you as a DJ can pick and choose from, as well as your other favourites. This helps the station have some defined identity, as network bosses generally feel that, were DJs to play the diverse records they wanted to, no one would tune into the station because they'd have no idea what to expect.

There is no one set route to radio DJing. Some DJs come through from journalism, others from more officey-type jobs at the BBC; still more work their way up through the role of production assistant at **local radio** stations. Commercial radio DJs may switch from local or national BBC radio, and vice versa. Almost everyone has started broadcasting with a passionate love for music and will find satisfaction in being able to talk to swarms of avid listeners.

Steve Lamacq is a BBC radio DJ. He started as a journalist, writing for *NME*. When he wrote a piece about the pirate station Q102 they were so impressed he was asked to join and did a show for almost three years. He skipped to XFM – London's indie station – then hopped over to the BBC to present the *Evening Session* with Jo Whiley when Mark Goodier was away doing the roadshow. Eventually he was given the job permanently.

He started his career on his local paper in Harlow before joining *NME* as a sub-editor, even though he says he can't spell. He gave almost ten years to the *Evening Session*.

'The job's gone back to being more about what I do, going out and finding groups again,' he says, ever gleeful at the thought of standing in a pool of cider at any given Camden venue,

watching some unknowns.

'After years of the *Evening Session* I found that I wasn't seeing support bands. It was getting to the point where it was more and more frustrating. The slot also needed a bit of renovation.'

He's also working for BBC's 6 Music and doing some writing again. But mainly it's about seeing those groups live – 'being able to shoot off for two days to go to Sheffield or somewhere is great.

'It's a strange addiction, I don't know what it is,' he continues. 'I'm not afflicted with anything else. I haven't found anything better than that warm sensation you get when the band you

RADIO DJ

first saw play in front of thirty people get on *Top of the Pops*, or go top five. Last year was such a brilliant time for British music. Loads of bands were coming through – it was so exciting again. You could see someone every couple of weeks, see someone you thought: I can't wait to play this on the radio. It's a big thrill.'

Lamacq does not have a remit to say he has to go out and find these bands himself.

'There's no job description. I guess I'm the A&R source for a certain type of music, but I'd never dare go in and ask for a remit because they might give you one. It's much better being New Bands Minister without portfolio, which is a very nice place to be.'

Has getting into radio got any more difficult, or easier, in Lamacq's opinion?

'To be honest I think it's opening up,' he says. 'There are just different ways in. A lot more people are coming into radio through student radio.'

There is also pirate radio, which has showcased yer more urban types. Obviously pirate radio is illegal, but thousands listen at the weekends and if you're passionate about music you might want to approach someone who's broadcasting from their Ford Capri.

The BBC's Talent directive also brings in, er, talent.

'They took on some people who had no radio experience, so these people had to learn while doing the job,' says Lamacq. 'One of them was a plumber who now works on 1Xtra – he was a huge music fan.'

Most people who start broadcasting work with a producer and a production assistant. Clare Sturgess, who now presents *X-Posure* on XFM, started out as a production assistant at the BBC. She had originally written to the corporation literally asking, 'Can I have a job please?' and managed to get a post filing and photocopying as a clerk in a small department in Broadcasting House. She saw an advert for production assistant for Radio One, applied, and got the job working for Simon Bates's morning show. Clare did a 'glorified secretary' job there, but it included some on-air and **OB reports** and she even managed to get old Simes to play Nirvana and The Pixies. After a week filling in for Mark Goodier on the *Evening Session*, she presented the *Rock Show*, which was in the middle of the night. Someone has to do it, after all.

'My doctor told me that, no matter what, your body will never be programmed to work at night and sleep all day,' says Clare. 'But I did get used to it. I had power naps in the afternoon. It's like a little club when you broadcast in the middle of the night because you have a dedicated crew of listeners. Though I must say some were a bit bonkers ...'

Being a radio DJ isn't all about this sort of glamour. You'll have to go through every new record before the show to ensure you haven't missed any brand-new gems. At Radio One, DJs used to have an engineer who would flick all the switches. Now DJs have to deal with the technical side and operate the studio themselves. This isn't a spectacularly brain-box job and you get taught along the way, but it does help if you're not too intimidated by machinery.

'I've stopped a few CDs while on air,' says Lamacq. 'When Jo Whiley and I were doing our trial period, I stopped the CD midway through Nirvana by mistake – and all the management people were listening in. I turned the **mic** on, and said, "Oh dear, a wire has come out of the back of the machine. What a shame." I got away with it.'

As a radio DJ you have to be reasonably polite so you don't get sued for slander, and it's obviously a career-shortening move to swear like a trouper. Clare Sturgess says she's never sworn on the radio. 'I'm sometimes tempted to say, "That was fucking brilliant!" but I've cultivated "fantastic" instead, and I think I'm overusing that . . .'

A bit about commercial radio:

Commercial radio is a different kettle of onions altogether – although you're still not advised to turn the air blue. Commercial radio needs to play music that everyone likes in order to maximise the station's popularity and ratings, because it survives through advertising and sponsorship deals. Commercial radio DJs also get paid a lot more than BBC DJs and are often more 'personality' inclined. Pat 'n' Mick, who worked for Capital Radio – London's mainstream commercial station – even released a string of singles in the late 80s. They got on telly well before the BBC had got round to creating such diversity and cross-media identity. Commercial radio has no shame, which is exactly why it is sometimes ever so good. And why it is sometimes awful.

Neil 'Foxy' Fox is probably the best-known commercial DJ in the country due to his involvement as a judge on *Pop Idol*, *Hit 40 UK* (formerly the Pepsi Chart) and his taste in bright shirts. He took a business degree, had a go on university radio in Bath, and then got 'a normal job' in Worcester. He landed a job at Radio Wyvern after entering a competition; he didn't win, but he became buddies with a DJ there and started helping him out. He then went to Radio Luxembourg, and moved to Capital two years later before moving again to Magic. Like Steve Lamacq, Foxy wouldn't do anything else.

'I love what I do,' he reflects. 'DJs are lucky because we get all the benefits – all the trappings of success without out the shit which goes with it. I travel, meet famous people and get free records.'

Foxy often invited the stars to play live in his studio, an invitation which was accepted by Bon Jovi, Sting, Bryan Adams and Noel Gallagher. He's met Madonna and Cindy Crawford. He also does the traditional DJ sidelines: **voice-overs** for adverts – 'I did a load of stuff for Cadbury's, so I got a load of chocolate,' he scoffs. He also DJs at corporate parties – 'Nice functions like dinner dances where I'm the star DJ. That's money in the bank.' He owns a helicopter too.

marverrific!
jolly good!
fabtastic!
oh sugar!
learn how to say more without swearing!
DICTIONARY OF ADJECTIVES
that's rotten!
bloomin' heck
gosh!

YOU ARE NOT ALLOWED TO SWEAR.

Nobody is exempt from these little earners, even if they are a 'cred' DJ. Steve Lamacq tells a story of John Peel taking him around to his house, pointing to each of his rare records stacked up alphabetically in a huge extension to the house, and reciting which advert voice-over paid for which.

Lamacq also has other interests – he co-founded the Indolent record label – home of Sleeper and Elastica. He is the Man on the Music Biz panel and writes for newspapers and has had his life and times published: *Going Deaf For A Living*. He's quite accustomed to being stared at when he goes to gigs and asked by people to play their mate's brother's band's cassette on his radio show.

DJs generally have a higher cred rating than a decade or so ago, when there was still a hangover from the wacky Smashie-and-Nicey poptastic Radio One days of the 70s and 80s. And radio isn't the plummy world of posh that it used to be. Regional accents make the stations seem more *with it*, nowadays.

Listen to the radio and find out who plays which sort of music, and note the different DJing styles. You'll notice that some DJs hardly ever say 'That was "Doing It With You" by Lincoln's finest, The Springy Mattresses' but rather '[Silence] "Doing It With You" [Pause] Springy Mattresses', which makes very little grammatical sense but at least serves to keep the DJ awake.

'I listened to radio and I think subconsciously I picked up when to talk and when to shut up,' says Steve Lamacq. He wishes there was more competition.

'There are some great DJs, but it's one of the things you worry about, you don't want to outstay your welcome – although I don't think I sound stale, I still have enthusiasm,' he says. 'But you also don't want to hand over your slot unless it's to someone you trust. Your apprentice, an indie sorcerer, if you like.'

What would Steve's advice to budding DJs be?

'Try and get as much experience as possible, and think about things that you can contribute that no one else can provide; you have to be better than someone we've already got. As well as being good across the board, find a specialist subject, become an authority – whether it's for record labels, magazines or radio, that's what they want.'

GLOSSARY
● **Local radio**
Commercial, pirate or run by the BBC. Always looking for people to help out.
● **OB reports**
'Outside broadcast' reports. The Radio One Roadshow is one big OB hell. Good experience.
● **Mic**
Microphone. Essential part of the DJ kit. Headphones, or cans, are a must as well. (If you DJ at parties and events, you have to bring your own.)
● **Voice-overs**
Providing a soothing, excited, sultry or informative commentary to go along with the visuals in the adverts. Good money.

SKILLS YOU'LL NEED
An ear for a nice tune, being able to talk reasonably coherently, an idea about what people want to listen to, being able to sound chirpy even when you feel glum.

TIPS

● University radio is a good place to start. So is hospital radio.

● Look for adverts from the BBC, in the Monday and Saturday *Guardian* job sections.

● DJ at friends' parties, then you get a good idea of what floor-fillers are and how to pace a set, man.

● A lot of people start by helping out at a local radio station for free.

● Make your own tapes and listen out for DJ competitions on local radio. If there are no competitions, send them in anyway.

● 'Decide what kind of DJ you're going to be,' says Neil 'Dr' Fox. 'A personality DJ, or a muso DJ where the music is the star.'

USEFUL ADDRESSES

● 95.8 Capital FM1, 30 Leicester Square, London, WC2H 7LA
TEL 020 7766 6000
FAX 020 7766 6044
WEBSITE www.capitalfm.co.uk

● BBC GMR, PO Box 951, New Broadcasting House, Oxford Road, Manchester, M60 1SD
TEL 0161 200 2020
FAX 0161 236 5804
WEBSITE www.bbc.co.uk/england/gmr

● BBC Radio 1, Yalding House, Great Portland Street, London, W1N 6AJ
TEL 020 7765 1439
FAX 020 7765 2471
WEBSITE www.bbc.co.uk/radio1

● GWR, PO Box 2000, 1 Passage Street, Bristol, BS99 7SN
TEL 0117 984 3200
FAX 0117 984 3202

● Kiss 100 FM, Emap Performance, Mappin House, 4 Winsley Street, London, W1W 8HF
TEL 020 7975 8100
FAX 020 7975 8150
WEBSITE www.kissonline.co.uk

● XFM, 30 Leicester Square, London, WC2H 7LA
TEL 020 7766 6600
FAX 020 7766 6601
WEBSITE www.xfm.co.uk

RADIO/TV PLUGGER

MONEY: The classic routine: start at around £15,000 p.a., average £25,000, then progress to a healthy wedge – around £50,000.

HOURS: Can be 9 a.m. to 10 p.m., including loads of gigs.

HEALTH RISK: 5/10. Keeps you fit because you run around a lot.

EQUIPMENT COSTS: All pluggers have those big, black record bags. From free (promotional item) to £50 for a sturdy one.

PRESSURE RATING: 8/10. It's your job to get records played by broadcasters locally and nationwide. There's a lot of pressure there.

GLAMOUR RATING: 6/10. Meeting radio and TV producers is obviously worthwhile and fulfilling, but it's not something to tell the grandchildren about.

TRAVEL RATING: 5/10. Regional pluggers hop about, but only to Burnley and the like.

Pluggers do the same job as a press officer – trying to get publicity for their given acts – but for broadcast media (radio and television) instead of newspapers and magazines.

Without pluggers you'd get Barry Manilow on Radio One instead of the thundering sounds of the revolution. Plugging, known to poshos as 'Music PR', gets new music heard by radio and television producers alike, who are always after the latest sounds to put in their respective programmes, as well as new videos and bands to interview on air. There are in-house pluggers in major record labels, and there are independent companies who work for smaller labels and bands that the record company sees as fit to have independent plugging.

A plugger has an individual roster of a number of artists and tries to get them exposure. What is different about plugging, as compared with magazine PR, is that the job involves far more legwork and is based not around mailouts but on actually hot-footing it out of the office to visit producers and physically hand over their CDs et al.

The record company will pay a plugger to work on a band, and once they've proved successful the plugger hopes to be asked to work on all the band's forthcoming stuff. Rob Lynch works for Anglo Plugging, covering London-based radio such as Virgin, Radio One and Capital. Kiss, Choice and Heart are covered by his colleagues. There's a regional department for local radio, and a TV department within the same company that deals with producers and band bookers if it's a programme like *Jools Holland*. There's also a web team who plug to music sites.

'The job isn't rocket science,' says Rob. 'People use us because we're the link between the record industry and the radio and TV world. They know we'll target the right people and we can provide them with a convincing case as to why they should choose to play that record over the 25 others they get that week. We're at the coalface, chipping away at the radio stations.'

At the start of the week, Anglo get ready for the playlists, which are decided upon mid-week by the majority of radio stations such as Radios One, Two and XFM. Rob is on the phone making appointments to make sure he's 'getting to the right people' and dropping records in the DJs' and their production team's **pigeonholes**. He works right through the week, and

'often weekends', covering band interviews and radio **sessions**, making sure the artist gets to the studio, has enough throat pastilles etc.

There is a hierarchy of sorts in radio, consisting of management, programmers, DJs, producers and broadcast assistants. However, everyone is important.

'I speak to the DJs like Steve Lamacq and Zane Lowe,' says Rob. 'You do need to have a good relationship with the producers, too – no one is more important than anyone else. You have to do a thorough job, you might find that one person knocks you back about a record on one show, but another person working on that show is a fan and can fight your corner. A good plugger will keep working on all **angles**. If the *NME* give a record a good review, that might change someone's mind.'

Pluggers come from 'all walks of life', as old people say. Lynch got a degree in law, took a year off, then started by stuffing records in envelopes at a Notting Hill reggae label for £50 a week. 'I worked my way up from there to radio promotion,' he explains. He then worked independently for Warners plugging their compilation albums. In 1999 he sent an email to the Director of Promotions at Anglo, Dylan White.

RADIO PLUGGER

'My timing was spot on as he always reminds me,' says Rob. 'There was a job coming up, I came in, did a month or so – and was taken on.'

Rob started as a regional plugger – often the first rung on the ladder – travelling the length and breadth of the land, visiting commercial radio and regional BBC stations. The remit is different for such a commercial station, who have advertising revenue to attract as much as listeners. The result is a more mainstream music policy and clearly defined play lists. Rob had his heart set on national radio – yer Radio One, Two, 6 Music and XFM (not strictly a national, but ...)

The job is one where you have to sell, sell, sell. The product might be something that you love, but you are the person who has to translate your enthusiasm for a record into airplay. But you can't be too pushy.

'You have to be aware of the situation,' says Rob. 'You can overdo it and piss someone off. If you see someone at a gig, you have to think: Do they look like they want to be plugged? The key opportunity is appointments at the stations. I'm not the only radio plugger in the world, there's a lot of people like me out there trying to get their records on a show which only has space for, say, ten new tunes. You can't bullshit or waste someone's time. If the reaction is positive straight off, you're on the right track to airplay. If it's indifferent the whole plugging thing kicks in when you're convincing and cajoling someone to play it. You can't bully or beg someone to play a record – that's not the professional way to do it.'

The pressure is intense. The record companies pay you to get results, and it's no good boasting that you had a tasty sandwich at lunchtime with Bono when you didn't get his record on the Radio 1 A list. A single costs around £5,000 to plug, plus there are bonuses for getting it into the Airplay chart, and in the real charts. If a plugger is really into a band who have no money, he or she will do it for less, or for expenses-only – with the proviso that if the band sign a good record deal the plugger will get the 'gig'.

Records are generally played less up-front than they were. That means radio stations usually playlist a single three to four weeks before the release date, as opposed to six to eight, unless it's from a stadium-type band. Radio still holds the upper hand over TV, interestingly enough. Television people are far less likely to go with broadcasting a single if it hasn't cut any sway with their radio colleagues.

Says Rob: 'There's a lot less music on TV than radio and it's mainly mainstream shows which deal with hits. I can take a record to a DJ and he can play it that night, whereas the TV plugger will have an awful lot of waiting and working on people to get them into bands and book them.'

At Anglo, which has a staff made up of fifteen people, the pluggers can all bring in bands and records to be plugged by the company. They also listen to a lot of records, which are sent in directly by bands, managers and record companies, to decide if Anglo is up for doing the plugging. Honesty is a big factor. Pluggers have to be honest with record companies about what they think the band's expectations are media-wise, to ensure nobody is expecting Dumpy's Rusty Nuts to go on *Jonathan Ross*.

Pluggers work extremely long hours

and are expected to go to all the happening gigs, but the joy of hearing a record that you've successfully worked on the radio is a real bonus. Plus, there are other career opportunities. Once you're in and know the business you can decide where to go next. Plugging has changed a great deal from the payola-laden days of the 50s to the 70s, when pluggers would fly radio producers to America or give them various promotional 'incentives' to break their records. Those notorious days are gone: now, the only way to be successful is to be upfront about good music. Indeed.

'It sounds like a very glamorous job – it does have some fantastic moments and perks but it's hard work,' says Mr Lynch. 'There's a lot of music out there trying to get on radio, and there's not enough space for everyone. To be a plugger you have to be disciplined, organised and have good enough social skills to deliver a product to someone who's been phoned a thousand times already that day.'

Rob recommends trying to get some experience in the plugging or promotion department in a major record label or independent promotions company.

'See how the guys in there operate, listen to them on the phone, try and shadow them when they go and do appointments – see how they target the right people.'

Rob's greatest coup was taking the unknown Liam Lynch and helping make his 'United States of Whatever' song a hit.

'That was a record that came from nowhere. Gary Crowley and Jim Lahat at BBC London thought it was fantastic and alerted me to it. We knew a guy

who ran a label and he put it out. There was no marketing money, no hype – the record literally stood or fell on its own merits. Radio One and XFM took it on, and we were off and running. The momentum built and built and suddenly we had a top-ten record from nowhere. We deal with big acts, which is great – U2, Oasis, Franz Ferdinand – but this made me feel that if you strip it down, essentially this job is about the record. You can have all the reviews, all the TV performances, all the buzz – but people will still have to listen to the record and like it.'

Rob takes a breath.

'It inspired me and made me remember that this was a really great job to have – the record came from nowhere and connected with people.'

GLOSSARY
● **Pigeonholes**
Wooden boxes where faxes, incoming mail and pluggers' jiffy bags full of hot CDs are left. No pigeons, all being well.
● **Sessions**
When a band goes into the studio to record some tunes. The BBC sessions with The Beatles in the 60s were repackaged by EMI in 1995 and sold by the million. Cult John Peel sessions still sell.
● **Angle**
The particular slant, or story, a magazine will use when covering a band. 'My drug hell' or 'When I was a woman' are two such angles.

SKILLS YOU'LL NEED
Energy; diplomacy; persistence – but not so as it becomes annoying; dedication; awareness of all media and what other bands are up to.

TIPS

● Get a job somewhere in the business if you can, and get to know the plugger types.

● Any PR work experience will give you an idea of this side of the industry.

● Practise playing your friends tracks they think they won't like, and persuading them that they do.

● If they don't like the records, don't try and force them to by dipping their ears in jam or anything.

● Or putting their elbows in pigeon-holes with hungry pigeons in them.

USEFUL ADDRESSES

● Anglo Plugging, Fulham Palace, Bishops Avenue, London, SW6 6EA
TEL 020 7800 4488
FAX 020 7371 9490
WEBSITE www.anglopluggin.co.uk

● Intermedia, Byron House, 112A Shirland Road, London, W9 2EQ
TEL 020 7266 0777
FAX 020 7266 1293

● Phuture Trax, 11 Savant House, 63–65 Camden High Street, London, NW1 7JL
TEL 020 7387 2545
FAX 020 7387 2392

● Power Promotions, Unit 11, Impress House, Mansell Road, London, W3 7QH
TEL 020 8932 3030
FAX 020 8932 3031

RADIO PRODUCER

MONEY: Can be anything from volunteering to do it for nowt to a good wage of over £30,000 p.a. It depends what level you're at. Oh, and independent radio pays more.

HOURS: Few jobs are 10 a.m. to 6 p.m. and there are definitely a lot of late nights here.

HEALTH RISK: 8/10. Similar to radio DJ, except the responsibility for the programme is all yours.

PRESSURE RATING: 8/10. Having to see that a live show is running smoothly is some stress indeed. Mr Pop Star will invariably turn up late.

GLAMOUR RATING: 2/10. It's not glamorous. Full stop.

TRAVEL RATING: 7/10. All those roadshows and special broadcasts live from the Reading Festival! Yes, the world of standing in the rain with a tape recorder in your hand trying to get the bassist from Jack to talk about his favourite sort of tent is, most likely, as good as it gets.

The radio producer is responsible for a specific radio show, dealing with content, style and format of the whole thing. Producers have to be responsible for everything, as it's them wot gets told off if things go wrong.

The world of radio would be precisely nil if it were not for reliable producers slaving away behind the scenes to bring you your daily load of smashing tunes and time checks. The actual skill of the job is precisely that – if you noticed the producer butting in or heard long ominous spells of silence, something would be up and the producer wouldn't be doing his/her job properly.

A radio producer will typically work on a specific time-slot and is involved in every show that goes out within it. The nature of the job depends on the nature of the show, but producers do follow similar ways of working. They will make sure that the station's playlist is adhered to, book guests for interviews and studio sessions, and where appropriate often edit the pre-recorded sections, too. It's a long, time-consuming business and means far longer hours than the dead famous, high-profile DJ has to keep.

You have to be an organised old beggar to do this job, and not mind taking all the responsibility for things. Most producers start with some experience of radio. Local radio is good, as many have programmes in which youngsters can volunteer their services, and learn how to produce and broadcast. The same goes for **hospital radio**.

Emma Lyne has enjoyed success as a freelance radio producer. She started at Radio Stoke at the age of sixteen, helping to make a magazine show that was staffed by volunteers. She interviewed and reviewed bands, put stories together, and learned technical and interviewing skills, while doing A levels at the same time. A couple of years later she saw an advert for a trainee producer at the BBC, applied for the job, and was offered five weeks of work experience on the Steve Wright show. She asked for more time at the end of it, because she was enjoying herself so much, and got three weeks extra. Emma was convinced that she had found her calling.

'I heard that a production assistant was taking leave for three months, so I rang up my boss and said, "Can I have Lisa's job?" He replied, "That's not how it works, Emma," but half an hour later he rang me back and told me the job was mine.'

A production assistant is a rung down from being a producer. It has a higher secretarial quotient (as noted in the 'Radio DJ' chapter by Ms Clare Sturgess, who had the very same job title). Emma worked for Jackie Brambles and then Gary Davies's lunchtime show. When she told him that the new Verve single was brilliant, back in the early 90s, he listened to it and then played it on his show – so the position is certainly not without influence.

Emma soon found herself travelling in vans to obscure towns nationwide, finding people in hairdressers who were willing to talk to Gary Davies – no easy task – and setting up pop stars for outside broadcasts: Take That in the underwear department of Marks and Spencer in Warrington, for example.

Virtually all radio producers begin as assistants, performing every lofty and menial task needed to keep the show going. In Emma's case, she had wanted to work for Mark Goodier's *Evening Session* on Radio One for a while, and after much badgering the men in suits gave her a job as his **PA**. When Goodier set up Wise Buddah Productions, he offered Emma a job as producer on *The Hit Parade* – the new releases show presented by ex-*NME* journalists Collins and Maconie. It's the eternal story of a foot in the door and talent leading to that all-important break.

There are several similar production companies in this deregulated age, such as West End, who make *The Essential Mix* and Danny Rampling's show. Many people prefer to work in this smaller, more intimate environment, but in these cases the producers liaise as much with Radio One as they would were they employed purely by the old-style corporation. Independent radio

RADIO PRODUCER

producers have to be a little more ratings-conscious, as the stations need to be as populist as possible, seeing as they have advertisers who want to reach all those consumers who are obviously listening to the radio between shopping.

Producer satisfaction lies in a top-rated programme, which is doing as much with the medium in the slot that it's in as possible. Producers can influence what goes on the playlist, can bring in new voices (often music journalists) for individual sections of their programmes, and overall have a chance to really shape an exciting radio experience. **Feedback** is very swift on radio, as listeners love writing letters and emailing in their thoughts, whether they're relevant or not. It's all a lot more immediate than TV. Direct.

There are courses in radio engineering and production at university, and these provide a good grounding, but it's experience that will really get you in. And, as ever, you can get this only by badgering radio stations or production companies to give you work experience – for nothing, or for a pittance.

'The job can be really stressful,' says Emma, who has spent some of her working life sleeping under her desk – the days were so long. 'But I really enjoy it. You can go out and see lots of bands, and then the next thing you know you might be putting their record on the radio. I always wanted to work in music.'

GLOSSARY
● **Hospital radio**
Large hospitals have their own radio station and it's an excellent place to learn your craft. It doesn't pay well, though, if at all. Many 'names' started by playing Elton John to people in traction.
● **PA**
Personal assistant. Does the filing, answers letters, goes to get a sandwich from the corner shop for the DJ, etc. A step on the ladder.
● **Feedback**
All radio stations use this term. Listeners ringing up to complain about rude jokes is 'feedback'. Has nothing to do with musical feedback, which is about electrics and 80s punk rock.

SKILLS YOU'LL NEED
Good organisational skills, ability to work under pressure with people who are often late (i.e. pop stars), thoroughness, some technical knowledge, knowing a good tune.

TIPS
● Look out for courses in engineering and production. Many local colleges do basic qualification courses.
● Try to spot BBC ads in the Monday and Saturday *Guardian*. They'll train you if they spot potential.
● If your college/place of learning has a radio station, get your experience there. You don't have to be a DJ to get involved. If there's no station, badger them to start one up.
● Local and hospital radio is always looking for people.
● Help any pals who want to be DJs to put together their own tapes to send out to local radio – then you have something to show for yourself.

USEFUL ADDRESSES
● 95.8 Capital FMl, 30 Leicester Square, London, WC2H 7LA
TEL 020 7766 6000

FAX 020 7766 6044
WEBSITE www.capitalfm.co.uk
● BBC GMR, PO Box 951, New
Broadcasting House, Oxford Road,
Manchester, M60 1SD
TEL 0161 200 2020
FAX 0161 236 5804
WEBSITE www.bbc.co.uk/england/gmr
● BBC Radio 1, Yalding House, Great
Portland Street, London, W1N 6AJ
TEL 020 7765 1439
FAX 020 7765 2471
WEBSITE www.bbc.co.uk/radio1
● Kiss 100 FM, Emap Performance,
Mappin House, 4 Winsley Street,
London, W1W 8HF
TEL 020 7975 8100
FAX 020 7975 8150
WEBSITE www.kissonline.co.uk
● XFM, 30 Leicester Square, London,
WC2H 7LA
TEL 020 7766 6600
FAX 020 7766 6601
WEBSITE www.xfm.co.uk

RECORD-COMPANY MANAGING DIRECTOR

💰 **MONEY**: From very little at a small company to a few hundred thousand at the majors. You may find yourself in those *Sunday Times* 'Very Very Rich People' lists if you're not careful.

⏰ **HOURS**: From 8.30 or 9 a.m. till late every evening – seeing bands (yes, MDs do) or having top-flight meetings with top-flight people in top-flight restaurants.

➕ **HEALTH RISK**: 7/10. All those fat-cat exec lunches might lead to obesity and heart problems.

✋ **PRESSURE RATING**: 10/10. You have to translate *grrreat* talent into *grrreat* big amounts of cash. Even MDs have bosses.

🍸 **GLAMOUR RATING**: 8/10. You get to go to **award ceremonies**, wear penguin suits, and get photographed with Sting in *Music Week*.

The managing director is responsible for every single move his/her record company makes in a given territory. From creative decisions to financial ones, and all the bits in between, the MD is pretty much the boss.

Some record companies divide their artists into three categories: newly signed; established, which are those acts with a gold album under their belt; and superstars, which are people with a few gold and platinum albums who've been around for a while. It's the job of a good MD to turn the first category into the third.

It should be pointed out at this juncture, in case it is not violently obvious, that there is a certain quantum leap between a) deciding that a career in the music business is for you and b) becoming a record-company MD. It's all very well to aim for the heights, but it takes bloody ages to become an MD. You have to be very, very good and you have to understand, and excel in, just about every area of the industry (except, possibly, roadie). There is, of course, the short cut – starting up your own record label and getting access to a photocopier to do your headed notepaper. That way, you can be MD as soon as you like. But, for real, serious players, there's no substitute for years and years of hard slog, dedication, conviction, and inspiration before you start earning sums of money which even Sting or Elton John will gawp at.

There is one question which springs to mind when pondering the sheer enormity of the job that is managing director. What on earth do they actually do, these big be-suited fellows? Do they charge around looking important and frightening the office juniors? Do they sit behind a desk doodling caricatures of Mariah Carey? Do they sit around George Michael's talking about traditional cheeses? No – none of the above (except maybe the first one). They do a demanding job like everyone else. It's just that they're a teensy bit more responsible for everything than anyone else, and the first to tick other people off for doodling those Mariah cartoons.

'I think the main job of the MD is to get an idea of the vision for the company,' says Tony Wadsworth, since 2002 chairman and CEO of EMI Recorded Music UK and Ireland, whose artists include Coldplay, Kylie, Radiohead, Robbie Williams and Queen. Labels include Parlophone, Virgin, Mute, Heavenly and Positiva.

Formerly MD of Parlophone Records for five years, the job has moved up a scale. As label MD 'you co-ordinate various elements of the label, and ensure everybody is moving in the same direction and understands the same **priorities**'. As CEO, the vision has to be that much stronger.

Wadsworth deals with every label MD as and when he needs to. If the label MD is a 'bridge between the corporate part of the business ... and the actual creative workings of the label' then Wadsworth has moved into the more corporate end, while retaining his fervour for music. In his office hangs an original poster for the Sex Pistols' 'Anarchy in the UK'.

'You have to be tough on the way you divide up your time,' he says. 'If I've gone through the day and not listened to much music I reckon I've failed, this is why I'm in this business.'

Wadsworth will also deal with his head of Business Affairs, the head of Finance, and head of Communications. That's a lot of meetings. The few months running up to Christmas, he says, he deals with the head of Sales, because that's when most records are sold.

Tony reports to the president of EMI Europe, who answers to the president of EMI Records Music Worldwide. Also up in the stratosphere is the president of EMI Worldwide, who also deals with the publishing side. The top dog is the chairman of EMI Group plc. Essentially, record companies contain the same corporate hierarchy as do

MD

multinational firms in every other comparable industry.

A CEO has to understand global markets as much as what on earth Emma Bunton is singing about in one of her Latino-inspired tunes. In March 2004 there was a major 'reorganisation' of EMI Europe. Music industry press reports were dramatic – jobs were cut. Was this a contributing factor to the end of the music business? Well no, it wasn't. Wadsworth clarifies.

'A significant number of people in continental Europe were let go,' says Tony. 'But hardly anybody in the UK. Virgin and "EMI" had been one company for years, but it had been running under two separate managements. We brought them together and were able to make economies. I wanted to do it once and once only. It unsettles staff and it's not good for business. Unfortunately, continental Europe as a marketplace has suffered a hell of a lot more than the UK. The UK has survived best of all the major music markets around the world, America included.'

Perhaps we should mention the Internet. Although Wadsworth claims 'more CD albums have been sold in the UK this year than in any previous year in history' they're being sold more and more cheaply, and this has had a striking effect on the record companies.

'It's great for the consumer,' he says. 'But it means we've got to actually watch our profit margins. The record industry is in transition and that's not unusual – the games industry is in transition from one format to another almost every four years. The new format for music is via the web. The challenge there is that many people are consuming music that way, but many people aren't paying money for it. And it's illegal.'

Tony's job is to 'protect' EMI's music and 'to start making some viable business models available'. Sounds fancy. Doesn't this just mean suing some children? Annie Leith, a fourteen-year-old from Staten Island, New York, had to pay $3,000 for downloading 960 songs. In just one week in May 2004, US record companies filed close to 500 lawsuits against Internet users.

'The biggest publicity goes to suing people but that's the smallest part of it,' he says. 'The main part of it is encouraging as many deals as possible so the consumer has the opportunity to buy their music in the way they seem to like it, which is online. By the end of this year the sales of online music in the UK will have increased several times over.'

With iTunes (Apple's music site), the new legal version of Napster launched in May 2004, Sony Connect in the US and Microsoft coming in with their offering, music downloads are becoming respectable. Record companies and artists get a royalty on sales – fine. However, it's not as cut and dried as that. Oh no. Some companies are still cynical, explaining that profit margins tend to be slim on downloads. Wadsworth is pragmatic.

'One thing we have to do is get our music cleared and available in a digitised form so that all this can happen,' he explains. 'There are also certain things not totally in our control we lobby for. Incompatible formats within the electronics industry – if you've got an iPod and buy music from MSN it doesn't work. Which is irritating in the extreme. So a great part of my time is spent on trying to get this transition from CD sales to selling electronic online music as quickly as possible, so we have a business back up to previous levels and higher. And I'm optimistic about it: a) I'm usually optimistic, and b) more people are consuming music in more places than they've ever done before. It's just we don't get the money for it.'

The trouble with being an MD in this day and age is that you spend all that time getting to a position of power, only to find you need some of the skills that teenagers have.

'Understanding the technology and understanding the possibilities is essential, but not in any great detail,' Tony admits. 'I can't write computer code – I'm not even at the level of my fifteen-year-old son – but I'm probably better than most forty-seven-year-old blokes.'

OPTIONAL.

So how do you ascend to such a rarefied position of power as MD? Well, Tony completed an economics degree ('which was handy'), spent some time in a band he steadfastly refuses to name, then after they split decided that he liked the music industry enough to pursue a career on the other side of the fence. He 'glossed up' his past in his CV – went on about his degree and not about spending two years in a Transit van – then applied for a job as product manager at Warwick Records. His job there was primarily concerned with getting CDs manufactured on time, but he later moved on to RCA before fetching up at EMI.

'I made people aware when I arrived at EMI that I was someone who could do more than just phone up the factory and get ten thousand records made,' he says. 'I sold myself a bit and they created a new job for me and called me the catalogue marketing manager. I got hold of the **back catalogue** and started re-releasing albums. It worked like a dream – it started with a couple per month and ended with a hundred per year.'

This success story propelled him into marketing. 'I guess they thought: Maybe Tony can deal with people who are living as well,' he says. 'I just made people aware I was there and didn't sit in the corner doing my job like a shrinking violet.'

Wadsworth says the toughest part of being an MD is holding on to your initial vision. 'It's hard to keep a level head in a business which is full of people who shout,' he expands. 'A lot of people have short-term ideas and you're trying to maintain a **long-term plan** and vision. The other thing is that there literally aren't enough hours in the day. I could live in my office and not have any personal life whatsoever. You have to know when to stop working. Working non-stop doesn't make you good at the job, and you lose everything when you lose your job, if it's all you've got.

'The big difference in the last five years', he continues, 'is that I've just spent a lot more time thinking about change. Change, if not dealt with properly, can be quite uncomfortable for staff that work for you. If they manage it well then it can be really exciting as opposed to being frightening. You've got to take people by the hand through it.'

The music business changes from year to year. There is the perception that it's just about pure commerce now, not the music, man. In fact, it's **the man** that's made it a business.

Tony is reflective. 'It was a relatively immature business in the late 50s, a boom business in the 60s and 70s, and it consolidated and matured in 80s and 90s. It's now an industry that is established but you're dealing with a product that you love. You're dealing with something that people buy cos they enjoy it; it makes them feel better. It's not a hard product, a generic product – no one piece of music is the same as the other.'

Some MDs are shouty folk who have a vision and make everyone do what they say; others work on more of a consensus approach, which is what Tony aims to do. Rival managing directors may be chummy enough with each other socially but: 'You go back to your office and it's war again,' says Tony, who doesn't wear a suit unless he's going to an awards ceremony or popping out for a pint with Tina Turner.

'I think I've got a different style from other people in my role,' he says. (Tony is known for being down-to-earth.) 'But as the industry consolidates, there are fewer people in my job. There are now five in the UK – the others are at Universal, Sony, Warners and BMG. And, yeah, they've all got a different style. Far be it for me to describe them.'

Tony spends a little time with ver stars, although he's typically modest, and won't say if any of them have ever thrown up on his sofa.

'Most of the dealings with the artists go through the labels – within that, the label MD, A&R people, marketing. Certain artists I still have direct dealings with for various reasons – be they historical or whatever. Artists will tend to gravitate with people they know and trust. If someone has a problem you can talk to them about it and they can explain their way through it. I deal with most artists but at different times.'

So what happens when people stop being managing directors? Well, some go on up the corporate ladder and become an MD in another country. Others may move into managing a band or artist. One former MD at Warner Brothers went back to being a writer and press officer. There is, however, a stigma attached to moving back 'down' the ladder in this country – whereas in America it's far more common.

Still, who's to worry, eh? Most managing directors can't be worrying about what's next or they wouldn't have time to do the job in hand. They have to be positive to motivate all the people at the label, and to run their company teeth-gleamingly well.

What's the last thing Wadsworth thinks about when he puts his head on his pillow at night?

'Hm . . . good question,' he muses. 'I don't worry about things, things very rarely keep me awake. And I've usually got a piece of music going through my head. And often it's still there in the morning.'

GLOSSARY
● Award ceremonies

Awful big parties where pop stars get a trophy for still living in the country and not going off to Sweden for tax purposes.

● **Priorities**

In all companies, some artists are prioritised. It generally means more money is spent recording and promoting them.

● **Back catalogue**

The old records that have been released through the years on the record label. Companies make a bit of cash re-releasing them on CD when they think the market is ripe for a particular artist.

● **Long-term plan**

While everyone else is talking about the flavour of the month, the MD must concentrate on the next few years' output on the label.

● **The man**

The corporate entity that controls our lives – apparently.

SKILLS YOU'LL NEED

Numeracy, literacy, vision, communication skills, boundless confidence.

TIPS

● Tony Wadsworth: 'As the Clash said, you turn rebellion into money. I think one of the skills of a good MD is being able to have a good conversation with an eighteen-year-old kid in a band you're about to sign as well as being able to connect with the finance director. You go from one extreme to another.'

● A lot of MDs are promoted through the legal and business affairs department. A good knowledge of this side of the business is worthwhile. Train as a lawyer!

● Any degree will stand you in good stead. Serious stuff like politics, sociology or economics helps.

● A wide experience of the music industry is required. Be prepared to work for different departments within the record company.

RECORD PRODUCER

MONEY: You get paid per job, which can be £75,000+ for an album, up front. And percentage points on every album sold.

HOURS: You can work twelve- to sixteen-hour days if you're the intensive type. Sensible sorts go for an 11 a.m. to 10.30 p.m. day. Which is still quite a lot.

HEALTH RISK: 9/10. Sitting down in a smoky studio all hours of the day with only tapping toes for exercise.

PRESSURE RATING: 9/10. You've got to come up with the goods, for the band, management and bloomin' record company.

GLAMOUR RATING: 8/10. You get to sit in a room with the stars for hours and hours, and they think you're tops if their tunes sound great. It's still sitting in a room, though, when all is said and done.

TRAVEL RATING: 7/10. You can get to go all over the shop when you're a famous producer. But you'll end up in a studio with no windows, wherever you go.

You work in the recording studio producing recorded sound with the band or artist that you've been asked to create with. Singles, albums, spook tracks for bizarre compilation LPs – you have to turn your wizard hand to all sorts of sounds.

Record producers sell millions of records and their artistry is heard by hordes of folk across the land: on the radio, telly, adverts, and in the background on *EastEnders*. Yet they are rarely noticed when walking down the street or buying pants in Marks & Spencer. Being a producer is just as creative and satisfying as being a musician, but you don't get the aggro and you do get to talk about plectrums with the stars. It's not at all bad, really, but it's a lot of hard work.

What producers do can vary, but there is a general job pattern. Generally, producers are commissioned by a record company's A&R department to go into the studio with a band or artist to record a single or album tracks. This can be from one day in the studio to several months, depending on the project. Most established producers have an agent or manager who maintains their clients' diaries and will negotiate a fee. Fees are variable: if the producer really likes a band, but they have no money, then he might waive his usual charge and go for something they can afford; with a major-label deal, the A&R department will have already set a budget that the band cannot go over.

The producer hears demos by the band, usually many more tracks than will land on the album, and decides whether he likes the stuff. S/he then cites which studio is preferable, and decides which engineer to work with – often the two will see themselves as a team. These details are sorted out by the A&R co-ordinator of the record company, who also checks whether supercool backing singers or any accordion soloists will have to be booked, and makes sure their fee is included in the A&R budget as well.

Most albums with a bit of major-label finance behind them will go through pre-production. This is rehearsals with producer and engineer, working out the ace guitar licks and swirlaway drum solos that might be appearing in the track. If any choruses need changing, the **key** altered, or the **intro** fiddled about with, this is the time to do it. Not all songs are quite 'there' when a band goes into the studio. Some of them are over in a corner and need to be coaxed out. The producer gets a feel of the tunes, decides an order in which they should be done, and is able to have a coffee and a Hobnob with the people he'll be trapped in a room with for weeks.

Then the production starts. The band, if we're talking a basic guitar-band set-up, files into the studio every day. Each member does their individual bits and the track is built up from there. The band playing together and performing a song straight through doesn't happen much any more. Instead, a microphone is set up each time an instrument is plugged in, and all those buttons on the mixing desk tweaked to get it going through a channel. For pop bands, each singer goes into the vocal booth individually and records their track/s over a backing track, which may well be almost complete. Some singers walk into a studio, spend ten minutes on a take, then go shopping. Others spend time listening to the mix, suggesting currazy new ideas for harmonies and backing

vocals, and perhaps slapping down a bit of bass for good effect.

Desks can have between 8 and 48 tracks, although 24 is the average in a reasonable studio. Each track is given a channel, between 1 and 24, for instance. Those desk buttons can boost the lower frequencies and higher frequencies and are known as the EQ (equaliser). Bass gets a lower boost; sometimes guitars get a higher frequency treat. It all depends. The producer just tries to get the sound s/he and the band like the best, that they think will fit the track.

The producer and band then go through all the tracks, choosing when the best time to do them is, according to how they're feeling and whatnot. It's obviously no use trying to sing a song about children being hurt in road accidents when the singer's just had a lovely slice of cake, and hopeless trying to persuade the guitarist to play the 'poppy number' when he's just found out the Cup footie has been cancelled. Producers aren't just there to twiddle knobs; they're there to get on with the artists and draw the beast inside right out of them.

'A producer is like a director of a film,' says Stephen Street, world-renowned producer who's worked with the likes of The Smiths, Morrissey, The Cranberries and Blur. 'You're working very closely with an artist and you've got to make sure that they're in the right frame of mind. You make decisions which aren't purely technical decisions. There are some songs you don't touch, but that's a skill: if it ain't broken, don't try to fix it.'

Stephen Street started off as a musician, playing with different groups who weren't very successful. He didn't

RECORD PRODUCER

reckon he was much cop at the guitar or bass, his chosen instruments, but he liked being in the studio. He decided to write to lots of studios and get a job as an assistant engineer, learn how to use the desk and progress up the proverbial ladder. He didn't get many replies, but a friend told him the Island Records studio, situated in the basement under their offices in London, was looking for someone. He went and saw them that same day, made out that another studio was interested in employing him, and got the job.

Stephen was the only assistant there for a time – a lot of studios have more than one – so he worked on almost every session. Often 'assistant' is just another term for 'tea boy' and you are allowed to do precisely zero good stuff but, because Mr Street had been in a studio before with his band chums, the engineers there let him be a little more 'hands on' (i.e. touch things), and within a couple of years he

was a house engineer working with whoever came into the studio.

'Then,' he says, 'you've just got to wait for that lucky break. When something comes along and you do a good job, you may hopefully hang on the coat-tails of their success.' Stephen's big break was The Smiths in 1984. The studio manager told him they were coming in and asked him if he wanted to do the session. He jumped at the chance as he'd heard their first single and loved it. They came in to record the single 'Heaven Knows I'm Miserable Now', produced by John Porter.

'I think my natural enthusiasm pleased them,' he says. 'Morrissey and Marr took my number. Then they did the next single without me and I thought: Oh, they've forgotten about me! Then I got a phone call from their manager saying that they wanted to record and produce the *Meat Is Murder* album themselves, but would I be prepared to go along and engineer it? That was my first step into something that was beginning to take off.'

When you're an engineer, says Street, it's inevitable that sooner or later you begin to make production decisions. The more knowledge you have gained, the more input you have. The trick is making sure you're recording everything in the best way possible. Ultimately, you have to please the record company, as they have employed you, although most producers would rather go with what they and the artist are happy with.

Once the recording has been done, the record is mixed: this is the stage which always seems a whole lot of hassle. The volume levels on every instrument have to be perfect. Some volumes will change as the song progresses. Most guitarists want their fingerwork nice and loud, and most singers will insist that you can't hear them and demand that you turn them up. Get the mix wrong, and the track won't sound right. It's like when you hear so-called 'critics' saying a track has been 'over-produced', because all the squelchy 'I am an alien' extra noises have been turned

up too high and no one can hear the tune. Thus producers are always listening to the songs they've produced and wondering whether the drums should have kicked in earlier, or the bleeps sound too New Romantic. Stephen admits: 'Yes, I have been known to say, "Those hi-hats are a bit toppy." I can't bear to listen to my own stuff at home. I'm never completely happy.'

Record companies can be a nightmare to work with, especially if the A&R man wants to have his or her say about what the album should sound like. Then you've got the artists who might think they're the latest hot cheese and storm about the studio trying to look powerful and not switching off their mobile phone when the poor keyboard player is trying to find middle C. A producer's life is not always a happy one.

'Sometimes the most intense people who have a natural-genius ability can be frustrating,' says Street. 'You can't expect everyone to be easy-going. If they're not entirely happy about the conditions they're in at the time, they can make the day really feel quite awkward. Look at the way George Martin worked with The Beatles. If they wanted to be they could be bouncing off the walls, and Martin was always there as the sober straight one, keeping the lid on the pot as it were. I don't believe in getting out of my brains while I'm in the studio, cos I don't think anything works that way, to be honest.' Street refuses to work deep into the night, as many producers do, because he says you lose the ability to make the right decisions and make

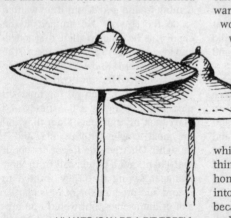

HI-HATS (CAN BE A BIT TOPPY).

them quickly. He says some singers do like to have a snifter before they sing because they get nervous, but personally he's content with a beer after the session.

Street has worked with Blur since the beginning, but still finds it a wheeze. 'I worked on Blur's fifth album,' he says, 'and people think that by then it's going to be business as usual, but I was just as het up about making that album as any of the others. I enjoyed the challenges. We went to Iceland for a couple of weeks to work out there.' Yes, if you have the **budget**, recording one album in a few places keeps the excitement up.

Would Stephen advise anyone to do the job?

'No, there's enough competition out there as it is!' he laughs. 'It's all about lucky breaks and being in the right place at the right time. I still do it because I still enjoy it. Perhaps you might just be a great engineer and that's your thing. It's up to you to know your limits.'

Richard X is an artist and producer, who first came to notoriety with his 'bootleg' version of Adina Howard's 'Freak Like Me' and Gary Numan's electronic classic 'Are "Friends" Electric?' – which was then recorded by the Sugababes and got to the magic number one spot. He later welded Chaka Khan's 'Ain't Nobody' and the Human League's 'Being Boiled' for the Liberty X single 'Being Nobody'. He's also worked with Rachel Stevens, Kelis, Puff Daddy/P Diddy/Ken Doddy and Jarvis Cocker. But not all together.

'I'm not sure how it all happened,' he says of his rise up the career ladder. 'I despise bands, probably that's why it's turned out like it has. At school I was in

a duo, we made cassette albums for our friends, but we never did all that live rubbish. We never had a name, either. It seemed so unimportant. All our songs were about celebrities. Being in our early teens there was nothing else to sing about – no love lost.

'I've always done music,' he continues. 'I'm a child of the electronic and dance era. It's always listening to Warp Records stuff, doing similar things, but singing about Daphne from *Neighbours*.'

Richard left school and did 'a bit of engineering' in studios and worked for various independent labels. At that point, bedroom studios were beginning to spring up everywhere. People started making spooky dance music, like the Aphex Twin, for next to nothing and putting it out to an eager listening public.

Mr X thinks you need to have an understanding of the business side of the music industry as much as you know how to twiddle a few knobs.

'One of the things I saw from being around musicians and studios was how ignorant people are,' he mutters, northernly. 'The business side isn't natural to any musician, it's like the other side of the brain. There's lots of stories about the record that sold lots of copies but mysteriously no one got paid, the person who's tied to an endless deal ... Some musicians say, "The business side has nothing to do with me," – but do you really want to end up not being able to make a record for five years? There's no excuse to be naïve.'

Wise words. Richard X signed as an artist to Virgin Records – allowing him to freely produce for other acts on different labels. He finds promotional duties 'hilarious': 'Last year it was straight onto *Ant and Dec*. And to meet

Lorraine Kelly and just have a casual chat. I loved it. Physically it's quite hard work, especially if you're a work-shy fop like me.'

Richard has his own ideas about art-work for his own albums, an area he would not have control over if he was a faceless producer. He 'went a bit mad' when a record company person told him record sleeves were 'just advertising'.

'Although I know he was trying to convey the fact that it's a commercial world, the artist has to make some compromise, so we came to a happy medium. His phrase was then stick-ered over the next promo single that came out.'

Richard wanted his sleeves to reveal the behind-the-scenes world of yer recording artist. He tried to print a record company royalty statement in the booklet, which showed him to be hundreds of thousands of pounds in deficit – but wasn't allowed.

'I thought that would be pulling away at the pop music façade,' he mumbles. 'The idea was it wasn't nega-tive. It wasn't moaning, "I haven't got any money," cos fortunately I haven't done badly out of it all.'

Richard's advice for those record producery/artisty types is simple. Get off your bottom and do it.

'To get a deal or get noticed, you have to get something released,' he states. 'People in the press might review it and talk about it – and in the Internet world. Never ever wait for someone to come along and put a record out for you. Most of the people I know who are signed did it by putting out 300 records themselves ... or being signed to a small independent, which isn't that hard if you're any good. There are a lot more people who want to put your record out

than there were ten years ago. I pressed up my first two seven-inch singles – the 'Girls On Top' bootleggy things – which got me all my original press. It cost me £600. I was working, saved up and did it. It's a lot of money if you want to do something, but without it no one's going to notice what you do.

'Make sure you're not depending on it for money,' he continues. 'If I was originally thinking, This is going to make me loads of cash! I doubt I would have mixed Whitney Houston with Kraftwerk. It wasn't about that. Don't let money cloud your vision. Until you've got your major label deal, and then it doesn't fucking matter.'

Richard would give the music busi-ness twenty out of twenty: 'It has its downsides but it's so much better than any other job. I saw Westlife on TV recently, and they looked so incredibly cynical, the whole thing is just massive business for them – but they don't even hide it any more. The music industry is a great place although there are so many shattered dreams down the rocky road. I like it. But I'm a very pos-itive person.'

A bit about engineers:

Engineers help the producer on the more technical side of production, learning their trade as they go on. They're responsible for setting up the equipment for the day: checking the tape that the band record onto, labelling tape boxes, loading samples, anything that needs to be done in preparation. Engineers can earn from around £100 a day to £20,000 a year and over. They often start as tea boys working for free, having done a studio engineering course at college. They have to make sure the band don't walk away with any equipment – which they are prone to do.

Says Street, of his engineering past: 'Often you're determining what the drums sound like, what reverb you need – you are making some production decisions. Whether you as a person have the wherewithal to carry on and develop that and turn into a producer is another thing, but there's sometimes no clear division between engineer and producer.'

GLOSSARY

● **Key**

The range of notes the song is written in. The key of C, for instance, has no sharp or flat notes. The key of B, conversely, is a bugger with semi-tones all over the shop.

● **Intro**

Start of the tune. 'Wooooooosh!' it often goes, or 'Brrrrrrr!' to give the song momentum.

● **Budget**

Set by the A&R department of the record company and governed by how many records they think they'll sell. Some albums are recorded in space-age technology studios in Jamaica (Happy Mondays) and others are made in bedroom studios in Wolverhampton (lots of dance types).

SKILLS YOU'LL NEED

Diplomacy; a bit of technical knowledge; ability to bone up on all new music – and old music; being nice to people; letting your ears, not your brain, do the thinking; reliability; creativity.

TIPS

● Ring up studios and see if they need anyone to help out doing anything at all.

● More and more colleges have sound-engineering courses which will give a basic know-how. Check with your local authority.

● Listen to records and see what extra bits are added that are not part of the main 'tune' – riffs, twinkly sounds, cymbal hits. This is how producers listen to music.

● If you have friends with equipment, offer to help them out and learn your way around. More and more people have home studios, and experience really is invaluable.

USEFUL ADDRESSES

● Abbey Road Studios, 3 Abbey Road, London, NW8 9AY
TEL 020 7266 7000
FAX 020 7266 7250
WEBSITE www.abbeyroad.com
● Air Studios, Lyndhurst Hall, Lyndhurst Road, London, NW3 5NG
TEL 020 7794 0660
FAX 020 7794 8518
WEBSITE www.airstudios.com
● Rockfield Studios, Amberley Court, Rockfield Road, Monmouth, Monmouthshire, NP25 5ST
TEL 01600 712449
FAX 01600 714421
WEBSITE www.rockfieldstudios.com
● Sarm West, 8–10 Basing Street, London, W11 1ET
TEL 020 7229 1229
FAX 020 7221 9247
WEBSITE www.sarmstudios.com
● Black Melody, PO Box 43683, London, SE22 8ZD
WEBSITE www.blackmelody.com

ROADIE

MONEY: From around £100 per day, to £1,000 per week and over for the U2 roadies of this world.

HOURS: Eighteen or more every day when you're on the road.

HEALTH RISK: 7/10. Lots of running around, but lots of fags 'n' booze late nights as well.

PRESSURE RATING: 7/10. If you barge into Noel and knock him over as you hand him his best Rickenbacker on stage, he won't be best pleased.

GLAMOUR RATING: 5/10. Scrabbling around at the feet of the stars and trying to fix their effects pedals. Hm.

TRAVEL RATING: 10/10. Your very job is on the road ... So, yes.

The roadie is responsible for the practical smooth running of the tour – from loading equipment to stopping the audience being sick on the artist's shoes.

'**G**oing on the road.' Ah. The Road is the magical land of tour buses, defective leads, and cans of beer. It is a Camelot, a mysterious place that doesn't exist to anyone but those who are in it. A bit like being drunk. Which people on the road normally are.

'Roadie' is a very un-now term. 'Backline technician' is the phrase du jour. When a group goes on tour, they employ backline technician people to carry and polish their guitars. These people are jolly sorts who enjoy the road lifestyle that bands lead – the moving about, the interesting people, the booze, and the pies at service stations. You get all the good bits of being in a band, but without having ever to utter the phrase 'Good evening, Leicester!'

Digby Cleaver wanted to be a roadie from the time he first found out what one was as a teenager. 'I tried to play guitar, but I was appalling at making chord shapes. Then I suddenly realised there were things called roadies. I thought: What a brilliant job! From then on I was intent on doing it. So I am actually a career roadie.'

Cleaver was working in a record shop and working three nights a week in a pub to earn extra money. The drummer of a rock band (UFO, old rock fans) used to drink in the pub, and that's where Digby got his break. Old drummer bloke happened to share a flat with **Hawkwind**'s head roadie and knew he needed someone.

'This roadie chap immediately took me under his wing,' says Digby. 'He showed me which end of the plug went into the wall and which one to the back of the amp.' A couple of months later, Digby was in Sweden, crawling around with leads and things.

A roadie is employed for a tour either by an artist's management or by a tour manager already commissioned to do the job. His employment starts with pre-tour rehearsals, checking the equipment which is going on the road. You have to make sure the leads are good, find out which guitar strings are used, and order picks and enough parts to get you through the tour. You may find you're asked to go to the launderette for a bassist who's forgotten to wash his smalls and is too busy trading football cards with the keyboard player to go himself. When the band are having an argument about how the song ends at the end of the rehearsal, you have to get them out, turn everything off, clean up, and perhaps drive half of them home. Then next day you're on the motorway again in search of the next Ginster's pie. Digby calls the whole process 'submarine living': living on a big tour bus until 'once a day you up periscope at a gig'.

↑
pop star

↓
important bit of
live equipment

ROADIE

Between 8 and 9 a.m. the first truck rolls into the loading bay at the chosen venue, but you may begin earlier if there's lots to sort out. The trucks full of equipment and crew (caterers, sound and lighting, backline technicians) will have been travelling all night to get to the venue, if it's a long way from the previous night's gig. (If it's less than twenty miles away, the crew might hotel it for the night.)

There will be a local stage crew, employed by the promoter, who unload the first truck with the lighting equipment on it. They hang all the lights up in a dandy fashion on the rig that eventually towers over the stage. Then the sound truck arrives and the sound boxes are unloaded, the **PA** built and the **monitors** for the band to hear set up. Then the band's equipment lumbers on stage. Digby will be making sure nothing is dropped or thrown around. He'll devote attention to the guitars: putting them on their stands, cleaning them, and checking the strings are all in place. The lights are positioned on the **rig** and the crew members who are milling around scoff breakfast courtesy of the caterers; the catering equipment is always the first gear off the trucks and the last back on.

The band or artist arrives in the early afternoon and does their soundcheck. Some hate this ritual and go through one or two songs while snarling or chewing gum - American thrash/grunge band Babes In Toyland (if you remember them) were known to soundcheck for a mere three minutes. Others love them and jam for hours – indie perennials The Wedding Present have played soundchecks which were longer than their actual gigs. Primal Scream like to 'jam', i.e. play none of their songs but old blues nonsense. Any technical problems are cleared up at this point, using the roadies' expansive knowledge, and then grub's up for everyone. And so the show begins.

We've all seen a bloke with his bottom hanging out of his trousers fiddling around at the ankles of some surly guitarist during a gig. That is a guitar roadie trying to fix an electrical problem. Backline technicians have to be alert all through the gig, ready to pounce upon a problem as soon as it occurs. Although, as Mark Radcliffe once famously asked on Radio One, 'Why do roadies always bend double when they come running on stage during a show? Do they think it makes them invisible and if they stood upright we'd all see them?'

After the show, the procedure is repeated in reverse as the roadies reload all the equipment on to the trucks as quickly as possible while the band and all their hangers-on are swanning around backstage drinking Cognac and smoking unfiltered cigarettes. The crew eventually climb into their own vehicle and put the video recorder on, play some hot tunes, drink lager, play cards, and whatever else.

'No one tells anyone to go to bed,' says Digby. 'But you have to be self-disciplined, because no one will come along and say, "You're not doing that very well," – they'll just sack you. You have to do the job because you're proud of what you do.' You won't last if you're a slug-a-bed surly bloke who likes kissing strange women. No, you have to be keen on the job.

It must be said at this stage that there aren't very many female roadies. Women minded towards the on-the-road technical side of the music business are far more likely to become lighting or sound engineers. Roadieing unfortunately remains very much a laddish, all-blokes-together calling and, although this situation may change, it's going to take time.

Roadieing is not without its in-built travails. Vehicle breakdowns can throw a tour into turmoil, as can equipment breaking when you don't

YOU TEND TO GET YOUR GRUB FROM SERVICE STATIONS.

have the budget to fix it, and truck drivers getting busted at borders for drugs. You have to be as diplomatic as the tour manager in order to be part of the team. You can't just go off and sulk because the drummer beat you at cards the night before. You have to be friendly: you're living with twenty strangers in confined conditions for weeks on end.

Digby philosophises about his job. 'You have to be incredibly diplomatic and very courteous, to know when to joke and when to be sympathetic. Half of the job is handling people, whether it's musicians or the idiot jobsworth in the village hall who's hired four children as the stage crew. And, to be successful, you have to really want to do it. No one says, "Thank you very much, you've done a good job." You know you have when you haven't been sacked.'

Roadies spend a lot of time polishing Rickenbackers and Les Pauls (a guitar, not a bloke) – bands love to have their guitars shining in the glare of the spotlights. You will also need a good knowledge of basic electrics – how much electricity comes out of the wall and the difference between 'alternate' or 'direct' current. Mm.

'Being a roadie is harder to get into than you might think,' continues Digby. 'The level of professionalism is higher than it used to be. Fewer bands will take a chance on a nineteen-year-old who's dead keen on working for them.' Like any business, roadieing is quite insular: friends of friends get jobs, or else people who have mates in groups. Bands will recommend their favourite roadies to each other, as will tour managers. It's all about reputation. Digby has worked with bands such as Madness, The Clash, The Only Ones and Black Box Recorder.

When is he happiest?

'The day the cheque clears, to be brutally honest,' he says. 'But also, you'll never feel anything else in your life like the buzz of 80,000 people screaming as your band come running on to the stage. I experienced that with The Clash at Shea Stadium, and most of the audience hadn't come to see them – they were supporting The Who! On the other hand, there are days when I wish I was a chartered accountant with a pension and a secure future. But there are plenty of guys who are envious of me and say, "You don't know how lucky you are!" and I always answer, "Yes, I do."'

GLOSSARY

● **Hawkwind**
Dodgy 70s rock band which once used to contain Lemmy.

● **PA**
Literally, public address system. The big speakers which stand on the stage and pipe out the music to the fans and headbangers out front.

● **Monitors**
Those boxes on stage that you see by everyone's feet. They play back the sound the band are making so that they can hear the music themselves.

● **Rig**
The bar over the stage which the lights are hung from. It has to be raised above the stage before each and every show.

SKILLS YOU'LL NEED

Diplomacy, knowledge of basic electrics, being handy with a screwdriver, enthusiasm, being willing to get up early in the morning even if you've had a late night, being nice to fans who are frequently profoundly annoying.

TIPS

● Help out local bands for free and see if you like it.
● Many colleges have technical drama courses where you can learn about lighting and sound for plays: the principle for gigs is basically the same.
● Local venues often hire local crew: you can start there, loading and unloading equipment.
● Ask a roadie at a gig for a few hints – if you're lucky, they'll feel flattered

you're taking an interest, as they're normally the unsung heroes of the show.

● Practise carrying your hi-fi speakers up and down the stairs and around your house. But only if you're really bored.

ROCK HOTELIER

MONEY: From peanuts to millions. Depends whether it's Margate or the Strand.

HOURS: Eighteen hours a day, in some cases. Hotels never close. Therefore they never stop having problems.

HEALTH RISK: 8/10. You may get flattened in your car park by a television thrown from the penthouse suite by a rock star.

PRESSURE RATING: 9/10. Keeping everything running smoothly and being able to make a profit in today's competitive market ain't easy.

GLAMOUR RATING: 3/10. You work for people you may never see again. They come and go and nick your towels.

TRAVEL RATING: 2/10. Perhaps down the road to go to a conference centre for the Dealing With Tricky Guests hotel summit.

The rock hotelier deals with tricky guests. And Portishead and Massive Attack, ho ho.

The Columbia Hotel in Bayswater, central London, is known in some circles as the rock hotel. Bands flock to it. Partly, perhaps, because it's known as the rock hotel and they want to keep within the fine tradition of being a bit rock and not staying with their auntie.

If you own such a place, you've got to put up with a lot. Musicians keep different hours from normal people and they also like to drink during these different hours and perhaps invite a friend or two to join them. They like to get up and check out late. They used to like throwing televisions out of windows, and sometimes enjoy 'accidentally' smashing into mirrors. They are the bane of the sane hotelier's life, but they bring in business.

The Columbia is relatively cheap with single rooms from £70 per night, and has rooms that sleep three or four so that bands can bed down even more cheaply. 'About 15 per cent of our clientele are people in the music industry at any given time,' says hotelier Michael Rose. 'There is nothing to suggest that they upset the other 85 per cent. Ninety per cent of the pop groups are polite and reasonably turned out. They stay and they go. Only a minute proportion produce incidents, and no one tries chucking televisions out of windows any more. Teenagers from Europe actually cause us more problems.'

Rose is very dismissive of people who come in hoping to see pop stars whooping it up all over the shop. 'If they get up late and keep different hours the other guests will have gone out anyway so they won't disturb them.' However, he does say, 'Pop groups are popular with the staff and the front desk enjoy having pop stars here.'

Some pop stars are awful. They get back from a gig and want to drink all night with several thousand 'close friends', some of whom may be ladies of dubious morality. Allegedly. They're sick in bins and order **room service** for ten people at 5 a.m. and then deny it when the night porter knocks on the door. They cram in seventeen to a room when all their 'friends' realise they can't get home and need somewhere to kip for the night. Or they play parlour games in the lobby until 6 a.m.

However, Rose is giving nothing away. Part of the skill of hotel business is to be discreet. 'We don't have an all-night bar, despite what some people have said,' says Rose. 'A group might bring one or two friends back, which they are entitled to do, but if it turns into a private party no more liquor is served. The problems that arise are very, very rare. We treat all pop stars who stay here in exactly the same way as other customers. We offer them the same services and facilities.'

If you're a hotelier, you can always chuck the offenders out and bar them for good. Or you can charge them lots of money for the wrecked hotel room, the ketchup on the walls, and the broken

mirrors. (Shampoo used to have to pay for all of these things – good job they made lots of money in Japan, eh?) You really are on top. The bands that you like will come back when you're tolerant, and develop into loyal customers. Some hotels, it is true, don't like having pop stars staying, but most adore it. It gives them something to talk about, for one thing. The only thing you must ensure is that the **less discreet members of staff** don't leak secrets to the press. There is no surer way of losing celebrities' custom – and your hard-earned credibility.

GLOSSARY
● Room service
Pop stars are particularly fond of ordering room service, particularly in liquid form. However, hotels prefer them to use the mini-bar: it earns the hotel more money and means the staff aren't so harassed.

CRASH!

warble!

MR. HOTEL MANAGER

HOTELIER

● **Less discreet members of staff**

Newspapers will always try to speak to hotel staff where bands/artists are staying. A place like the Hyde Park Hotel in London, where Madonna frequently stays, will be besieged with calls and the press will book rooms and stand outside all day. You have to ensure your staff aren't going to the *Sun* to reveal all about Maddie's 5 a.m. mooning in the bar.

SKILLS YOU'LL NEED

Discretion, organisational skills, single-mindedness, tolerance.

TIPS

● Take a hotel-management course.
● Learn to cope with irresponsible, immature people. Some time spent in charge of a crèche may prove invaluable.
● Or maybe as a warder in a young offenders' centre.
● The only thing to suggest would be to let your friends stay in your room overnight, and charge them if they break any furniture.

SECURITY PERSON

MONEY: Around £4.50 an hour up to £40,000 p.a. and over for management positions after years of work. Masses if you own your own company.

HOURS: Any time from very early in the morning to very late at night.

HEALTH RISK: 8/10. You have to avoid getting brained by over-excited fans.

PRESSURE RATING: 8/10. You have to protect the star and the fans. This can mean ensuring the safety of a crowd at Wembley stadium. Without losing your temper.

GLAMOUR RATING: 3/10. Showing people to their seat or making sure that no kiddies fall into the road at a record signing is not the most chintzy thing to do on a Saturday night.

TRAVEL RATING: 9/10. It's one of those jobs – if you get in with a nice, rich artist you can travel the globe helping them to walk through airports.

Safety is the mantra and gospel of security workers. From top-notch star to wide-eyed schoolchild fan, the security person has to make sure that no one is getting pulled about, roughed up, or is fainting or jumping from a great height. This includes the pop star. Oh, and shiny jackets are optional.

Increasing numbers of people are attracted to rock security work. The trade is fast losing its previous, exceedingly dodgy, reputation. In the past, too many venues and promoters would pick up their **bouncers** dirt-cheap and not bother to check their CVs and career histories. People with criminal records and GBH convictions were manning doors, and **dodgy dealers** used to abound. In old Dickensian times, security people at Ma Purseshifty's Olde Coffee House would duff you up before you came in the door, set fire to your eyelashes and nick your hat. Now it's a respectable job.

All kinds of different people now get into the security line. One of the biggest event-safety companies in England, ShowSec, carefully vets all its prospective employees in case they just want the chance to shout at and bully people. They have their own training and safety department to put recruits through their paces.

'With gigs, we deal direct with promoters or record companies,' says JC, who runs the ShowSec training centre. 'If it's a band we know, then we'll quote them the standard arrangement. With boy bands like Boyzone you're assured a young female audience, so you make sure plenty of first aid is available and bring a trained team who can look for the first signs of distress and hysteria. You can have thousands of young girls, so you need barriers outside. You have to keep people from getting knocked over.'

There are also security people backstage. If the venue doesn't have its own staff to collect tickets, ShowSec will also perform this duty. It's hard work. Around 400 security staff are generally required to man an arena show of 20,000 people. They need a multitude of skills, from being able to be calm when someone's being rude to them to knowing the exact whereabouts of the telephones in every venue they work at.

'When the seats collapsed at the Pink Floyd show at Earl's Court,' recalls JC, '1,100 people suddenly had a flying lesson. It was down to us to help the people who were trapped and you need a calm temperament in a crisis. A lot of people think the job's all about violence and martial arts but we don't carry guns; we carry first-aid kits.'

And it's all right, you shorties! You only need to be burly if you are at the front of the stage lifting fainting girls over a barrier. Otherwise, you can actually be quite tiny – and you get to wear the nice shiny jacket so that people can see you.

Personal security guards are not needed as much as you might think, but they do need to be hyper-professional and very well trained – it's not all free albums and luxury-liner travel. If an artist is touring there'll be a team of people around them who are **crowd-management** specialists. In Japan, Italy and many other countries, security teams will liaise with the local police to discuss how big the crowds

SECURITY

will be. The job involves far more than just being an intimidating man-mountain walking around next to Britney Spears.

However, some misguided people try to get into rock security purely because they think it's a short cut to meeting the stars. 'They think they can get their photo taken with George Michael,' continues JC. 'But George doesn't want that; he wants efficient people who can help him. He gets that other rubbish all the time. And don't think you'll always be backstage or can get anybody you want backstage. A lot of girls – especially at boy-band gigs – will come up and say, "I've written a card – can I take it into the dressing room? It'll be OK, four years ago they said hello to my sister!" You have to be polite but firmly insist that no one comes backstage. The artist doesn't want to be seen in the dressing room putting his feet up, without his wig, by anyone. Keeping them out can involve huge amounts of diplomacy.'

JC is realistic about promotion prospects within the security world. 'I'd be reluctant to say you can make a career out of security,' says JC. 'In our company there are only eight people who earn really good money and tour round the world. It can take years before a band will put their trust in you. But there are prospects for progression, and if you're smart, efficient and polite you can be made into a supervisor.'

On the whole, JC enjoys the life of a rock security person. 'To me, it's the best job in the world,' he enthuses. 'You meet so many different people, and there's a great feeling of satisfaction when people leave a show, shake hands and say, "Thanks, we had a great time."'

GLOSSARY
● **Bouncers**
Slang for security people, because they 'bounce' people out of a building.
● **Dodgy dealers**
People who get involved in schemes and scams which are illegal and would have them banged up in chokey were they to be found out.
● **Crowd management**
What security people are skilled at. They like to use this kind of term.

SKILLS YOU'LL NEED
Being calm – especially under pressure; being patient; liking those shiny jackets; efficiency; politeness; looking a bit scary sometimes.

TIPS
● There are some dodgy companies out there. Before joining any company, ask these questions: Do they have a health and safety policy? A training policy? Are they registered in the UK? Do they have insurance for their staff? (If you get smacked around the bonce by some deranged Metallica fan, you will quite fancy the idea of receiving some compensation.) And, remember, be careful: anyone can set up a security firm.

SLEEVE DESIGNER

💰 MONEY: From £30 an hour if you work freelance. In-house designers get a standard wage from £12,000 to £30,000 p.a. and over.

⏱ HOURS: From 10 a.m. till sometimes very late, because the deadline demands it.

➕ HEALTH RISK: 6/10. You might accidentally whip off a finger with a scalpel knife.

✋ PRESSURE RATING: 8/10. The turnaround time for sleeves is very short, so you might be working against the clock. And you might have to change things quickly because the marketing person 'isn't happy with red'.

🍸 GLAMOUR RATING: 4/10. You might get to drink with someone who wants a horse on their cover, but you have to be really in with your stars to stay on their ranches.

The sleeve designer is commissioned to design the covers for record releases in all formats by specific acts. They either work for an independent company or in-house for a record company.

Sleeve design can define a decade. The *With The Beatles* cover which has the four mop-tops, in black and white, peering down a stairwell. Seminal. The Velvet Underground album with the banana on it. Epoch-making. Bruce Springsteen's *Born In The USA* with his bottom representing the death of the American Dream. Hm. The Rolling Stones' *Sticky Fingers* album with, er, a crotch representing the sexual decadence of the 70s. Um. The Smiths' archive sepia snaps of long-dead stars. Ooh. Radiohead's childlike drawing

SOME BANDS HAVE A PROBLEM WITH CERTAIN COLOURS.

things. Nnnn. Design a good sleeve and it will help zoom records into higher chart placings as part of the overall marketing package – and you'll receive both artistic and professional satisfaction. And you get to use computers and jiggle things around, which is far better than the felt-tip pens which were the height of design innovation many moons ago.

Most designers start with an interest in art, graphic design or illustration, and do a foundation art course at college, then specialise for their degree. Some sleeve designers come from a fashion background and some from graphic design; some just 'fall into it'. Junior jobs at design companies and for in-house designers at record companies are regularly advertised.

Brian Cannon designed all of Oasis's and The Verve's sleeves. He did a degree in graphic design at Leeds

Polytechnic, but went about things his own way. 'I was a fan of the **electro and hip-hop scene** in the mid 80s,' says Brian. 'I wasn't musical and I couldn't breakdance, but one night I drew this big graffiti mural in Wigan, where I'm from. A Manchester band – Kermit from Black Grape's old band, The Ruthless Rap Assassins – noticed this and nearly crashed their car!

'I heard word on the grapevine about this, met them, and did their artwork from then on,' says Brian. 'Then I was at a party in Wigan in 1989 and a spotty student wearing funny clothes started chatting to me. It turned out to be Richard Ashcroft and he promised me I'd do his artwork when his band got famous. I bumped into him at a petrol station in Wigan, and he'd just signed to Hut Records. It started from there.'

Brian never wanted to work for anyone else or be answerable to anybody, so he got office space in Manchester, where he bumped into a bushy-eyebrowed bloke who was working with Inspiral Carpets in the same building. They talked about his obscure Adidas trainers and the guy said, 'When my band get signed you can do my artwork.' It was Noel Gallagher and he proved true to his word. Brian's company, Microdot, is based in London, and he has now diversified into directing videos. Yes.

Sleeve designers will generally begin by listening to the songs they are working with and seeing what ideas spring to mind. 'If you look at my previous work you can see the stuff I'm not into,' confesses Cannon. 'I designed Inspiral Carpets' stuff because I was skint, and on Noel's recommendation.' The designer and the

band will then come up with an initial idea, and plot it out: commissioning a photographer, choosing graphics, providing a logo if the band don't already have one. The Verve's cover for *Urban Hymns* was taken before the shoot had even been set up, but it had that natural feel, man, and so the band preferred it to the other, more formal shots.

Brian also likes to go overboard on Oasis's covers and make them a spectacular roller-coaster ride of allusions to old Beatles records, Noel's pub gags, friends of the band, and some other stuff. They certainly go to town. The famous cover of *Be Here Now* cost £20,000 to shoot. Cannon hired a swimming pool and bought a knackered Rolls Royce for £1,500. The shoot took three months to sort out – from start to finished product. This, however, is classic old-school decadence. Most bands don't have that sort of money. By the same token, you can only make a lot of money as a designer if you have your own company or are at the top of an in-house team.

'I always tell people,' says Brian, 'forget going to a record company, because they're not interested in sleeve design. They don't know what the fuck they're talking about. Why on earth would they give a kid who's **wet behind the ears** the new Oasis sleeve? Get well in with bands when they're unsigned and do stuff for nothing. Noel and Richard are personal friends of mine and that's the best way – I wouldn't bother with people I don't like.'

Sleeve designers have to produce computer-processed artwork, on the whole. It has to be clear, eye-catching, and work well within the whole context of the band. They have to know where the music is coming from, and what imagery is suitable. Sometimes the stars are too busy to say what they want or give you any clues, though, so you have to be sharp. It's no use putting a photo of a car crashing into a swimming pool on the new Beyoncé album when she might think that's a bit outré. Likewise, George Michael won't want some fat bloke in a hat on his covers – it's all models round his way, you know. Stereolab are best left painting singles sleeves in their bedroom, which they do because of their individualistic nature. (Whether design is anti-individualistic per se is another matter entirely, and not one to be pursued here.)

In-house designers are given projects by the company they work for, rather then being able to choose them, so sometimes the job is rather more stifling. However, in this role you will work on a broader selection of music and related design, which means more variety for the easily bored. In-house designers have the advantage of being able to hear some releases a long time before they come out, and can build up exciting visual treats in their head before they go down on paper. All in-housers agree the most boring thing is thinking up covers for anonymous compilation albums. This task can be inspiration-free, but at least the money is regular, whereas designers working for independent companies are paid by the hour and fill in timesheets for every job they do.

Vaughan Oliver worked for 4AD Records for over seventeen years, first on a part-time basis then as in-house designer. He studied graphics at Newcastle University and decided he didn't fancy that, but still had a longing to do sleeve design. He began freelanc-

← record sleeve

SLEEVE DESIGNER

ing for Ivo Watts-Russell, who was then engaged in setting up 4AD, in 1980. Together they created a continuity within the label's design which is now world-famous and has been exhibited all over the place. The Victoria and Albert Museum even bought a **limited-edition sleeve** a few years back (*Lonely Is An Eyesore* by This Mortal Coil). Oliver's sleeves, often looking like nothing you'd ever recognise – mainly out-of-focus swirlings, helping bring back the word 'ethereal' into modern pop parlance – are a good example of sleeve design which suggests more than dictates a mood.

'I like to put a bit of mystery in,' says Vaughan. 'The sleeve has to be instantly seductive or attractive. It may not be an idea you get immediately but something more open-ended. A lot of sleeve design is trend-orientated, and I never wanted that. I don't enjoy stuff that joins in. You look around now and you can't tell the difference between Echobelly and Echo and the Bunnymen.'

Oliver now finds that the budgets for sleeve design have shrunk in recent years. The money tends to be allocated to videos and remixes. 'In record companies there are no art directors now and nobody who comes in with an art aesthetic,' he says. 'Apple Mac computers (used widely by designers in the industry) give a certain level of surface finish all round, but there are no "ideas" buttons on those machines. Maybe it's old-fashioned but I don't think people dealing with design appreciate the difference between traditional and computer-based design.'

Now Oliver has once again gone freelance, he still gets first choice on 4AD work but also works on corporate identities, logos, brochures and posters – including the graphics for the Young Vic's performance of *Hamlet*. Vaughan is famously pro-aesthetic and likes to spend as much time as possible on sleeves because he thinks they're so important. He's built his career on purist grounds, while Brian Cannon is another type entirely. But both can exist in the art-pop world, you know.

Cannon says he believes arrogance does help you to get in with the stars and get work. But he doesn't consider he has a glamorous existence. At least, not all the time: 'At the minute I'm in a dingy basement with two sweaty northerners – the sort of thing I find myself doing far too much. But I get to travel all over the world and I'm paid a lot of money, which I guess you can call glamorous. It's better than working in a bank.'

Designers, like all music-business people, also have to work around the fragile egos of pop stars – whether they are your pals down the pub or not. 'I love both Oasis and The Verve, but I am scared of them!' Cannon admits, ruefully. 'I've had severe dressing-downs from both of them.'

GLOSSARY

● **Electro and hip-hop scene**
American-led stuff that inspired DJs over here who liked spinning on their head mid-set. Trendy reference point.

● **Wet behind the ears**
Term for 'not being very experienced'. Not exclusive to the music industry but well used within it. It can have a positive or a negative sense: fresh naivety brought to a tired situation, or some godawful mistake by someone who should still be in school. People 'in power' use the phrase.

● Limited-edition sleeve

Like some records are limited edition. 4AD used to put out a luxury, fold-it-out, open-it-up sleeve once in a while, only making around a thousand, for instance. The sleeve in question here was made out of wood. A beauty.

SKILLS YOU'LL NEED

Artistic abilities ('I can't really draw,' says Brian Cannon, 'but I'm a good draughtsman'); some knowledge of computers; ability to work well under pressure; some degree of neatness – all those important papers on your desk might get something spilt on them, you know.

TIPS

● Get an art degree. The London College of Communication is good for graphics.
● Try to get to know some bands if you want to be a Brian Cannon type and call them your mates.
● Apply to record companies.
● Assemble a portfolio to show record companies and managers. Include work that might suit sleeve design. They are always keen to see new ideas.

USEFUL ADDRESSES

● Goldsmiths College, University of London, New Cross, London, SE14 6NW
TEL 020 7919 7171
WEBSITE www.goldsmiths.ac.uk

SONGWRITER

MONEY: You may be writing songs for nothing, until someone picks them up, but most songwriters at least have a publishing deal. When you get a hit (and as long as you're properly credited), you shouldn't be scrabbling at change for the bus.

HOURS: Can be from 10 a.m. to midnight, working on that hot middle eight.

HEALTH RISK: 3/10. Unless you're chewing a pencil, ready to write a top lyric, and you accidentally choke on it.

EQUIPMENT COSTS: Some writers start on a four-track tape machine, which you can get for about £100 upwards. Hard disk recording is pricier, and not always necessary.

PRESSURE RATING: 10/10. You are the machine that makes the charts go round. You are a 24/7 songwriting leviathan and you're only as good as your last hit single.

GLAMOUR RATING: 8/10. You may not be in front of the camera, but you get to go to the Ivor Novello awards and hang out with musicians and smoke tabs etc.

TRAVEL RATING: 3/10. You might go to a country retreat to work with some other songwriters, you may be sent on one of the many songwriting courses in Nashville. But all you'll be doing is sitting in a studio, man.

Songwriters are the people behind ver hits, crafting the tunes that we all hear.

In the past few years the songwriter has reigned as a real force behind chart music. Most recently, pop records have sold not for who the artist is, but whether the song they're singing is any good. Britney's version of Joan Jett and the Blackhearts' 'I Love Rock 'n' Roll' barely nudged the top fifteen, but when Cathy Dennis wrote 'Toxic' – more suited to Britney's persona – it was number one. Westlife penned a tune themselves called 'Whatever' – it lumped into the chart at a 'disappointing' number four. They followed this up with a cover of Barry Manilow's 'Mandy' – which went straight to number one. This latter release was at the suggestion of Simon Cowell, their A&R manager, who knew that Westlife fans bought ballads. With songwriting, you have to keep the dreaded brand intact.

Karen Poole – formerly one half of Alisha's Attic, is now a songwriter. She penned Kylie's 'Red Blooded Woman' and has worked with Sugababes, Jamelia and Will Young.

The first song Karen wrote was as a teenager with sister Shellie (the other half of Alisha's Attic).

'It was called something like "Dance On ..."' she says. 'Let's just say that it was pretty hideous. Shellie and I wrote it in her bedroom on a Casio organ from Argos. We were dancing around the room. I remember we thought we had rewritten "Listen to the Music of the Band" by Neil Sedaka, and "Crackling Rosie" by Neil Diamond. It was more S Club really.'

One of Karen's influences was Prince: 'I was in love with his harmonies, his vocal arrangements … and just his weirdness.' She also cites 'Kate Bush, Blondie, Olivia Newton John, Adam Ant, Hollywood musicals and *The Wizard of Oz*. I hadn't yet discovered Bowie, Dylan, Paul Simon … they were too sophisticated for me.'

She and Shellie bought a **four track** from a Romford music shop 'with the money that we both got from singing in the church choir. I think we got 60p per wedding – we'd been saving!'

Eventually they moved on to a Fostex eight-track recorder.

'Because we loved singing tons of vocals, we got very good at singing together, so there was no margin for error,' she says. 'We would be keeping each other in order and we used to use those tracks wisely. One of us would be playing the tambourine, and the other finger-snapping or whatever … while in perfect harmony! We definitely got good like that.'

Alisha's Attic made two albums and garnered a lot of praise from types who liked involved lyrics like 'You've listened to too many T Rex LPs for me to think I could tame you' and enjoyed the feisty female angle, long before the Spice Girls nicked the phrase Girl Power from Shampoo.

Karen's favourite song from that period was 'The Incidentals' – 'If you can imagine sitting with a guitar and something just being given to you, like a piece of sparkly magic. That was the moment. I knew it was special.'

Eventually the band were dropped from their label and had no publishing deal. Karen decided to write songs for other people. 'Basically I was back at the bottom of the ladder,' she admits. 'To make another record as Alisha's Attic with the same concept was too tired, so it was just a matter of crawling my way back up … by using my contacts, forcing myself into people's studios, cold calling, hassling people. I got myself in by just

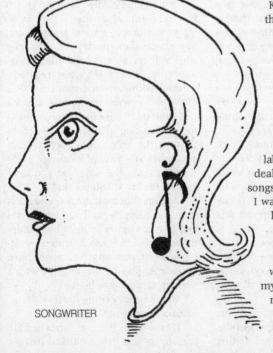

SONGWRITER

talking myself up. Luckily, I pulled it off.'

Cathy Dennis, one of the UK's most successful songwriters, was a featured artist in a combo called D-Mob, and then made records under her own name. She is notoriously shy of publicity, and currently enjoys a life of unrivalled credibility while sippin' lots of cocktails (perhaps) and going to Waitrose without being recognised.

Bernie Taupin is Elton's John longtime musical partner; he writes the lyrics while Elt does the tunes. He is not known for being big on self-publicity. Do you know what he looks like? Thought not.

The songwriter's role has changed over the last few decades. Artists want in on the action – there is not only credibility saying you wrote your own song, but also cash. Some call it 'change a word, take a third' – meaning all you have to do is alter something tiny and be in on a third (or whatever percentage it is) of the publishing royalties.

This might mean that you have a stroppy type who – because of one hit single – thinks they can start writing their own material. This happens *a lot*. One sniff of success and Timmy from top boyband Boyzerk is deluded; he thinks he's George Michael who wrote 'Careless Whisper' on this bus when he was seventeen (apparently) so Timmy reckons he can pen a number-one single in 45 minutes. But no.

'Everyone in the charts seems to be under seventeen,' says one insider. 'But most kids don't write good songs. It's all people with experience in their mid 30s writing the hits.'

One imagines Cathy Dennis writing 'Toxic' while taking a look at a cigarette packet thinking, 'Ooh, I'm *not* getting any younger.' Dennis's work is very knowing. 'Can't Get You Out Of My Head' – which was a song you couldn't get out of your head. That's her genius. If you could bottle it etc etc.

One thing that Cathy and Karen both have in common – they can sing. It is important to be able to hold a note because you can demonstrate parts of the melody and inflections easily. It's also very handy for your demo. Someone has to sing the melody line as a **guide vocal** for the artist. And insiders say you can often still (or only) hear the guide vocal throughout a finished track – it can be stronger than the artist's own warbling. Let's mention no names, eh?

Karen has advice for aspiring songwriters:

'Don't necessarily always go to record companies first,' she says. 'Approach producers and songwriters. The chances are much higher that the stuff will get a listen and most songwriters/producers who are regularly working with current artists know lots of people in record companies, so it's a real short cut. These people are waiting for something amazing to come through the door. Obviously, I don't encourage any form of hassling ...'

What about the style? Do you have to have the latest equipment?

'Be disciplined but don't spend a fortune on equipment. Four tracks are just fine. It's better to have less equipment and learn to use it in an interesting and different way. You might have to resort to playing the table top with a wooden spoon ... so be it.'

And the songwriting itself? How on earth do you present yourself?

'If you are only a lyric/melody person, try and find a musical partner who you can work with,' Karen reckons. 'Listen to loads of current music, see gigs, be aware of what's happening in the charts, get inspired. I know that publishers are becoming more and more choosy, they don't just sign anyone. Get into action, write loads and loads.'

Another industry insider mentions that in the music business songwriting is seen as the new growth industry, but this cannot last. 'Literally every producer is now a songwriter too,' he says. 'It's the only way to survive, to deliver the whole package. And so many artists have been dropped by their publishers, because *they've* all become songwriters, it's insane.

'The top songwriters are churning them out,' he continues. 'The people who are really successful employ loads of other people to help them write. There's a big house in the country where they invite people down all time. There are five studios, a production workshop and every day they're working on the same songs. They take the best **hooks** and incorporate them in one song.'

The more names you see on the writing credits to any one song, the more likely it is that the song is composed of the best parts of several songs. But the percentage of royalties isn't always split equally. Some (the big names) might get more than others (the less established persons). Or the

OLD-SCHOOL FOUR-TRACK
CASSETTE RECORDER.

big name might release the finished product under their name solely.

Stargate – the top Norwegian songwriting team who write with the likes of Britney and Gareth Gates – are also said to work on several songs at once: all best **topline** writers go out there. It has to be almost a production line, this job. There is a high demand, and you've got to supply.

If you're in a band, you have to decide how you're going to split your songwriting royalties. If there are five of you – as in The Rolling Stones – and only two write, do you credit just the songwriters and risk ill-feeling from the others? Or do you split it equally? Bill Wyman was in The Stones for twenty years, rockin' and rollin'. When they stopped touring in '82 he stopped earning. Jagger and Richards – the credited songwriters – still earned tons through royalties. It took him seven years to get them to tour again.

Even The Beatles were not the egalitarian love-in some fans might suggest. When they split in 1969 it was rumoured that John and Paul were each ten times richer than Ringo, although their non-songwriting profits had been divided equally. Hm.

Once you have a record deal, you will get a publishing deal (although sometimes it works the other way round). It's the job of the publisher to pay you songwriting royalties – collected from each CD sale – which are collected by worldwide collection (hence the name) agencies such as ASCAP, BASCA and BMI. You will also get royalties from the Performing Rights Society (PRS) for every time your record is on the radio or on telly (it gets more complicated as publishers do deals with TV channels giving them a package – so you might just get a percentage of that). If you are an artist with no songwriting credits, you will simply get mechanical royalties – a percentage of the cost of each CD sold. Internet sales/downloads use a percentage system just like CD sales. Unless it's those evil pirate sites, wot rob artists of their cash. Fortunately record companies are cracking down on such felony, with the result that eight-year-olds in Utah are being prosecuted for illegal downloading.

Songwriters may not start out knowing much about technology, but they soon become au fait with cutting edge computer programs and gimmickry. Once upon a time, Atari computers were used for dancey-boy music, and programs like Cubase were the height of technical wizardry. Now these are *well* old-school (but still the preferred method of some dancey-boys, and still cool). Pro-Tools is *the* music computer program which is expensive (it costs tens of thousands of pounds) but used almost universally in the digital studios of the world. Only the so-old-school-it's-no-school types like Toerag Studios, whose clients have included the White Stripes, use only analogue technology – but many studios use both. Other songwriting programs include Logic and Cakewalk.

'I should be a lot better at the technology than I am,' says Karen. 'But

hey! I like it all emotion; pen and paper. It's just me, my thirty or so lyric books (a huge kit bag), and a cassette Dictaphone. I should get learning but part of me thinks I don't really want to know too much ... it's like when you have a hundred different effects to choose from, you lose the vibe of what you actually want. Simplicity is the key. They write songs like that in Nashville!'

Ah, Nashville, home of country music – and as many songwriting courses as you can wave your iPod at. Many music publishers suggest a quick trip to Nashville for either their artists or songwriters. But are these courses any good? It depends on whether you like sitting in a seminar room, being told about classic Dolly Parton arrangements, rather than propping up the bar.

One person we spoke to found the world of songwriting 'a bit of a closed shop ... even though I got some introductions because I have a lot of studio connections'. It is true that a lot of successful songwriters have been artists or established producers themselves, but this isn't always the case. And sometimes, too, it becomes the cliché. Little David Sneddon, winner of the first series of *Fame Academy*, quit 'pop stardom' after a year to become a songwriter. When Gary Barlow's solo career stalled *he* became a songwriter. Has no one ever heard of gardening or interior design? Or indeed, a post-fame period of recreational drugs (Nico from The Velvet Underground, Billy Idol, Jason Donovan ...)?

'Perks of the job?' asks Karen Poole. 'I wouldn't want any. My work is my life. I get to do the thing I am most passionate about, work with my pals and get good money for it. I am very lucky, and I never forget it.'

She says that she doesn't think of herself as a 'jobbing songwriter. I have to be into it or it turns out crap!

'It's very important to understand the artist,' she continues. 'After all, it's them you are writing for, which is a real personal thing. They all have different levels of involvement, ability, ideas etc. Sometimes my role can be minimal and sometimes it can be huge.'

Karen says she would love to work with wrinkly types like Paul Simon, Neil Sedaka or Neil Diamond. Let's face it, they're not Girls Aloud. 'And Prince ... actually –' She thinks for a second. 'No! I wouldn't want to work with him. It would kill the fantasy ...'

A bit about copyright:

Some young songwriters worry about copyright. Will the tape you send out end up in the hands of someone keen to rip off your ideas and claim them as their own?

A song is copyrighted the moment you complete it. All you have to do is prove that you wrote it ... The classic advice writers used to receive was to record your songs onto a cassette, then send them registered post to your own address, remembering not to open the envelope. The date stamp on the package will serve as proof of when you completed the song.

An insider from songwriter management tells us that in the UK there 'isn't really a problem' with posting your CD to A&R or publishers and then getting your songs ripped off. 'As long as you don't send the master copy out you will always have proof that something is your copyright should a problem arise.'

In the US, they don't allow unsolicited mail for this exact reason – just in case they do get into legal problems. And lawyers in the US are keener than mustard. Our insider does go on to admit that she's never 'discovered anything sent through the post. Most writers come recommended by other writers or managers or producers.' She states that most unsolicited material they get is not of a high standard – it's more like fifteen-year-old girls in their bedroom singing along to Mariah Carey records rather than having the potential to be the new Ms Dynamite.

Some artists get shirty about their credit. Paul McCartney decided, a thousand years after the event, to change certain Beatles' credits from Lennon/McCartney to McCartney/Lennon – because they were essentially *his* songs and he wanted recognition. Some might call this immature. Others might call it ... overly precious. No listener really gives a toss about the writing credit, do they?

GLOSSARY
- **Four track**

Recording equipment. Originally a reel-to-reel system which recorded four separate tracks onto tape. Then became a cassette recording system; now you can record onto mini disc or hard disk – from four to sixteen tracks. Everyone starts with one of these.

- **Guide vocal**

Literally, the vocal line is sung as a guide for the artist, who sings over the top to get the melody and lyrics right.

- **Hooks**

The parts of a song that are the catchiest. Kylie's 'Can't Get You Out

Of My Head' has loads of them. *Popstars: The Rivals* winners One True Voice had many fewer. Between all five of them.

● **Topline**
The melody line and lyrics of a particular song.

TIPS
● Just get writing. Experience is the mother of, er, being really good at something.
● It doesn't matter if you're using old equipment, being snazzy is not going to help you craft that middle eight. And you have to read the manual.
● Try writing on different instruments to see how they dictate style and structure. Writing on guitar is not the same as writing on piano.
● There are books with handy rhymes and programs you can download online. You might need a bit of help if you end a line with 'orange'.
● For fun, look up Courtney Love's Royalties Manifesto on the web and read her venom towards the music industry. Weep with the tragedy then just get on with it.

SKILLS YOU'LL NEED
Handy with a tune, good at teamwork, flexible, single-minded, extremely creative – you have to find ideas from thin air, mate.

USEFUL ADDRESSES
● www.songwriter.co.uk has advice for would-be tunesmiths.
● Native Management, 32 Ransomes Dock, 35–37 Parkgate Road, London SW11 4NP

TEL 020 7801 1919
FAX 020 7738 1819
EMAIL info@nativemanagement.com
● www.vocalist.org.uk/ songwriting.html gives advice for songwriters.

STUDIO MANAGER

The studio manager looks after the recording studio, taking bookings and ensuring the day-to-day running of the studio goes smoothly. As smoothly as possible, that is.

It's all very well musicians creating hot licks and putting them down on to tape while the producer looks on, nodding in time with the axemanship and smirking at the tape operator in an acknowledgement of universal musical healing. It's all very well, but who's there to order the producer a cab when they want to go home? Who has to try to find a bit of pluggy lead when the engineer's gone sick? And who's going to step in when some mate of the band in the studio is trying to nick the sampler?

The answer is the studio manager – which is a far more exciting job than it sounds. The good studio manager is a wily beast who looks after the artists, producers, engineers, technical people, and anyone else coming and going around the recording process. Their job is a hectic one, rather akin to being a headmaster at a school for rock 'n' rollers. Studio managers must govern their domain, make the rules, slap wrists, hire and fire, and still get on with the record companies. They have to 'sell' their studio and make sure everyone knows it's good, fine and happening to be in. They take out the swanks of the A&R departments to lunch (but only sometimes), laugh at really bad jokes by engineers, look interested when someone's talking about the EQ, and try not to shout at people who are complaining about **effects pedals**.

Studio managers arrive from all walks of life, many following the simple route of working on studio receptions then being promoted. Some are ex-managers, ex-engineers and the like. It's rarely a job people plan to do.

Trisha Wegg is the studio manager at RAK Studios in London. She initially applied for a post with legendary record producer Mickie Most when he bought a mobile studio in the early 70s, which went round the world recording pop concerts and tours. Coming from an advertising background, Trisha's job was to 'oversee all the bookings, making sure the studio got to gigs, crewing it, booking travel, liaising with tour managers – the whole thing'.

Mickie Most decided to build his own London studio and opened RAK in 1976. Initially there were only two studios, but now the building is larger and houses three, plus accommodation. Artists such as Radiohead, Robbie Williams, Beth Orton, Paul McCartney and Whitney Houston have all recorded there. When we visit, an indie band called U-Turn, a female duo signed to Warners called Caesar, and Rod Stewart (doing vocal overdubs) are in. Cor. Trisha's job from managing the mobile studio to this permanent base did not differ.

Like all studio managers, Trisha also liaises with A&R co-ordinators to negotiate studio prices and supplementary expenses such as cab costs and hiring equipment. Bands never arrive with all the gear they need: they're always deciding to add a fancy kazoo solo to a B-side then finding they don't have the Fender Rhodes electric piano to go with it. Hiring equipment is never ending. That is, until the budget your record company has set has been exhausted. And it's the studio manager's job to track down the gear and stay within budget, but not necessarily know all about **EQ**.

'I find out what each artist wants,' says Trisha. 'I'm not a technical person at all, but I am aware of technology and what things do. I do stick my nose in and read tech magazines.'

RAK houses the two original American API **mixing desks** – 'the Rolls Royce of desks in the 70s' that they started with, as much as they are 'kept running on a wing and a prayer'. There's a Neve 51 in studio three, another retro desk but with an automation system for mixing.

'We've got the only two working APIs in the country,' says Trisha. 'They're classic desks, with a rich, warm sound which is part of the reason we have a lot of return business. I may not see someone for five years, they end up producing someone else and ring me and ask: "Still got that desk?"'

Trisha will check what time every session needs to start and exactly what sort of budget the artists have at their disposal. She is the link between every area of practical recording, and therefore has to be nice to everybody. (Interestingly, most studio managers are women. Trisha reckons this is because 'men are competitive with each other – they don't see us as wanting to step into their shoes in any shape or form – we're not vying for their job'.) Sometimes being nice can be difficult, as everyone gets demanding at times. Some more than others.

'Most people who come in here to record are absolutely fine,' says Trisha. 'I hate to generalise, but if anything I would say maybe some American clients are more demanding. It's not an ego thing, they have very specific requirements and expect everything yesterday.'

If a studio has a fish tank, music-biz legend says: Don't count on a complete set of guppies after a band has been in. (RAK has a budgie which looks pretty healthy.) In this writer's opinion, you are essentially playing host to a bunch of stoned, mindless, fun-loving eternal students. RAK's apartments see a few parties. 'Funnily enough, the worst mess was made by a female band,' says

STUDIO MANAGER

Trisha. 'They wrote on the walls and ruined the carpet.'

The studio manager has to ensure the studio is as profitable as possible. Studios these days aren't as well off as they used to be, as technology changes with frightening regularity and it's imperative for studio managers to update equipment and monitors or producers will go somewhere else. It's the producers, more than the bands, who call the shots: they (and engineers) will have favourite studios and can influence record-company choice by passing on their opinions. Location is important, and parking.

Typically a modern studio spends around £75,000 per year on coloured leads and black boxes with buttons on them. All the studios, recording and rehearsal spaces need to be booked up consistently in order for the place to

have the means to buy these extra goodies. Trisha's main job – as much as making sure everyone has had their lunch – is to persuade record companies to book RAK. The studios cost from around £600–900 a day, with special rates for block bookings.

'A&R people love wheeling and dealing – they're all at it. They say the same to all studios – "How many hours can you give me, can I have this, can't I have that, can you throw in **Pro Tools**?" It's very competitive.

'In the 80s,' she continues, 'studios wouldn't talk to each other, but eventually we saw the way things were going and we formed what's called the Studio Accord which brought everybody together. Suddenly we're all talking. Initially the record companies were terrified, they thought we were forming a cartel to fix prices and said they weren't going to deal with any of us until we made our agenda plain. They used to play one studio off against the other but now we can exchange ideas, and develop a symbiotic relationship that benefits everybody. We help each other out.'

Mickie's widow Christina Most owns the business. The staff also include a financial director, a royalties manager, publishing company manager, publishing A&R, technical manager, two assistant engineers and a 'pool of freelance people'. And this is what Trisha calls small (Abbey Road employ around seventy people). The studio manager and technical director are the folk who decide what new equipment they'd like – and the assistants have an input too, actually.

It is a stressful job. You are in a position of responsibility. If you double-book you have to deal with it. If a tape gets wiped (analogue recording) or a computer crashes (digital) then you have to pick up the pieces, even if it's not strictly your fault. And some people get very batey.

'Mickie – bless 'im – was so level headed,' says Trisha. 'He used to say, "Some people take themselves so seriously! We're not finding a cure for cancer here, we're only making music." That was great – I've always got that mantra in my head. Yes, it's important to handle responsibility, but within what you're doing, you can't overreact.'

Trisha doesn't think it's glamorous. 'Someone like Rod Stewart or McCartney, they're here to do a job and you're here to help them. It has its perks – there was a time I used to go to all the parties, and go backstage. Great, but after a time you just want to go home and watch the gardening programmes.'

Successful acts often build their own studio – it keeps costs down and you're always top of the waiting list, so you don't have to wait months to get in there. A top-flight mixing desk can easily cost £250,000, so you need a bit of capital to start with (although – hey – it's tax deductible, isn't it?). Bedroom studios are cheap and so many acts use big studios as a start and end point – using their own equipment in between.

Trisha thinks that you need to have some technical knowledge if you want to be a studio manager. There are business courses in corporate studios and management.

'I'm lucky in as much as I don't have a big board to answer to,' says Trisha. 'I know that other studios that are held by a corporate entity have to do forecasts. But I'm aware each month of the target figure and whether we're achieving it or not. In that aspect, it is a business.'

When studio managers leave the job they often move on to managing producers or artists or A&R. Trisha Wegg jokes that the two jobs she'd be ideal for are hotel landlady or brothel madam.

'But it's very much a team effort,' she adds. 'One comment that I get is that the people are so friendly here. We take what we do seriously but we're not above ourselves.'

A bit about studios:

Studios are bizarre places which are just full of wires and twiddly knobs and never have posters or windows or anything remotely reminding you that you are in the outside world. (RAK is one of the few studios I've been to that has windows.) They also look completely inconspicuous on the outside, so that robbers are put off nicking the pricey equipment inside. There are no worldly distractions: studios are very boring places, which ensures that nobody gets too excited about anything but the music. Man.

The building will contain a lounge and a pool table. There is always a pool table. You have to like pool or video games if you are in a band, because there's always a great deal of time when you won't be doing anything at all but waiting for the tambourine player to **lay down the middle eight.**

There are residential studios like Mono Valley in Wales, for people recording albums. The advantage of recording away is that you can get drunk in the countryside and have someone make your meals for you. However, artists can get distracted there: the Stone Roses famously went into the studio to record their second LP in 1990 and didn't emerge for four years. Essentially, though, being in a studio is a laborious and tedious process. Anyone who's visited a studio and said that it was 'Great!! Really, really interesting and wiiiiild!!!, man!' is lying.

GLOSSARY
● **Effects pedals**
Put them on your guitar and hey! It sounds like a squirrel is gnawing the wires!!
● **EQ**
Equaliser. Something to do with making the bass less toppy, the high sound less piercing. Linked with a frightening word called 'compression', which is similar, and often linked with vocals. So they don't sound as if they've been recorded in a bin.

● **Mixing desks**
The big table with all the knobs on. Controls the sound coming in from live recording, like vocals, and from digital sound generators – those machines that make techno beeps. Used for volume and frequency effects – making the bass less 'toppy'.
● **Pro Tools**
Industry standard computer program which makes records sound so glossy.
● **Lay down the middle eight**
Nothing to do with taking a quick forty winks; it means putting down on to tape (i.e. recording) the middle section (often eight bars) of a song.

SKILLS YOU'LL NEED
Ability to get on with people, being a good salesperson, ability to cope under pressure, persuasive skills, general chirpy manner; not yawning when someone mentions patch leads.

TIPS
● Apply for jobs answering the phones at studios. Secretarial skills might be useful.
● Apply for jobs at equipment and instrument hire places so you can get to know the studios.
● Tea boy/girl jobs at a studio can show you the ropes. You can work your way up to sound engineer or studio manager.
● Sound-engineering courses will show you how to use a mixing desk and all the other equipment. Useful training.
● Practise charging your friends for using your stereo and see how far you get.

USEFUL ADDRESSES

● Abbey Road Studios, 3 Abbey Road,
London, NW8 9AY
TEL 020 7266 7000
FAX 020 7266 7250
WEBSITE www.abbeyroad.com

● Air Studios, Lyndhurst Hall,
Lyndhurst Road, London, NW3 5NG
TEL 020 7794 0660
FAX 020 7794 8518
WEBSITE www.airstudios.com

● Sanctuary Pro Tools Studio, 45–53
Sinclair Road, London, W14 ONS
TEL 020 7602 6351
FAX 020 7300 6515
WEBSITE www.sanctuarygroup.com

● Rockfield Studios, Amberley Court,
Rockfield Road, Monmouth,
Monmouthshire, NP25 5ST
TEL 01600 712449
FAX 01600 714421
WEBSITE www.rockfieldstudios.com

● Sarm West, 8–10 Basing Street,
London, W11 1ET
TEL 020 7229 1229
FAX 020 7221 9247
WEBSITE www.sarmstudios.com

STYLIST

MONEY: From 'helping out a friend' for nothing, to hundreds of pounds per day just to bring along a pair of gloves. The average wage is around £250 per day if you're established, and can be as high as £600 and beyond if you're a bit of a name on the **scene**.

HOURS: Can be any amount of time, as you'll be a freelancer and thus expected to turn up as and when you're needed – for photo shoots, video shoots, TV shows, etc.

HEALTH RISK: 7/10. You may become so trendy you die.

PRESSURE RATING: 8/10. If the backing singer is shouting at you because you didn't get the purple feather boa, quite high. If you lose all the stuff the shop's lent you, very high.

GLAMOUR RATING: 5/10. You might be shopping with the stars one minute, then having to pin plastic fish on to hemlines the next.

TRAVEL RATING: 7/10. Good if you get in with a successful band and they like you and can afford to take you on the road to the US. Otherwise, it may be another trip to Top Shop or Camden Market.

The stylist is in charge of getting the right sort of shirt to dress pop stars in – so that they are vaguely presentable for photo and video shoots.

In the music business of the 70s, stylists didn't exist. Bands wore clothes they'd just bought down the market or nicked from their girlfriend and, quite frequently, looked absolutely rubbish. Then everything changed. Once the first poncey picture was taken by a style magazine – *The Face*, who were at the forefront of the early part of the decade's **wafty blouson** movement – record companies realised that the kids liked bands who looked trendy. Something had to be done. The first stylists appeared when promo videos started. They put tea towels on people's heads and the New Romantic movement was born (even though Duran Duran claim to have styled themselves).

YOU FIND YOURSELF GETTING POP STARS TO WEAR TEA TOWELS ON THEIR HEADS.

At this time, the bands getting styled all pretended it wasn't really happening, because they were *ashamed* of the whole business. It also went against the grain of 'raw', 'street', punk authenticity. Artists wanted fans to regard them as bleeding soul and honesty from their veins, not clotheshorses or manipulated puppets. Even now, when Blur came out dressed in shellsuits during the *Parklife* era, the music press sneered copiously: they had a stylist who went to Cobra Sports for them! How dare they! Now, cynics claim that you hardly need a tune to cut a swathe in music these days, just a nice pair of wellingtons or the one-trouser-leg-up, one-trouser-leg-down rap style.

Most stylists start out through a friend of a friend because someone needs a favour, or they meet someone influential by accident. It's a difficult thing to get into and also very competitive. You don't earn much cash at first – you spend your time doing favours and assisting other stylists on shoots for precisely nought pence. Try to view it as a learning process and that all-important first break.

Stylists are invariably required for photo sessions, whether for promotional photos, record sleeves or magazine shoots. They are hired by record companies. The stylist is either given a budget to trail around the shops for puffy jackets and silver boob tubes, or else borrows clothes from designers, which you obviously have to give back later. You're best advised to keep a record of every single item, as you'll be asked to fork out for the clothes you lose, especially if Jenny Pop Star decides to nick a couple of tops.

It's a myth that you'll be given free trainers for every day of the week, and you can often only borrow stuff if it's credited in a magazine; this worked at *The Face* but doesn't at *Smash Hits*, who don't give credits. Some stylists like to boast that they go to charity shops and jumbles for their 'funky' gear as such anti-elitism has a certain hip cachet.

Stephanie Kaye, who lives in New York, became a stylist by accident. 'It wasn't until I was actually in the midst of this big job earning big bucks that I even realised I was a stylist,' she marvels. 'I'd never even heard of the job before. I went to stage school in order to be an actress.'

Stephanie did many things before she found herself dressing the stars. She invented a model agency 'for weird faces' that saw her dressing as an elf for Petland Discount. She was in a band which was 'more about changing our costumes for every song than music' and had fancy bohemian musician friends. Then she became friends with acoustic singer-songwriter Suzanne Vega.

'We didn't think she'd be big, because she was one of our friends and none of us ever did anything!' admits Kaye. 'I would always shop with her, and by the way she tipped her beret I knew there was this fashion beast waiting to come out, even though all she ever wore were cords.'

Vega's record company were ready to release the single 'Luka' and put a bit of cash behind it because they thought it would be a hit. 'They said, "We'll give you oodles of money to do a stupid video!"' giggles Stephanie. 'Suzanne asked me, "Will you be my stylist? They told me they want one, will you do it?" And I replied, "Of course!" We had a virtually unlimited budget, so we went to a department store and bought some expensive clothes. I thought: Well, this is great!'

At the end of the shoot, someone stuck a **time sheet** under her nose and the baffled Kaye wrote 'fashion stylist' in the space left for job description. There was a blank space for her to fill in her fee. 'I thought: Well, I didn't do anything – I just sat and drank a lot of coffee! So I wrote down $125. The video producer came over to me with the form later and asked, "Is this a joke? It should be around $650 shouldn't it?" So I said, "Er, yeah."'

Stephanie was given more work, essentially because the producer liked her and her fancy way with stripey tops. She was next given the task of styling a **Debbie Gibson** video. 'It was no easy job,' she recalls. 'I had to begin by trying to get the palm tree out of her hair. Had I known what I was getting into, I may well have thought twice.'

Once you are at least slightly established, you may find yourself on a roll. People know your name and pop stars learn to like your tricks with leggings, and you should get regular work. However, there are a few things to understand: primarily that the job isn't just shopping for a living.

'It's weird, but

stylists have to virtually be psychologists,' says Kaye. 'With pop stars you have to hang out and be friends and find out what their biggest fears are about how they look – that's what stylists get paid for. With **Edie Brickell** she'd never worn anything but a pair of jeans and it was my mission to get her into leggings and a jacket.'

It can be tricky stuff. However, nice elements about styling include being given a small budget for extras, and going to markets and haberdashers to buy feathers and ribbons and pieces of old curtain to dress them up in. On the other side of the sartorial coin, it can be a chore to find out exactly what size everyone is and exactly how many extras there will be on the set.

One of the trickiest tasks is styling bands who have an identity already but need a bit of tweaking. Ms Kaye has had to help out Heavy Metal 'big-hair bands' like Mötley Crüe: 'Obviously, my idea of what they looked good in wasn't their idea of what they looked good in. You have to know when to step back. It's not your creation – it ultimately comes from the artist.'

You also have to look reasonable yourself. This doesn't have to cost much money, as we live in a world where jumble sales and charity shops virtually litter the pavements with cheap tat which can look fairly swingin'. Some styl-

MANY ITEMS HANG FROM THE STYLIST'S LOW-BOTTOMED JEANS.

ists are relatively poncey (remember, they are, when all is said, a similar breed to the hair and make-up personages) and they like their rucksacks to be Prada, but it's not necessary. There's no real need to swank about – you especially shouldn't do it in front of your artists, or they'll get the hump that you're better dressed than they are.

Maria is a stylist who works in London. She originally studied illustration, then got a job with model agency Storm and helped them put together their *New Faces* magazine – a tome full of young models which is sent out to clients. She got in via her best friend, who worked for another model agency. The owner of Storm suggested Maria should do styling because she was 'good at borrowing clothes from top names'. However, Maria hates carrying bags of clothes around and thinks the greatest crime of styling is 'over-accessorising'.

You will easily notice when a band has been over-styled – they will look like they have been dressed by a short-sighted kipper after a few too many sherries. Kris Kross, child rap stars from Los Angeles, made the grave mistake of trusting their stylist, who told them to wear their dads' dungarees backwards, the crotches of which billowed by their ankles. They were not to worry the charts again after their first hit, 'Jump'. A coincidence? Who can say? Dannii Minogue has always teetered on the edge of high fashion

STYLIST

and complete disaster – one imagines she does a lot of her own 'styling'. Unlike her sister Kylie, who some claim was reinvented thanks almost *solely* to her stylist, William Baker – who is now as much a name as she is. Well, a bit. He doesn't agree that a stylist should stamp their own brand on an artist.

'You're the medium between the artist and their ideas; making them a reality, he says. 'You have to extract their best points, you're creating an environment which allows them to do what they do best.'

Many stylists will actually move on from dressing pop stars for photo shoots and videos to advertising work, which is on the whole better paid but may involve the soul-destroying element of promoting a product you have utter contempt for.

Stephanie Kaye is honest about what you can do after you've styled the stars. 'I believe in music and that's why I love the job,' she says. 'On the other hand, it's hard to believe in yet another deodorant. That rubs me up the wrong way. Styling work can be surprisingly tiring, though, and now the field is so saturated. You have to work for free if you want to be a stylist's assistant. Everybody wants to be a stylist these days because people perceive it to be an easy job – but it isn't.'

Alice is a full-time stylist for MTV in London. She got a job as assistant fashion editor on *Brides* magazine, of all things, did a spot of freelance assistant styling, then heard there was a job going at MTV. She had built up a portfolio through assisting and this helped land her the job.

TV styling is different from magazine styling. For a start, Alice works full time and not on a freelance basis. She styles nine of the VJs – they each get a budget and she takes them out shopping twice a month. Bizarrely, she can't buy them anything blue, or that's got a bit of blue in it, in case they have to stand in front of one of those **chroma key** screens, in which case their clothing would merge into the wildly swirling graphics superimposed behind them. Small stripes and checks are also out, because on screen they make your eyes go funny. Because television doesn't 'credit' the clothes, designers are loath to lend out fancy threads. The lovely VJs (all of whom are picked for not only being chirpy but also looking like supermodels) might sometimes mention what they're wearing, but it's fairly unlikely.

Alice agrees that the job is mainly psychological. 'Someone's not going to look happy if they're not feeling happy, and everyone has their bad days. Presenters have got to go on screen and convince people they look good and feel good, which is quite demanding sometimes.'

Alice doesn't dress too many pop stars because when they come in they've generally already had their styling persons fluttering around them. 'But stars can ask for advice – some celebrity came in the other day and didn't know what shoes to wear.' And what happens if Coolio comes in and his trousers are falling apart? One crucial point you should never neglect if styling is your calling – stylists always carry a lot of safety pins. Remember that, and you won't go too wrong.

GLOSSARY

● **Scene**
All stylists want to be part of this. It is a make-believe group of trendy people and places, and is a load of rubbish.

● **Wafty blouson**
As worn by Morrissey of The Smiths and Robert Smith of The Cure. Even Tom Thingy from The Thomson Twins wafted a bit. Very 80s.

● **Time sheet**
Freelancers have to fill in one of these to show how many hours they spent on a project and what they are owed.

● **Debbie Gibson**
Tousle-haired singer of the late 80s who shot to fame with 'Only In My Dreams'. Starred in the stage version of the musical *Grease*. Goody-goody image.

● **Edie Brickell**
American hippy dippy singer of the late 80s.

● **Chroma key**
TV device that can superimpose an object on to a different background, e.g. a TV presenter looks like she's standing by a waterfall. Looks naff now, in comparison with new computer graphics, man.

SKILLS YOU'LL NEED

An interest in clothes, knowledge of what doesn't make people's tums and bums look too big (pop stars are very vain), persuasiveness, organisational and communication skills.

TIPS

● Do whatever work you can when you start out. You don't know what it might lead to.
● Fashion or styling courses at college may be a way in.
● Moonboots don't look good on everyone.

SUCCESSFUL EX-POP STAR

💲 MONEY: From zero, apart from a few royalty cheques coming in, to a hefty wedge if you suddenly become a top media businessperson, like Bob Geldof.

🕐 HOURS: A full-time occupation.

➕ HEALTH RISK: 10/10. You could get depressed and start taking 'to the bottle' and all sorts of other things. Beware.

PRESSURE RATING: 10/10. Living up to expectations once you've left a group or lost a record contract is extremely stressful.

🍸 GLAMOUR RATING: 1/10. Well, obviously.

✈ TRAVEL RATING: 5/10. Your band might re-form and then you can play Leicester's Princess Charlotte for years and years. No, come back, you really can!

Send in the clowns, for the ex-pop star is the modern phenomenon that fascinates everyone. They used to hog the limelight; now they can't even get a light for a solitary cigarette down a dark street. Unless they get themselves together and find a proper job – hooray! Or appear on reality TV and are reborn anew.

It's difficult being a pop star. Everyone thinks you're great for ten minutes and then they suddenly get into computer games and you're left wondering what happened. Well, this isn't the case for U2 or Tina Turner, but how many people get into the charts and then swiftly fly straight out of them? It is the pop star's greatest fear – The End. But it's like worrying about when it starts to rain, because it will eventually start to rain, and then life will still go on, philosophy fans. Anyway, pop stardom is not always what it's cracked up to be if you're a sensitive soul and is mostly quite useless and damaging to one's sense of self and social life. Probably.

Ex-pop stars are an odd breed but they do share certain traits. Either they are teetotal, no drugs, organic-carrots-type people, newly converted to the idea of 'normality' and thus getting the wrong end of the stick completely, or they remain wild, abandoned ultra-heroes of rock who still don't know when to go to bed or anything.

EX-POP STARS TAKE UP HOBBIES.

SOME WANT TO PRETEND THEY
WERE NEVER IN A BAND.

Ultimately, these are two sides of the same coin. Some do settle down and pretend to be like everyone else, but it can be hard, especially if you had such a wonderful time and were in a band that enjoyed the fruits of pop success and had everything done for you.

Clare Grogan was the lead singer of Scots pop band Altered Images for five years in the early 80s. She was on the cover of glossy magazines, on *Top of the Pops*, toured the world, and did the whole much coveted pop-star routine. She then left the band and embarked upon a solo career which was 'a kind of half-hearted attempt'.

'I've only myself to blame for it being totally ineffective,' she says. 'I don't really think it was what I wanted

to do. People said, "Why did you leave the band? To have a solo career?" And, in fact, that was the furthest thing from my mind. I wanted to have a boyfriend, I wanted to have my girl pals back, and I wanted to go out on Saturday night.'

These are the things that are denied to the pop star – any sense of having a life. Pop stars work so very hard that they never stop being their perky/smiling/surly/grimacing selves, 24 hours a day. Then, when they decide they want a real life, they get offered another stab at doing the same old thing on their own, and end up deciding that it would seem a bit stupid to turn down such a courteous offer. Holly Johnson from Frankie Goes To Hollywood, all of Take That, Matt Goss from Bros, even Andrew Ridgeley, who was never the wholly musical one in Wham!, released their own solo records.

After a while, however, sensible ex-pop-star types realise this is not the way forward, if it's going badly, and settle for something slightly different. Boy George became a top DJ, remixer, label boss (More Protein), as well as making his own club records under the name Jesus Loves You. Craig Logan left Bros and became a successful record producer and now manages Pink. Keith Duffy from Boyzone was in *Coronation Street*. For many former pop stars the choice seems to come down to acting or TV presenting – and that's where we find Clare Grogan.

Ms Grogan released a solo single and recorded an album for London Records but the latter did not see the light of day. 'I guess that put me off considerably,' she says. 'I felt maybe someone was trying to tell me something, and because through other circumstances I was pulled in other directions – acting and presenting – it didn't become such a big deal that the record wasn't being released. It got further and further down my list of priorities.'

Before joining Altered Images, Clare had appeared in Bill Forsyth's film *Gregory's Girl*, and after they split she was in the same director's *Comfort and Joy*. She was also approached for both presenting and acting roles after she left Altered Images, and was even offered an American sitcom which she refused to do because it meant going away for six months. She puts this refusal down to 'naivety rather than arrogance'.

'I started at the top, so none of it was a struggle,' she says. 'But that gives you a false expectation of what the future will be like. I really did believe that my whole life would continue in that trend – I'd be literally bumping into people who just happened to be film directors. When I left the band, for the first time I had to go out and sell myself, which in the long term has done me absolutely no harm, but it was quite terrifying. I had got comfortable with people handing things to me on a plate.'

Clare is still acting, and she also regularly presents music shows on VH-1, MTV's more 'mature' counterpoint. She appeared on the 80s 'comeback' tour 'Here and Now' with the likes of The Human League. She's acted in *Blott On The Landscape*, *EastEnders* and *Doctors*, and in *Father Ted* …. as a rock star.

'To be honest, it was obvious to me that when I left Altered Images I would be asked to play rock stars, which I said I'd never do. But I loved *Father Ted* to bits, so I thought it would be really great to play an obnoxious rock star. It

SOME WANT TO PRETEND
THEY'RE STILL IN A BAND.

was a very affectionate thing – it was meant to be a bit Sinead [O'Connor], a bit Dolores [from The Cranberries] – basically a "bonkers chick in rock", which I'm more than happy to label myself as.

'I think it's too easy to view life after pop stardom as a bit sad,' continues Clare. 'I know from my point of view that I have no desire to get caught up in that pop-star lifestyle again, but I can't go to see a group I like without wishing I could storm the stage and grab the microphone. Once you've had a taste of that, you never get over it. I never will. It's the biggest buzz ever.'

Clare's old Altered Images compadre, Johnny, is now in **Texas**. The rest of the band have settled down to domesticity. Clare is quite happy with what she's doing and, although she never has a plan, 'if I happen to win an Oscar then I'll be delighted! I don't regret that my life has moved on,' she reflects. 'I don't mind being older and doing what I do at all. But I think there is a snobbery in this business to an extent – when you've been a pop star people aren't always convinced that you can be anything else but that. I truly believe that, no matter how much people around you try to put you off, if in the face of all this you think I'm going to do this, you've every chance of succeeding.'

GLOSSARY

● **Texas**

Not the state in North America, but the resuscitated rawk band with a woman singer wot everyone fancies.

SKILLS YOU'LL NEED

To have been a pop star and managed not to become a bitter, twisted individual. It can happen.

TIPS

● Don't cry; think of what you can do instead.

● Look at Edwyn Collins! He kept going and then had more hits.

● Look at Texas, come to think of it.

TOUR MANAGER

MONEY: From around £500 per week when you're starting out, to £1,000 a week for a well-established tour manager, and around £2,000+ for yer Elton or Madonna tours.

HOURS: 24 hours per day for the length of a tour: you're always on call to sort out a mishap.

HEALTH RISK: 7/10. Ver Road might take its toll a bit. Eat fresh vegetables.

PRESSURE RATING: 10/10. Tough. You have to move a small army of music types (notoriously unreliable) around the four corners of the earth amid language barriers, changing currencies, and different people with confusing customs.

GLAMOUR RATING: 3/10. Waking up pop stars and trying to get them on a coach is not the most illustrious of tasks. Ringing up railways stations and airports isn't the most glimmering pleasure either.

TRAVEL RATING: 10/10. You get to go everywhere! Places you'd planned, and sometimes places you didn't expect. Oh, and a lot of service stations.

The tour manager sorts out all logistical problems during a band's tour. That is, booking crew, trucks, hotels and extra transport, and sorting out the budget and any other day-by-day requirements that your spoilt pop star might have (e.g. paying for wrecked hotel rooms).

Nobody ever really grows up wanting to be a tour manager. Imagine you are a nanny taking the kids on holiday, a holiday where the kids try to get as drunk as possible every night, snog strangers and ruin the camper van. But also take into account that the kids have to work every night, and need to be kept as well as possible despite the ice cream and chip diet.

Being a tour manager is, frankly, a mug's job. It is only for the very most Mary Poppins of people, who have a strong constitution and an unshakeable calm in the face of inevitable disaster. Consequently, frightening people do the job because they are good at getting people out of bed in the morning, imposing fines for oversleepers, and taking what they call 'no shit' from anyone. As you can imagine, once you get yourself together and manage a few high-profile tours, the money becomes very good. There is fun to be had, you can be a roaming Jack Kerouac-style free spirit – you don't have to have permanent accommodation back at home to do it, unlike most jobs. But it is a lot of hassle.

Tour managers normally start through helping out friends, managing bands themselves, or moving up from being part of a touring crew – sound, lighting or **backline crew**. Obviously, you have to have some interest in music and not mind going to bed late. You also have to be able to organise yourself out of a civil war, if the need arises.

You start when you're asked by the artist's management or record company to do the job, as their band has just announced a tour which they've put together with a booking agent. Obviously, this can range from ten dates in Britain to a year-long trek round the world. You're given a **budget** and from there you contact everyone involved, including backdrop companies and stage-set designers, if you have that sort of cash for a big bonanza tour.

TOUR MANAGER

You find a production manager, lighting and sound engineers, and backline persons. These are most often people you've worked with before, or types recommended by people you've worked with before, just so you know they won't sulk in a corner when everyone else is playing charades. You have to negotiate the wages for all these people – you have to say a lot of 'I'm not paying you that!'s. You book the hotels and flights for everyone, with the help of a travel agent – and there are music travel agents who are used to this sort of thing and pick out the hotels that have late bars and are more tolerant of pop-starry behaviour. You'll need at least one tour bus, and one with beds if not everyone is staying in hotels.

Then you may have to hire trucks – there are certain music-biz transport companies that have the right insurance – book equipment for when you're there, and contact venues to check they've got a stage, lights etc. (sometimes they haven't). You also have to make sure your band gets their rider in the dressing room: from ten cigars to eight pairs of individually monogrammed pyjamas. You have to arrange the **per diems** for everyone, too.

Steev Toth has tour managed Erasure, Spandau Ballet and Alice Cooper, plus other top names. He started as a sound engineer. He did school gigs then promoted gigs in his home town in Somerset. He did the sound for an Erasure concert, then started tour managing the band he was managing, brutal dance fiends Nitzer Ebb.

'Once you've got the information, you put it in an itinerary, which is known in the trade as **The Book of Lies**,' says Steev, drily, who got his real name – Steve – changed by deed poll because he thought it wasn't exciting enough. This 'book' is doled out to the band, crew, management, record company, press office, and wifey and husbandy types who need to know where their loved ones will be for the next few months. You should also have your tour **laminates** to bung about, too.

Hey! You're on the road! Here's where the proper work starts. You have to do the accounts, unless you're going with a dead famous band, who'll have the money to bring a special accountant along with them. Tour managers pay for everything as they go along: bus drivers, hotel bills, even little plastic souvenirs for the folks back home. If a show is cancelled, for instance, you'll lose thousands of pounds; if a bus breaks down, you have to get it fixed, so you have to put a bit aside for emergencies. After every gig you sit down with the promoter and work out how many people came along, what the promoter's advertising costs were and, if the band is at a reasonable level, you split the chunk of profit between promoter and band. There's a guaranteed minimum fee for each show, and you almost always get paid in cash. After the tour is over you have to go back to the artist's management or accountant with a set of accounts.

Sounds OK so far? Not too bad, is it? Well, there's more. You have to sort out different currencies and look after the well-being of everybody – people get sick or homesick or start to hate each other. Then you have to liaise with the record label, as they are sure to arrange on-the-road press and promotional schedules for the artist. Making sure the band get to these contractual commitments on time, like in-store record signings, radio and TV interviews, is obviously pretty darn important. Then explaining the fact that they nicked half the record shop's stock of Alternative Rock because they were bored is another thing. This is why a lot of tours are like a chaotic kids' holiday, where the children are **fined** for being late and are literally carted around being told what to do.

Steev Toth is very matter of fact about it. 'You get to have a method, and you do all tours the same. You find a good way of doing it. Bands do make the tour manager wake them up, to get to the airport on time. It's a bit "Let's see how far we can push him." I do issue warnings: the band must remember you're the boss – they must respect that.'

The job isn't for the weak of heart. You can be detained at customs when you touch down in a new city because they know you're with a rock band and that rock bands are renowned for taking drugs. You have to arrange work permits for everyone to enter some countries, and your promoter may forget to get them, or the authorities may not give them to you. There're all these things at stake. It's a rough ride and only for the insane, in all honesty.

'Two weeks in Russia in '92 was the most depressing tour of my life,' says Steev. 'Nitzer Ebb went to Siberia. There was no toilet roll or food – just vodka. It was a culture shock because we'd just arrived straight from America. You had to book a telephone call two days in advance. My wife desperately tried to get food and water out to us but failed. It was really frightening, so we trashed a hotel room out of frustration and had to pay for it. It was $80. A year's salary to them; to us it was pocket change. The whole bathroom, toilet and bed went out from the eighth floor. I thought that was quite a bargain, really.'

Steev can recall times when he's had to separate warring members of bands who are waging fist fights just before they're about to go on stage: 'Renegade Soundwave had a fight before a performance in Macedonia in front of fifty journalists. It makes a good story, but they were trying to kill each other.'

And, of course, there are also groupies to fend off. 'They get tedious,' he laments. 'They'll always be so sycophantic because they think music is a glamorous industry, and so will spend their time just hanging around. It's not just females – it's males as well. In the

A TELEVISION ACCIDENTALLY 'FALLING' OUT OF A WINDOW.

early days of Erasure, there were all these spotty youths hanging around trying to ask what kind of keyboard Vince plays. You become hardened and can be quite rude. And I do find I end up having to lie for the artists. Lying to wives isn't my favourite part of the job.'

And, to top it all, bands never make much money touring unless they play from stadium to stadium. The **shortfall** is picked up by the record company. You have to be playing arenas and stadiums to start raking it in, and if you want a light-show extravaganza or someone dressed as an anteater dancing to the left during the encore, you've blown your budget. The merchandise sales provide revenue, but the record

company has nothing to do with this side so it can't pay for the tour.

But! There is a good side. You get to hang out with pop stars in strange hotels getting drunk on dodgy liquor. You get to cross people you don't like off guest lists – even famous people. You get to spend your PD on sweets and crisps and make typically caustic remarks about bands and/or touring all the time. You can go on business-class flights, stay at the fanciest hotels, and you're not actually spending any money. All your wage goes in your bank account as everything on tour is paid out of the tour budget. And, if you can do the job properly, there should always be work.

'Most bands prefer a British tour manager,' says Steev. 'Americans insist on them because they're used to festivals and different types of venue. We tend to be more used to different currencies and languages. American tours are a piece of cake – it's either a club, an arena, or a shed. Over here you have to be a lot more versatile.'

GLOSSARY
● **Backline crew**
The guitar and drum technicians who you see faffing about with pedals and leads before a band goes on stage. They always look grumpy.
● **Budget**
All tours are based on a budget, which doesn't alter. It is set by the management and record company and allows for the fact that the tour might not break even. The budget is rarely optimistically extravagant, thus ensuring that the shortfall should be as little as possible.
● **Per diem/PD**
'Per day' – amount of money every

member of the tour contingent gets for sweets, pipe cleaners and copies of *That's My Plectrum!* magazine. Sometimes spent in the pub. No, not sometimes. Always.

● **The Book of Lies**

Contains every date, venue, telephone number, hotel detail, stage size etc. Called thus because the schedule will invariably change from one minute to the next.

● **Laminates**

The magical laminated cards on strings which get you access to parts, or all, of backstage. Eagerly sought after. They now have pictures on them so you can't nick one and pretend to be the sound engineer.

● **Fined**

A lot of bands have to be threatened before they'll behave themselves on tour. They are fined for being late in a lot of cases, because it wastes everyone's time, doesn't it?

● **Shortfall**

The money owed at the end of the tour – that falls short of the budget. It is always paid by the record company. They might ask for it back in some cases, if the band suddenly makes a lot of cash through record sales.

SKILLS YOU'LL NEED

Common sense; 'people management' skills; a desire to look after other people all the time; a bloody good organisational mind; ability to get going even when feeling a bit peaky; diplomacy, plus being dead strict, too. Sort of headmistressy skills, really.

TIPS

● Get to know about tours, by helping out friends in bands.

● Engineers often get into it. Plus truck drivers. Any job involved with touring will help you to do it.

● You have to start at the bottom. The Rolling Stones may employ four tour managers, but they've all had masses of experience. Patience, patience.

● Don't even bother if you're a bit of a dosser. It's a complete nightmare of unearthly hours and hard work. The tour manager is not a job for slackers, quite frankly.

TOUR PROMOTER

The tour promoter's job is to try to sell as many tickets as possible for a given artist's live performances. Promoters deal with the advertising and organisation once the tour is booked.

Ah, the world of touring. It is a veritable monster and many music-industry jobs are connected solely to this netherworld. The tour promoter is an essential prop to the industry, and no signed band can even remotely begin to survive without one. The tour promoter takes over once the booking agent has arranged a band's jaunt around the country, and sets about telling the world about the dates until, hopefully, they are totally and utterly sold out.

Promoters occasionally work with bands who are not yet even signed, but it's more normal for them to become involved when an artist has signed a record deal or is on the verge of doing so. Surprisingly, promoters can become just as involved in bidding wars as record labels and publishers, as competition to promote tours by much-touted upcoming bands is very fierce.

Essentially, the tour promoter buys up all the tickets for a date cheaply, and then tries to sell them on to the public at a higher price. Promoters can deal either with one show or the whole tour. However, it's very rare for a promoter to attempt to cross international boundaries: virtually all promoters below the absolute giants of the industry work dates only inside their own country.

Ticket sales are the key to making money on tours, or at least breaking even (tours, like singles, are generally regarded as promotional devices for albums, not money-making entities in themselves). The main task of the promoter is to ensure that the publicity reaches the right people: there would be little point in advertising Cliff Richard in *Kerrang!*, or Ozzy Osbourne in the *People's Friend*. The tour promoter, rather than the band, loses money if tickets for a tour don't sell. Although, if a record company loses money on a tour which is particularly unsuccessful, the band may well find themselves having to recoup the loss from their advance. This, however, is another story.

There are venues to accommodate all audiences, from small pub gigs like Barfly at the Camden Monarch, through medium-sized clubs like the legendary Buckley Tivoli and Dudley JB's, up to Wembley and the Docklands Arena. Before the promoter becomes involved, the booking agent (see 'Booking Agent' chapter) should have carefully estimated the likely appeal of the tour and chosen venues accordingly. However, bands do sometimes upgrade or downgrade at a late stage if ticket sales have been much higher or lower than anticipated – the latter scenario, which was wonderfully depicted in the seminal Spinal Tap, is deeply humiliating for the artist concerned, and will unquestionably be accompanied by loud crowing and sneering from the music press. On the other hand, extra nights may be added if **demand** is overwhelming. Sometimes venue ownership and tour promotion overlap – the mighty Mean Fiddler group owns five venues in London and promotes all gigs staged there themselves, as well as the Reading and Phoenix Festivals and a host of other events.

So, let's say you have a moderately successful band who would like to do a twenty-date tour of Britain in about four months' time. The booking agent arranges the venues and then the promoter steps in. The promoter, who is aware of the tour budget, firstly contacts all the venue managers, confirms that the venue is hired, and pays a fee to do so – which can be anything from a couple of hundred pounds to thousands of smackers, depending on the venue size and the date of the gig.

The next task for the promoter is to arrange the printing of tickets (although very occasionally individual venues may handle this task) and place adverts in newspapers, magazines and periodicals to promote the shows. Naturally, the *NME* is pretty much essential for any tours of an indie or slightly alternative nature, and advertising space may be booked in these mags as much as ten weeks consecutively to publicise one tour. The prodigious cost means that television advertising is effectively a no-no for any act smaller than Kenny Rogers or The Rolling Stones, but radio stations such as Kiss FM are handy for dancier gigs. Most promoters also make use of **flyers** and will employ a host of students and part-time workers to stand outside gigs freezing their socks off and giving out bits of paper to drunk fans rolling out at midnight.

Flyposting is still technically illegal but all the major record companies and promoters do it and hold huge accounts with the poster companies. It's a vital part of the publicity process and can really boost a promotional campaign. Few offenders ever actually get pulled up by the police, unless their unfortunate operatives are caught red-handed. Like prostitution, flyposting is generally tolerated due to the vague belief held by the authorities that, were they to clamp down, something far worse would probably replace this fairly minor misdemeanour.

The next stage for the promoter is to liaise with the artist's tour manager to discuss stage size, lighting, the **PA**, forklift-truck hiring, security etc. Normally the tour manager is the first port of call here, although extravaganzas such as U2's PopMart tour or The Rolling Stones' Voodoo Lounge monstrosity will have their own production manager, who in turn will have a host of staff. The promoter and tour manager will discuss finance, and also the sacred **guest list**.

Here is an example of how the finances of a live date might work:

A band may be performing at a small but esteemed venue with a capacity of 350 people. Selling tickets at £17 each means the promoter makes £5,950 if the show is sold out. After VAT, £5,000 or so is left. The venue hire is £1,000 leaving £4,000. You then have to pay for the PA, crew, catering, the press adverts, staff, security, support band, PRS, artwork and insurance which is at least another £3,000. The money left over is £1,000 artist's/band's. Booking agent gets 10–15 per cent of this and the tour promoter gets the change between door money and costs (including band fee), so in this case they got £200. [The artist/band has to pay all their costs out of their £850–£900 e.g. musicians, equipment rental, van hire, rehearsals, effects (projectors etc.), their own sound engineer, guitar techs etc. Tough, eh?]

Paul Hutton is a director at Metropolis Music, one of the major promoters in Britain. He started, as many do, as social secretary at his university. Then he went on to stage gigs, with a couple of friends, in the Fridge club in Brixton and at the long-defunct Hammersmith Clarendon (which is now a Tesco).

'It's hard for promoters to make a large profit,' he says. 'You are certain to promote some dates which lose thousands of pounds. Ask any promoter. If you made up a business plan based on promoting gigs and went to your bank manager, I'm certain he'd say, "No, no! Think of something else!"'

Most promoters begin at the lowest level, probably putting on gigs in pubs and small clubs as a hobby. Chances are you can meet an indie band you like, attract forty or fifty people, and earn about £60 on the night. The Camden Monarch have a club night called the Barfly which is run by a couple of people as a labour of love. Some of these people go on to be full-blown, large-scale promoters, but just as many head into being venue, band or tour managers, A&R people, or (more rarely) music journalists.

Promoters can find they spend half their life at rock gigs. The hours are very long, as it's important to be **on the circuit** and see not only your own shows but ones staged by rival promoters. You're always bumping into people at the bar, gabbing about The Next Big Things, making contacts and networking. The social side of the industry overlaps with and becomes indistinguishable from work, as per usual. You even have to enjoy talking to people about points on albums, in this line.

TOUR PROMOTER

There's a danger you may be made the scapegoat for a tour when the band have failed to attract the level of ticket sales they expected. Artists on the slide will often give their promoter or booking agent the boot after a flop tour rather than look at their own waning star as a reason for the poor attendances. The band manager will also look to dump someone else before being dumped him/herself. Paul Hutton summarises the worst elements of the job as the hours and losing money.

Tour promoters may find special, one-off gigs in unusual venues an interesting challenge. Some bands are minded to play art galleries, circus marquees or Battersea Power Station. Metropolis put on an Aphex Twin show at The Clink, an ex-prison in south London, but these kinds of event have their own problems. 'You have to remember that Johnny Punter can't always find his way to a lot of out-of-the-way places,' says Hutton. 'And one-off concerts cost a lot and rarely make money, so the record company has to be very much behind the band.

'I wouldn't necessarily recommend the job to anyone,' he summarises. 'You've got to be sure that you want to do it. I set out thinking: I don't want to have a nine-to-five job. But sometimes I sit here and wish I had one. Basically, you just have to have a bit of an entrepreneurial streak.'

GLOSSARY
● **Demand**
The number of tickets that are wanted. Demand is always 'overwhelming'. If it is underwhelming, it is simply not mentioned: it doesn't exist.

● **Flyers**
Pieces of paper which advertise forthcoming gigs, given to people coming out of similarly styled gigs. Flyers are also used to promote club nights, theatre events etc. No one is sure why they are called flyers, but they fly away in the wind if you let go of them.
● **PA**
Public address system. You can address your public in a musical style through the big speakers which sit on either side of the stage. Not to be confused with the PA that is personal assistant.
● **Guest list**
The most important word on a ligger's lips. The guest list is a terrifying list of all the people who are getting in free to a gig, or at a reduced price. These are all industry good-for-nothings who won't watch the bands but sit at the bar drinking cocktails and looking for famous people to talk to. Mostly.
● **On the circuit**
The 'rounds'. The endless toil of live gigs around the capital. Once you've been circuiting a while, you see the same faces everywhere. It is, as they say, a small world.

SKILLS YOU'LL NEED
The spirit of the entrepreneur; sociability, being able to organise, ability to do things at the last minute, friendliness, bossiness.

TIPS
● Many promoters start out at university student unions, where you learn the skills but are using other people's money.
● Some companies might take you on for work experience. Write to them.

● Local venues are often willing to put on gig nights for local bands. This is a good way to start and gain experience.

● Organise your friends to play in someone's garage, publicise it, and see if anyone turns up.

USEFUL ADDRESSES

● International Talent Booking, 27 Floral Street, London, WC2 9DQ
TEL 020 7379 1313
FAX 020 7379 1744

● MCP Promotions, 16 Birmingham Road, Walsall, West Midlands, WS1 2NA
TEL 01922 620123
FAX 01922 725654
WEBSITE www.mcptalent.com

VIDEO DIRECTOR

MONEY: For a video shoot where the budget is around £35,000, you'll be handed a tidy £3,500 (10 per cent). You can make two promos per year, or two hundred (weather permitting). But budgets do go beyond £100,000.

HOURS: Anything from an afternoon a week to every day of the week, either doing the video thing or going to see clients, pitching storyboards, hanging out around idiosyncratic scaffolding for inspiration ...

HEALTH RISK: 9/10. Trying to get anyone to stand still is difficult. And then matching them drink for drink afterwards is worse.

PRESSURE RATING: 8/10. You have to deliver a promo that band, record label, management and MTV will like. And you have to make ugly people look good on a depressingly regular basis.

GLAMOUR RATING: 9/10. Those above will love you for it. Video directors get given flash awards nowadays as well, and get to go to Rotterdam to receive them.

TRAVEL RATING: 9/10. Yes, if you hook up with a glossy boy-band-type who likes to lord it about in the Bahamas with nothing but a billowing pair of trousers to their name, ready to **lip-sync** at the drop of hat.

The video director comes up with the idea for, and is in charge of producing, a feisty little film to go with a band's track. Shots of the bassist are optional nowadays.

In the early 80s there were a certain number of snarling indie stars who liked to anticipate the demise of the pop video while spitting into their lager and lime. Such Luddite thinking proved to be hopelessly inaccurate and the use of the video as a promotional tool became more and more widespread. The birth of MTV meant the non-believers were scuppered. A new industry was born in which jobs were made, egos were expanded, money was spent on penguin costumes and careers were made or ruined by a little three-minute film.

A cheap video costs around £20,000. Yup, that's a cheap one. Around £100,000 is what you can pay if you're a swinging hellcat of an *artiste* and have sold a fair few units in your time. For a promising, hit-friendly single in the UK, £40,000 is a respectable amount. In the US it can be much more expensive: $200,000 and upward.

Someone called a 'video commissioner' at the record company will be aware that a band needs a video made for a top new single due out in a month or so, and will commission (hence the name) a director to work on it. Directors will either be known by the commissioner through their previous work or else s/he will have seen their **showreel**, which is full of their best work. The most suitable person, within the band's budget, will then be chosen.

Note: Bands do not generally enlist the help of a director who's made videos in which bloody chicken heads dance around plates of rotten sprouts if the band is a Gaelic folk trio with a song about knitting. Well, the band might want to, but the record company won't.

AN IMAGE NOT ACCEPTED BY MOST POP BANDS.

Often, several directors will pitch for an idea after hearing the tune in question. The idea that suits the artist, management and record company will be chosen and the director duly employed. Once commissioned, the director will shout 'Yippee!' then get on with the task in hand. They'll have a **recce** with a location manager in the glamour spots of the world for starters. They'll often find themselves in Berwick Street market in Soho, London – trillions of videos have been recorded next to the artichokes there. Many times, they'll record it all in a studio. Girls Aloud thought they'd be off to the Big Apple when they read 'New York

feel' in a video **treatment**. They ended up in a warehouse in London sitting next to some NY-style props.

The producer will be recruited and will work out a budget, and together with the director will find a crew and a casting director. The casting director is employed to get hold of any **models**, children or comedy fat/short people who may be needed. (Geri Halliwell once referred to the *people of restricted growth* in one of her god-awful videos as 'mini people'. Nice.) This process is all pre-production, which also includes meetings about what sort of lamps need to be used and how to make the triangle player look less morose.

Production is usually a one- or two-day shoot where the video is actually shot on film rather than video tape. The negatives of the film are then telecine-ed on to video; offline editing begins, and it all gets very technical. Luckily, your editor will sit in the editing suite with you and help you to pick the best bits. Then, once this process is completed, the finished article goes back to the record company. They may well make you do a different edit if the original has, for example, **cats on fire** in it.

There are many and varied routes for people to become video directors. Film school is an obvious one – the London College of Communication and Harrow College are just two places that provide degree courses in film-making. Walter Stern, who's made promos for bands including The Prodigy, The Verve and Massive Attack, started at Bournemouth College. He wanted to direct his own films from the start, but wryly says that the chances of that happening immediately were 'slim'. So he made some short films, and as a result filmed a commercial for *Time Out* listings magazine in London. 'I thought: At least if it's rubbish, it'll be short,' he remembers. 'Then a friend took my showreel around a few small production companies without telling me. Someone liked it, and thought I should go into music videos.'

Most music-video directors work alongside a production company and sign a contract so they don't flee to rival companies. The companies deal with getting the showreel shown around and sometimes fixing up editors and other technicians if necessary. On average, the director gets 10 per cent of the budget. The production company takes 15–20 per cent of the video's budget and the producer gets around 5 per cent.

Stern's first promo was for the re-release of 'Rock On' by David Essex. Well, we all start somewhere. He then made a video of some friends of his, a pub-band affair, which was more his style. 'As soon as I'd done one thing that represented my tastes, during the following six months my jobs got better and better,' he says.

One of his favourite jobs was doing the video for The Verve's 'Bitter Sweet Symphony' – although his original version, in which Richard Ashcroft gets beaten up, was rather different from the final cut which was shown on TV. The tale of how the vid for 'Bitter Sweet Symphony' developed is a good example of the way things work.

Walter initially wrote a treatment that was too expensive, so the record company told him to drop the idea and come back with another one. He then remembered a short film he'd wanted to make at college about a man trying to walk down the street in a straight line. 'Luckily, it fitted in with the band,' he says. 'Richard Ashcroft said that he didn't want to do any acting and wanted to keep the filming very low-key and private – just him, me and the cameraman – so he wouldn't be embarrassed. He agreed to my idea, then, the next thing he knew, he was surrounded by loads and loads of people – the exact opposite of what he'd wanted.'

Pop stars are difficult at the best of times. Getting them in a recording studio can be hard enough. Getting them to a film location on time is harder still. Then there's keeping them there. 'Drugs is the obvious problem,' says Stern. 'I've had bands leaving in the middle of a shot because they're out of it. My biggest nightmare – for a different reason – was with a band called World of Twist, who had previously made all their videos themselves. They didn't want an outside director but the record company insisted.

'They were very nervous of the camera so I had to shoot them secretly from a long way away. One band member left after the first day so the stuff I'd shot I couldn't use. They also kept wandering off all the time. What they really wanted was to film some guy in a bedroom listening to their track. I said this might get dull after a minute or two but they were saying, "No! You can zoom in on his belt and film a flare coming off it!" In the end I said, "Look, here's the camera, you finish it!" At which point they did. They were actually really nice people – but not to work with.'

Walter reckons promos use fewer effects now because they date quickly – and are now more story led. When you make a video you need to please the band, management, record company and television companies. MTV are notoriously picky. They particularly don't like flames, guns, smoking or drinking. They don't like body parts either. Most recently, that young filly Britney Spears got *well* into trouble when she filmed a 'suicide' for her video 'Everytime' by director/photographer posho David Lachapelle. It had to be severely edited so it was all a bit ambiguous. These directors eh? All about pushing back the boundaries, art and all. But since time began (sort of) artists have been controversial – not always through their songs, but through the medium of promo. Madonna's 'black Jesus' in 'Like A Prayer' caused waves (not real ones). George Michael's cartoon Bush 'n' Blair 'satire' for 'Shoot the Dog' caused more rumpus than the tune, which was a bit poor, wasn't it? Beats laydees snogging other laydees on the MTV awards.

VIDEO DIRECTOR

Video director Chris Cunningham filmed home-made mechanical masks in his garage with a school video camera, became a comic artist for 2000AD, then went back into films, working for Stanley Kubrick, among others, on special effects. At the time he was into bleepy electronic music, and approached the band Autechre at a party and persuaded them to let him make a video for them. Since then he's directed promos for The Auteurs, Aphex Twin, Madonna and Bjork. In

'Frozen' Madonna turned into a crow, and in Bjork's 'All is Full of Love' she became a white, shiny, snogging robot. Chris says he can find it difficult, because he has to make a video that he's proud of, and that the record company *and* MTV will like. This highlights the director's dilemma. Art versus commerce.

'I was sent a tape of one group's music and it wasn't really my cup of tea so I thought I'd try to make something really really commercial as an interesting experiment. I wish I hadn't done it now. People were thinking, He's lost it – he makes really normal videos now. I also did a Gene video for their single "Fighting Fit" but unfortunately it was crap because I was only given one day's notice so didn't have a chance to get my head together. With Aphex Twin I had the trust of the record company to do something I wanted and it ended up taking a month and a half.'

'You're only as good as your last piece of work,' says Walter Stern. 'I'm careful of my own image. Pretty much 99 per cent of what I'm offered I turn down.'

It is true that videos are often used to break in records. That (let's face it) awful 'Sledgehammer' video for Peter Gabriel was made in order to promote what the record company thought was an average song. Walter reckons that the promo for 'Bitter Sweet Symphony' broke The Verve in the States: they hadn't toured there for years or had much TV exposure. He also reckons that the same happened with The Prodigy's 'Firestarter', which didn't get exposure until Walter's video was shown repeatedly.

There can be bizarre problems which come along with this sudden wealth of acclaim. As ever, fame has its downside. 'There's a mad woman in Sweden,' says Stern. 'She rings up every time a Prodigy video comes on MTV and warns me that she'll do something crazy, something to do with Satan. "Firestarter" surprised people, which is what we wanted to do.'

The people who succeed in video directing believe that, if you try hard enough, you'll get there in the end. It seems it really is as simple as that. 'There's no big mystery,' says Cunningham. 'Any kid can buy or borrow a camera and make a film. You can edit it to a piece of music and next week you're doing a band's video.' It can also lead to feature film directing – Jonathan Glazer directed *Sexy Beast* after cutting his so-called teeth on Jamiroquai's 'Virtual Insanity' video (floors sliding round all over the place) and Radiohead's 'Karma Police' (where a man repeatedly gets run over). Mr Cunningham is currently working on commercials and short films for Warp Films.

However, don't expect to swap tips with any rival video directors when your career takes off. They simply don't mix. 'I've got a couple of friends who do the job,' says Chris Cunningham. 'But I'm not massively interested in what they're doing. I'm not being rude but I genuinely haven't

the time for it. I don't want to be distracted. Anyway, I think that 95 per cent of video directors are shit.'

GLOSSARY

● **Lip-sync**
Miming along to the soundtrack, while being filmed. Look closely at videos. Some pop stars are useless.

● **Showreel**
The collected works of a director on video tape. A 'best of' for potential clients e.g. record companies.

● **Recce**
'Reconnaissance', French word for surveying, as in looking at interesting locations, such as the Berwick Street market.

● **Treatment**
A short written outline of the overall video narrative – the plot, if you can call it a plot. NB: A storyboard is the plot, shot by shot, drawn roughly on consecutive squares.

● **Models**
Thin types. Often replace backing singers and lip-sync really badly.

● **Cats on fire**
Strictly not allowed. Neither are bleeding chicken heads.

SKILLS YOU'LL NEED

An eye for a good visual image; being a bit pushy – one has to admit; liking your music and being prepared to work on some ropey things before you hit the big time.

TIPS

● Start filming anything. The less you try to copy someone else, the better it will be. Video directors can be commissioned after someone's seen a piece of work that may not even have music on the soundtrack.

● The London College of Communication and other colleges do film courses for aspiring directors. However, they can be anti-promo and more full-length-movie based.

● An art course can be just as good as a pure film course. And all colleges have camera equipment to borrow, if you suck up to the teachers (it has to be done sometimes).

● If you need to get to know the ropes, a lot of production companies take on youngsters to copy tapes, gofer and make cups of tea. As in any job, this is a good foot in the door.

● Walk around holding up your hands in a square, as if you're looking through a camera lens. Directors do this in real life, and they say it helps. No, really ...

VOCAL COACH

MONEY: From £25 an hour to £80 for a freelance hourly rate. You can negotiate for block bookings, as it were. £££££s if you get a TV talent show.

HOURS: As many or as few as you please.

HEALTH RISK: 3/10. Strained tonsil, maybe?

EQUIPMENT COSTS: You need a piano, a keyboard, or something else to strike a note on.

PRESSURE RATING: 5/10. It's not your fault if they can't parple properly, is it?

GLAMOUR RATING: 7/10. You'll meet rising stars and if you're lucky they may bring you nice chocolates.

TRAVEL RATING: 3/10. You tend to sit in your house waiting for budding pop stars to tread grit into your carpet. You also get to the recording studio once in a while, and may be asked to help on an artist's tour. Hello, Wolverhampton!

You help the stars to sing out those lovely notes and bring out all the richness and timbre in their voices: notes they never knew they had, vibratos which have been locked inside from childhood. Or at least to hold a tune so that no one can tell they're teetering on a vocal precipice.

A vocal coach is essential to the music business. You are the pepper on the steak, the ketchup on the chip, the squirty cream on the trifle. You have to bring out the potential in all the top crooners, and some of the not-so-top ones. Almost every pop star goes to a vocal coach – and it's become more acceptable to admit it, although some only go because they're made to. Vocal coaches have to be cool and collected, because they live in a world of skylarks and melodies, unravaged by a cut-throat industry that is nasty to bands and eats kittens for breakfast. Going to a vocal coach (they're not really called singing teachers any more), if you're a nice pop star, is something like chancing upon a dappled glade in a country field when you've just come out of the Dublin Castle and someone has spilt bitter on your Alexander McQueen knee-pads. No, really . . .

Vocal coaches teach by the hour, and give weekly, fortnightly or 'once in a while' lessons, depending on the pupil and what's coming up. A lot of singers will go to a teacher before and during a tour, so they know how to cope with singing every night (v. difficult). Some get the coach in while they're in the recording studio to go through each line with them and get the best performance possible.

John and Ce Ce were made nationally famous by *Pop Idol* – they coached the final fifty down to the last two on the night of the final. Collectively they have also worked with Gareth Gates, Charlotte Church, Mel C, Will Young and plenty more. They work as a team, having met when David and Carrie Grant – former *Pop Idol* and *Fame Academy* vocal coaches – put a band together called United Colours of Sound. They all used a technique which they refer to as 'speech level singing' which uses the diaphragm, not the throat.

'I got introduced to the whole technique,' says Ce Ce. 'I started learning it and continued doing sessions and singing for different artists. I got into the band and it spiralled from there. Producers would ask me, "What's that technique about?" When they got another artist into the studio I'd get a phone call, asking me to come in and help them through.'

John and Ce Ce understand the singer's psyche because they've done the job themselves.

'Every time we work with an artist,' says Ce Ce. 'I always think – if it were me, how would I receive criticism or encouragement? I try to come at it like that. Artists are such emotional people, as coaches we've got to gain their trust – if we don't we can't do our job.'

Ce Ce worked with Carrie Grant on the first S Club 7 tour. Ce Ce had to listen to the records, pick out every single vocal line – be it melody, harmony or backing – and assign it to the best S Clubber for the job. Naturally, it took weeks (they were also not used to

VOCAL COACH

singing together, at once). She then went through the songs with the group through rehearsals up until the first night. She stayed with the tour to iron out any problems as and when they arose. It was, as she says, 'a huge job'. She couldn't pop off for a couple of pints between songs. John and Ce Ce started working together because it seemed easier.

'For one person, it's madness,' says Ce Ce, as John nods. 'The last S Club tour we did with the S Club Juniors [now S Club 8] too. At times we could just swap over, to give the other person a break.'

'It's always good being a male and female team,' says John. 'Ce Ce understands the female voice. If she sings a note, the guys might find it difficult so I come in. The combination works very well.'

It also works emotionally. Some singers gravitate towards Ce Ce's 'direct' approach, others towards John.

Although both felt they stumbled into coaching – they still sing as a duo and as backing vocalists – they think the key to being a good teacher is the experience and the passion to help other people bring out the best in themselves.

'If you can sing and you've got a level of success, you should pass it on,' says John.

Singing is emotional, it can make

people feel exposed, and coaching helps your charge come to terms with wider issues. John and Ce Ce don't just teach the technique, they often provide a shoulder to cry on.

'If someone comes in and they start singing and their mind's not focused, we talk and often they will break down and cry,' explains Ce Ce. 'If you want to work with top artists, you're talking about people who are sometimes getting just four hours of sleep a night for a month; they don't have perspective any more. They're tired; surrounded by Yes people who are there to get them coffee, tell them when to go to bed, when to wake up, where to be. I've been there, perhaps I've not been there on the level of some of the artists I've worked with, but I can relate on some levels to what they're going through.'

The other problem is people who just can't sing at all. And yes, John and Ce Ce have met a fair few of them. But they are nice.

'I don't like crushing people,' states John. 'It would be ignorant and arrogant of me to say, "That's your dream, you suck." There's a lot of people singing nowadays who can't sing, but they've made money.'

Adds Ce Ce: 'It's different if you're a record company person, you can say, "Get out of my office, you can't sing!" because you're investing a lot of money in someone. But for us ... I'd never *lie*, tell them it was good when it wasn't. I'll say, it's all right, but it's not fantastic.'

Tona de Brett is world famous for training the tonsils of the stars, and she has had to deal with non-singers as much as anyone else. While working at the City Lit in London she met Malcolm McClaren. He asked her if she could teach his young protégé to sing – Johnny Rotten. Tona was, appropriately, teaching musical-comedy vocals at the time.

'I thought: Well, a voice is a voice. And that's where my career teaching pop singers started. I taught Johnny, then Malcolm told everyone about me. One fine day before his film *The Great Rock 'n' Roll Swindle* came out, he rang up and asked if I could tell him how I taught Johnny Rotten. A camera crew came along for a couple of hours – it was all quite a laugh – and at the end they said they'd like to pay me £25. I thought this was rather good and I wasn't earning much in those days so I signed a receipt. Then, the next thing I knew, there was the film in the West End, with me in it! Still, at least it began to spread my name around ...'

Tona's son advised her to make a tape of her vocal exercises. The cassette cost a thousand pounds to make and has been selling ever since. She thinks it's important that 'any singer who's going to make a living out of singing should know how their voice works' and so gives people a basic grounding in voice production and tries to help them change any bad habits. She doesn't follow any one particular method or try to force people to change. And you have to be careful with singers.

'Even in the most dire cases you can find something to say that is positive.' Singers who are good to teach, according to de Brett, are the people who 'want to make a lasting career of it. Most people who come to me are basically nice. I've not met any "I'm the big rock star" types.'

There are a fair few charlatans in the business because you can start teaching singing whether you've had any experience or not. And, if you're a good teacher, you will get a lot of people coming to you who have already been taught to sing, but badly. A lot of the job involves correcting other people's mistakes. One pupil of Tona's admitted her last teacher had made her sing to the wall. One day she turned round before she'd finished and saw her teacher deep in a novel.

'The teacher jumped up and said, "I've been teaching for years! I can teach and read a book at the same time!"' says Tona. 'Another singer brought his teacher to the recording studio and the teacher couldn't sing himself – he was a failed dancer who thought he'd teach singing.'

Tona has all the relevant qualifications and is an Associate of the Royal College of Music. She works for three and a half hours per day, five days per week. 'I'm not making a vast amount of money,' she insists. She would most certainly never have wanted to be a pop star ('No fear, mate! It's a hell of a job!') and much prefers teaching.

De Brett finds it frustrating to listen to singers on records who she doesn't think make the most of their voices. 'People have wonderful gifts and they don't use them!' she complains. 'Brett Anderson from Suede has a fabulous baritone but doesn't use it – he uses his "pop voice". Skin from Skunk Anansie has a glorious voice but only uses it in bits. And I don't approve of that Jimmy Nail "Crocodile Shoes" style ...'

Essentially, though, Tona de Brett loves being a singing consultant to the stars. 'Yes, because you never know who's going to come through the door. Every individual has their own approach and way of doing things. Sometimes they can't string two notes together and it takes enormous patience on both parts. But it's an exciting and worthwhile job and I have no plans to stop.'

A vocal coach is always on call, day and night, when they're working with an artist. John and Ce Ce say they can't plan their holidays in advance; they have to be as flexible as possible. Sometimes the work comes in thick and fast, and sometimes there are points when it's a lot quieter. They both used to get nervous when their vocal students performed.

'I've learned to let that go,' says Ce Ce. 'When I first started doing really big jobs in pop music I'd be worried in case the management company were not happy. It was during *Pop Idol* I relaxed.'

'Everything you talk about in rehearsals goes out the window on the night,' adds John. 'If we've done our job to the best of our abilities we can't blame ourselves for what goes wrong.'

'Again, we draw strength from each other,' Ce Ce adds. 'When I'm having a down day, John's on top of the world.

YOUR VOCAL COACH WILL NOT RECOMMEND THESE.

And when we're both having a down
day I feel sorry for the student!'

SKILLS YOU'LL NEED

To be able to hold a note, patience,
understanding of the way the industry
and its stars work. A degree of
personal experience helps.

TIPS

● Get a qualification – a reasonably
high music grade or singing
qualification – to prove you're worth
your salt.
● Studying drama and movement as
well as singing helps.
● Once you have the requisite
qualifications, send your details,
address etc. to A&R managers at
major record labels.
● Ideally you should have been
singing for a while yourself, so you
can relate (man) to your students.

WIFE/HUSBAND/ LODGER

MONEY: Not a lot. Or loads. Depends on the state of your marriage, really.

HOURS: 24 per day, seven days per week.

HEALTH RISK: 10/10. You may end up with the same set of addictions as they have.

PRESSURE RATING: 7/10. Depending on how famous your spouse is.

GLAMOUR RATING: 8/10. You may become mates with the bassist's partner as well, unless you're married to Diana Ross, who obviously knows presidents and statesmen and business moguls and stuff.

TRAVEL RATING: 9/10. You can swirl around any place your beloved swirls, e.g. recording studios, rock venues, aeroplanes and posh hotels (when things are going well); Transit vans and B&Bs (when they're not). The Caribbean is a regular haunt for the Imans of this world. You know, David Bowie's bird.

The husband or wife is the sturdy rock of support for the fragile, tortured artist who is allowed to sulk about there being no milk in the fridge because they have been on Richard and Judy. Once.

Rock wives don't get a very good press. You're seen as a glamorous addition whose only role in life is to phone Selfridges on your mobile to see if they've got any chocolate-covered shrimps. You pout and preen on your spouse's arm and glow in reflected glory. But that glory means nought, because everyone hates you. Especially the fans. Rock wives are portrayed as bimbos and money-grabbers who start nosing around in professional matters when they should be inventing new ways of cooking with broccoli.

Yoko Ono was charged with splitting up The Beatles by pulling her besotted husband John Lennon under the influence of her cruel womanly wiles. Heather Mills McCartney is portrayed in the press as a spiky-nosed madam. Nancy Spungen was accused of egging on Sid Vicious in his heroin-taking and general deviant behaviour. Yasmin Le Bon was just left to do shampoo ads: no one worried about her because she was a model – and they're not threatening because they're thick.

Rock husbands don't have so much bother. More often that not, they have some power. They often tend to be managers, record-company people, footballers or fellow pop stars. There are few trophy husbands, just there to look dandy and hold cigarette lighters aloft for passing tabs.

But some rock spouses are fine people. Ozzy Osbourne's wife and manager, Sharon, brought the alleged bat-eater back from the edge of alcoholism. Belinda Carlisle's hubby helped her to stop taking cocaine. Gloria Estefan, on a more individual note, states that her husband gave her the freedom to be free, lose weight, or some such thing. These alliances can be fruitful.

Amelia* is married to a musician, Clem*, who was the singer of a band who had a moderate amount of success in the early 80s then were dropped and split up, although he's now '**working on a new project**'. She found little stress in rock-wifedom. 'I wasn't that friendly with the other rock wives of the band,' she says, 'although I did

⌐ BOUNCER.

'A ROCK HUSBAND'

spend a lot of time at home playing Sega with the girlfriend of the guitar tech. We'd hire games and sit and get the buns in. I also knew a "rock lodger" who lived with other members of the band so, instead of moping around on our own when the others were away on tour, we'd drink lots of red wine.'

The rock tour doesn't hold that much interest for peripheral people. There's either nothing to do at the soundcheck etc., or then there's unwanted attention after the gig. Being 'the girlfriend' is not all glamour. You end up trawling around record shops to see if their single's been placed in a prominent position, going around distribution warehouses putting flyers for the fan club in record sleeves, and having to listen to your other half witter on about middle eights.

Furthermore, you're always your spouse's **plus one**, and this can be wildly infuriating. Rock husbands/wives get fans coming up to them, but so that they can get close to their famous partner and not because they actually want to chew the cud with them. These accessories have to talk to the geeks from whom Mr/Ms Pop Star can simply waft away with a snooty flick of the hand. Plus, pop stars never get their round in because they're worried about looking 'flash'. Either that, or they're mean.

'People would just be asking me questions about B-sides all the time,' says Amelia of the rock-touring lifestyle she ultimately decided to eschew.

'They assumed all the songs were written about me. Clem wrote a song based on a meat commercial which was about ballroom dancers who argued a lot and the fans assumed it was about our relationship! I'd just tell them, "Leave me alone!" I didn't know what most of the songs were about anyway ...'

Amelia says her bloke didn't get all high and mighty when he signed a deal with a major record label – just a lot porkier. 'We suddenly had a lot more money so we went out and ate loads. We definitely drank a lot more – it was an **F. Scott Fitzgerald and Zelda** type situation for six months. I'm sure if Clem hadn't been dropped from the label he'd now be writing crass novels and I'd be in a sanatorium. But, actually, the fundamentals of life didn't change that much. There wasn't much scope for excess in Leicester. A six pack and a balti every night was about as far as we could go.'

YOU FIND YOURSELF DRINKING A LOT OF FOREIGN LAGER. GLAMOUR, THAT IS.

Poppy* has been going out with a pop star we'll call Ted* for seven years. She started seeing him when she was in the sixth form, so she reckons her life changed but would have done so around that point anyway. She is just as feet-on-the-ground about it all as Amelia. 'I would never hang around the studio: it's dead boring and you just get in the way,' she reflects. 'And, if the band go away, they take lots of other people who are now my friends, so I have people to talk to even if Ted isn't there.'

Poppy doesn't worry about the groupie situation and neither does Amelia. 'There weren't any!' Amelia splutters. 'And, anyway, I trusted Clem. I once heard that there had been a woman interested in him and he literally ran away – his coping mechanism was just "go and hide". In any case, at the level he was at it just wasn't glamorous. Girls who went backstage would find themselves surrounded by men drinking strong lager, which is not exactly conducive to romance. I never found the lifestyle glamorous. If we ever went to record-company parties the bassist would normally end up in a fight with someone and we'd have to leave. I went to Switzerland and Germany and it is more glamorous abroad, but only because you're drinking the foreign variety of strong lager.'

Clem once got annoyed because he was slagged off in an interview by another band, who claimed they'd seen him and Amelia in a clothes shop and she was saying, 'Darling, you'd look great in that jacket on stage.' They called her a floozy, or something. That's as difficult as it got, and Amelia wasn't terribly bothered. She was more irritated by flying out to see the last leg of the band's American tour and finding the journey took 24 hours each way because she'd made a late booking. People did occasionally find out their phone number and call up but would invariably put the phone down without speaking rather than saying, 'Hey, bitch! That guy's for me!' Oh, and a Japanese stalker once tried to find Clem, who by now was living in

Brighton. She found out where he hung out and spent a few weeks hiding behind lampposts because she was too shy to speak to him. He got a bit worried that she might find his house, but she eventually got bored and went away.

Poppy is also in a band herself, as yet unsigned, but doesn't feel there's an awful rivalry there between her and her boyfriend. 'His money pays our rent, and that's good,' she reflects. 'My sister's famous, so you get used to it. I hope one day to be successful myself so I'm not so bothered. The only thing that's a pain in the neck is when Ted goes away to Japan and he phones and either he's drunk or I am. I think sometimes I would prefer it if he had a nine-to-five job.'

There aren't many rock husbands who are not in bands or other such glamorous jobs. Most female musicians seem not to find lowly real people attractive, but perhaps this is something to do with the eternal balance of power – it's very difficult for a successful woman to go out with a less successful man.

Paul went out with a singer in a band for a few years but, for him, the relationship wasn't good. 'I think people in bands crave attention, on the whole, but also I went out with a particularly extreme example,' he says. 'She was a junior Courtney Love. Singers' egos are incredibly fragile and hers certainly was. I can't say I'd recommend it. I don't think I've recovered yet, years on.'

Paul says that, in his case, his partner's lifestyle affected their relationship in a negative way. Birds of a feather, in this case, certainly do hang out at the same nightspots. 'They go on

tour and it's amazing the way a lot of people in bands get satisfaction seeking the attention of other pop stars,' he claims. 'This may be a sad thing to say, but stars are very clannish. Oh, it was bloody awful. When I started out I didn't care what she did because I was in love with her, but over a long period of time it ground me down. There are long spells of boredom for musicians and then there's the thrill of doing something completely exciting – a show – and it only lasts an hour! After that you don't want to go to bed; you want to celebrate and get hammered. These people are living a graveyard life.'

Furthermore, when the press gets involved and splashes your personal life on their grimy pages, the game changes. Your private life becomes their private life and suddenly your godmother knows where your boyfriend's been before you do. Your mum will ring up and ask who the kiss-and-tell former girlfriend is, and the people in the corner shop will ask you about your holiday even if you haven't got a tan. It gets to the point sometimes where the spouses who try to act normally and want their private life to remain secret have to move house, or leave their jobs, or both, if any scandal is revealed. It can be tough at the Very Famous level. But, to be honest, most people don't get that far: there aren't that many pop stars who approach tabloid potential.

A lot of hangers-on and groupie-types do often go out with, and even wed, the stars, but a lot of women who couldn't give a toss about whether David Bowie is coming around to tea also become rock wives. However flippant this might seem, rock wife or husband is a job: you're permanently associated with the famous, and it's not an easy ride. Before you marry that megastar, make sure you realise what you're getting into.

GLOSSARY

● **Working on a new project**
What ex-pop stars do next. It can span from 'being in the pub by midday' to inventing quantum leaps in techno music under an assumed name.

● **Plus one**
As on a guest list, e.g. 'Lord Famous Person, plus one'. This chapter could have been called 'plus one' because that's essentially what we're dealing with.

● **F. Scott Fitzgerald and Zelda**
F. Scott Fitzgerald, author of *The Great Gatsby*, and his wife Zelda sank into an alcoholic abyss intensified by their habit of holding week-long parties. Zelda was finally certified insane.

SKILLS YOU'LL NEED

Getting on with your chosen one, not minding if they go out a lot, having a life, being able to bear hearing their songs over and over again, being a plus one.

TIPS

● Don't do it unless you really do want to hear those B-sides in full, each day every day for months.
● Don't do it unless you are completely not in awe of the other person or else they'll make you go to the shop for them all the time.
● Don't do it unless you want to be hanging around horrible cold and empty venues in Wolverhampton listening to roadies shouting 'Two! Two!' at soundchecks.

● Don't do it unless you don't mind your name being unofficially changed to P. One (see glossary above).

* All names have been changed. They're a sensitive bunch.